DENG XIAOPING:
THE MARXIST ROAD
TO
THE FORBIDDEN CITY

by **CHING HUA LEE**

With an Introduction by
JAMES C. HSIUNG

THE KINGSTON PRESS, INC.
P.O. Box 1456
Princeton, N.J. 08542

Copyright © 1985 by THE KINGSTON PRESS, INC., PRINCETON, NJ 08542

ISBN 0-940670-27-5

Library of Congress Catalog Card No. 85-050583

Published by

THE KINGSTON PRESS, INC.
P.O. BOX 1456
PRINCETON, NJ 08542 USA

Printed in the United States of America

Contents

To my wife, Heidi Hsiao Chin

Introduction

The significance of this book is invariably tied to the importance of its hero, Deng Xiaoping (Teng Hsiao-p'ing). If the history of the Chinese Communist revolution can be simplified, three names probably will stand out, among many others: Mao Zedong (Mao Tse-tung), Zhou Enlai (Chou En-lai), and Deng.

Mao, the home-spun Communist, was the romantic revolutionary whose vision was responsible for both the creation of the Chinese Communist state and for much of its dismal plight, not the least of which were the incessant upheavals culminating in the Cultural Revolution. Zhou, the super diplomat, will be remembered as the man who crafted the administrative structure of the new Chinese state, steared the statecraft through even the worst storms, and held the country together while the Maoist radicals aligned with Lin Biao (Lin Piao) were waging their merciless battles against the Party's senior leaders during the divisive Cultural Revolution. Deng, on the other hand, will probably go down in history as the hero who saved China, after Mao, from the earlier dogmatic straightjacket and ushered in an era of economic liberalization that brought to the Chinese people their first taste, since 1949, of a living free of hunger and despair.

Deng has lived a dramatic life. A landlord's son, he left home at the age of 16 to study in France, where he became a Communist revolutionary. At 25, he led a major Communist uprising in Guangxi (Kwangsi). For 12 years, including the period of China's war with Japan, he was the Political Commissar of the Red Army. During the civil war, Deng led the Communist forces in the most decisive campaign, known as the Huaihai battle (also called the

1

Xubang, or Hsu-pang, campaign), that broke the backbone of the Kuomintang (KMT) government troops. This victory paved the way for the unimpeded advance of the Communists across the Yangzi (Yangtze) River, the seizure of the remainder of the Chinese mainland in 1948-1949, and the expulsion of the KMT government to Taiwan. For 10 years he was General Secretary of the CCP (1956-1965). But it was during that period that Deng, a long-time ally of Mao, turned into one of the latter's arch-foes.

Purged and rehabilitated three times, Deng holds a record of political resilience unmatched in the history of the CCP, or, for that matter, of any Communist party. It is Deng who has proved to be Mao's nemesis, reversing Maoist programs and, more important, ending the grip of Mao's thought on the nation. It is Deng who finally has been able to routinize the Chinese Communist revolution, although Mao's spotty sympathizers in the West may deplore it as a Chinese "Thermidor." Most importantly, the Dengist economic liberalization, which sometimes borders on heresy because of its stress on private entrepreneurship, is beginning to pay off, like never before.

Despite Deng's importance, there have been few comprehensive studies of his political life, other than scattered episodic writings about him. Even his real name is often a subject of confusion for writers outside the mainland of China as Patrick Ching-hua Lee points out in the present volume. The paucity of the literature, nevertheless, offered a unique opportunity for a study of this nature. I first urged Patrick to undertake the study as his dissertation in 1979. Apprehensive at first, he gradually discovered more and more available sources, and pursued the topic in earnest. After much hunting and sweating, he has produced what is, to date, perhaps the most complete scholarly work on Mr. Deng's political career in any language.

As both the proponent of the topic and the supervising advisor, I am enormously satisfied with the shape and major findings of the dissertation, and most pleased with its speedy publication. Certain specific findings, such as Deng's real name, his role in the August 7 Conference, his participation as an observer in the 1935 Zunyi (Tsun-yi) conference, etc., are revealing and will add to our understading of CCP history. However, most important of all is Patrick's portrait of a real person that is peppery in temper, devoted as a Communist revolutionary, and practical and deft in his approach to problems, Emerging from the pages is a man whose unswerving conviction and pragmatism, only reinforced by his personal ordeals through 10 years of the radical reign of terror (1966-1976), provide a guiding force for China's present sweeping anti-Maoist reforms.

Unlike many a similar study, this political biography is, to say the least, not lopsided in its treatment of its hero. It shows no signs of an author being carried away by his own enthusiasm arising from his necessarily intense involvement with the subject. Patrick Lee offers, instead, a cool-headed and balanced analysis, while treating his reader to a massive parade of fascinatig facts about the fiery little man (under five feet tall) from Sichuan who, as Mao reputedly observed at one point, was to "shake the world." Among other things, our author finds Deng no great theoretician, which of course is no surprise in view of his pragmatic reputation ("It doesn't matter whether the cat is black or white, so long as it catches mice," as Deng is known to be fond of saying). Besides, Deng is found to be very different from both Mao and Zhou, which is also not surprising. But the author's discovery that Deng is economically liberal but politically conservative is, to me, refreshingly original. In the political domain, according to the author, Dent is at times more "orthodox" than Mao, such as on matters of Party discipline. Whereas Mao would occasionally go outside the Party to encourage external criticisms of Party cadres for their wrong attitudes or dereliction of duties, Deng would stick to the Leninist view that Party discipline is a matter purely within the Party itself.

This contrast may help explain why, contrary to the hopes of many for a Fifth Modernization (or democratization) in China, Deng ordered the abridgement of the Democratic Wall in Peking in late 1979, when it had turned from a vehicle for airing grievances against the Gang of Four into one for articulating the public's demands on the Dengist regime. The economic liberalization, nevertheless, persisted. This political-economic differentiation also provided a reason for our author's rather cautious conclusion regarding the future. The political conservative in Deng (namely, the Marxist ideological pull) may, in Patrick's view, work at odds with the economic liberal in him (the pull of his faith in private intrepreneurship).

The paradox allued to by Patrick Lee is not without its empir-

3

ical basis, in view of my own observations during a trip I made in the summer of 1984 as a guest of the Chinese National Academy of Social Sciences. I had expectations to meet with Mr. Deng in person and, in fact, was holding off writing this introduction until after the trip. In a last-minute change, however, I was received by Premier Zhao Ziyang, in the seashore resort of Beidaiho. I only hope that the switch had nothing to do with my involvement with this biographical study of Mr. Deng. Nonetheless, I was able to observe first-hand some very important and far-reaching changes, which gave me a more upbeat view of China for the moment, but also raised my concern about the reconciliation of what Mr. Deng is doing and what his ideology calls for.

I shall first report two important trends I observed. One was a deliberate modification or dilution of Marxist socialism, in favor of private entrepreneurship, which has led to the rise of a nascent, though still relatively insignificant, private sector of the economy. The other was the selective return of China's cultural legacy, obviously in support of the current Dengist efforts to "create a socialism best suited to Chinese circumstances and needs." Quite typical was the new prominence of traditional forms of art (like calligraphy and brush painting) and theater (such as Shaoxing Xi and renditions of historical dance and music, best captured in the "Tang: Changan" repertory). The intellectuals I met, besides, ostentatiously showed off their knowledge in traditional Chinese *belles lettres*.

The installation of the special economic zones (SEZ's), 14 of them throughout China, where greater elements of Western-type capitalism are allowed, further enhances the symbiosis of two different sectors competing with each other: one dominated by the state-own public enterprises, and the other by private enterprises.

As of the present, it seems, nobody, not even Mr. Deng himself, knows for sure what shape the competition between the two sectors will take and what the outcome will be. The Dengist team has embarked upon two measures to ensure that the trends just noted will continue beyond Deng's lifetime. One is a purposeful effort to widen the number of "beneficiaries" (and the extent of their benefits) from the Dengist reforms. The peasants are the first group to benefit from the new "responsibility system," in which they are allowed to keep the surplus they produce after meeting pre-set obligations. The next group of beneficiaries are the urban

4

workers, followed by the 15 million intellectuals and cadres. With the widening of the ranks of the beneficiaries, it is hoped that any future atempt to undo the Dengist reforms will run into opposition among the majority of the Chinese at all levels, who will have stakes in defending the Dengist system.

The other measure is a systematically staged and carefully managed decentralization, in the political sphere no less than in the economic. This measure is designed to make it extremely difficult for any opposing group to grab power in Peking and hope to carry the whole nation with them, as happened with the Gang of Four during the Cultural Revolution. If these measures work as expected, the Dengists can hope to make a much longer lastintg impact on China than did the Maoist era.

However, the unavoidable question still remains: At what point will the Dengist system, on the momentum of its own reforms, cease to be Marxist (socialist)? In other words when will the quantitative changes become a qualitative one? For example, peasants are now doing well because of the material incentives built in to the Dengist "responsibility system." Some peasants today, at least in Guangdong (Kwangtung), are well off enough not to have to till their land, but rent it out to "tenants" from poor areas. With the rent they collect, plus money remitted by overseas relatives in some cases, these well-off peasants individually or in groups are investing in small-scale enterprises producing consumer goods such as garments. Some other newly rich peasants, albeit in very special cases so far, had enough money to buy a second-hand "Shanghai" automobile and use it as a taxi in Guangzhou (Canton), bringing home the equivalent of U.S. $500 a month, nearly 10 times the wage of an unskilled worker before. If the trend continues, the private sector will inevitably expand.

Is it possible, then, that the private sector may become so large and unwieldly that, like the tail that wags the dog, it may eclipse the public sector? When that happens, will it in fact have transformed the socialist system into quite something else, while the name of "socialism" or even "Chinese socialism" may continue? I put this question to my hosts in China. Never once did I hear a satisfacory answer, although nobody took issue with me. The best official answer was that (a) the socialist economy, would not be overhelmed by the small private sector allowed to exist; and (b) before the private sector could grow to a position to threaten the primarily socialist economy, the government would have acted to maintain a controlled balance. Moreover, I was told, ownership and management (or utilization) are separate in the current Dengist dual system. The land is still state-owned, for example, although peasants are given the utilization rights.

Despite these official assurances, however, there seem to be two remote possibilities lying ahead for China after Deng. First, the bold dual-track system, which requires a very delicate balancing of the existing public sector and a growing private sector, may lose its balance when the latter becomes too robust for the former. The so called "Chinese socialism" the Dengists are now consciously building would, in that eventuality, be socialist only in name and become at best a mixed economy with a very weak or ineffectual public sector. The second possiblity is that *on the eve* of the qualitative transformation just mentioned, the Dengists could be most vulnerable to attacks by more dogmatic opponents who feel threatened when the system is perceived to be making that quantum leap to capitalism. Whether or not this dogmatist revolt would be successful depends on whether or not the Dengists will have created large enough numbers of "beneficiaries" from their ecomic liberalization program.

Between the two possible courses of development, it seems to me, the Dengists probably have better control over the second than the first, if one believes that economic forces, once released, like Genie out of the bottle, will have a power not likely to be contained. In fact, if that eventuality comes, that is, if China should ultimately acquire a private-enterprise-predominant economy, it would only be a blessing to the one billion Chinese people. Deng, in that event, would be remembered as their true "liberator" from the Communist yoke, however ironic it may sound,

In any event, Deng's impact will unquestionably be great. He will be remembered in history either as Mao's nemesis, at a minimum, or, at a maximum, as China's liberator from Communism. For the average Chinese, to paraphrase Deng's famous remark, the Dengist cat will do well as long as it catches mice. For the outside world, it means that it is incumbent upon us to gain a better and closer understanding of Deng and his program. For that purpose, this volume will prove to be an authoritative source.

James C. Hsiung
New York University

6

Foreword

This is a study of the political life of Teng Hsiao-p'ing (Deng Xiaoping).* While in Marxist theory the growth of Socialism is largely determined by economics, in practice it is the command of political power that determines the fate of Communist countries such as the Soviet Union and China. In a stable democracy, a change in leadership may be followed by a change of policy. Such changes are primarily reformist in nature. The value system and the fundamental structure of the society remain unchanged. This is not the case in the Communist world. Whenever there is a change of leadership in a Communist country, it may be followed by a radical change of policy that alters the entire system. Thus observers and researchers of Communist politics are frequently most interested in such issues as the succession of leaders and the background of an established leader. The reason is simple: in a totalitiarian system, the power of an established leader is enormous. Teng Hsiao-p'ing is no doubt the paramount leader of China today. What he does will touch the lives of 1,000,000,000 Chinese. He

---

* The Pinyin system of Chinese names and places was not adopted extensively by publishers when the author began writing this book. Thus the spellings of Chinese proper names in this book are in observance to the Wade-Giles system.

is determined to modernize the country by the end of the century.

Teng is a unique figure among Communist leaders. He has been purged, and then reinstated, three times. He is not a philosopher, but a quick-witted aphorism maker. His saying — "As long as the cat can catch mice, it doesn't matter whether it is white or black" — has been quoted frequently by friends and enemies alike. His refusal to assume a top formal position in the government and Party is highly unusual in the Communist world.

At age 16 Teng, the son of a landlord, left home and studied abroad. He converted to Marxism in France and returned to China to serve under the revolutionary Christian general Feng Yu-hsiang. At 25 he led a major uprising in Kwangsi. He became, and then remained for 12 years, the Political Commissar of the Red Army during the Japanese War. For ten years he was the General Secretary of the Chinese Communist Party. Once a confidant and a close friend of Mao Tse-tung, he became Mao's enemy during the Chairman's last years.

Teng belongs to the first generation of Chinese Communists. As early as the 1920s he actively participated in the Communist revolution. In addition to leading uprisings, he helped build communes in the interior of China, planned military campaigns, and participated in Party power struggles. Since the founding of the People's Republic, he has been absorbed in strengthening socialist Chinese society. He has occupied key positions in the Party, the government, and the army, giving him a wide range of leadership experience. Of the many important events in which he played a major role, some of the most critical were: the Kao Kang-jao Shu-shih case, the Eighth Party Congress, the economic reconstruction in the early sixties, the Sino-Soviet debate, the Four Modernizations, and the normalization of the Sino-U.S. relations. In 1977 he became the de facto ruler of China. He made a radical shift in the policy that was established by Mao and his followers.

The posts Teng formerly held included Vice Chairman of

the Chinese Communist Party, General Secretary of the Party, Vice Premier, Chairman of the Political Consultation Conference, Chief-of-Staff, Minister of Finance, and Political Commissar of the Second Field Army. His present positions include Director of the Party Central Advisory Council, Chairman of the Party Military Commission, and Chairman of the State Military Commission. An examination of Teng's career will not only provide us with deeper insight into the history of the Chinese Communist Party (CCP), but may also enable us to predict future developments with some degree of accuracy.

Although there have been numerous biographies on major CCP figures such as Mao Tse-tung, Chou En-lai, Lin Piao, Chu Te, Liu Shao-ch'i, and Chiang Ch'ing, to date no detailed scholarly biography of Teng Hsiao-p'ing has appeared. A special study of Teng's life is therefore absolutely necessary.

The author wishes to examine some of the controversial questions surrounding this complex figure. What kind of person is he? How deep is his understanding of the West? What is his relation with Mao? Who adheres more to Marxism, Mao or Teng, and what is the point of divergence? Why was Teng able to be reinstated after purges again and again? In terms of ideology, what is Teng's contribution to Chinese Communism and to Marxism in general? What is the outlook for success of Teng's Four Modernizations? The author also compares Teng with Chou En-lai, Liu Shao-chi'i, Lin Piao, and Hua Kuo-feng, all of whom had been prominent leaders of Chinese Communist politics.

In writing about communist figures the most difficult to overcome is the problem of reliable materials. China has never published documents concerning its leaders and their private lives. Teng is no exception. Even his real name and the date of his birth are subjects of debate among scholars. Fortunately, during the Cultural Revolution, the Red Guards, in their struggle against Teng — "the second greatest capitalist roader in the Party" — published many previously unknown facts about him. With Teng's reemergence in 1973, and especially after his second comeback in 1977, there have been an ever increasing number of reports about him coming from both Chinese and foreign sources.

The major sources of information in this book are drawn from Teng's writings, Red Guard pamphlets and related books and articles.

A word about the Red Guard pamphlets is necessary. The major problem with using these materials is that they were designed to descredit Teng, since the Red Guards regarded him as an enemy to be beaten at any cost. In using these materials it is necessary to corroborate them with other contemporary sources. If this is not possible they must be checked against facts established later. These materials are valuable because they were furnished by the Central Cultural Revolutionary Group headed by Chiang Ch'ing, the wife of Mao Tse-tung. The authors enjoyed access to secret files which contained materials found nowhere else. It is after weighing these considerations that I have utilized these documents.

I wish to express my gratitude to Professor James C. Hsiung of New York University for his advice and encouragement.

Ching Hua Lee

Chapter 1

The Family (1904-1920)

Accounts differ as to the birth place, the birth date, and the original name of Teng Hsiao-p'ing. It is generally agreed that Teng is Szechuanese, but the precise county in which he was born has been a subject of debate. Some writers indicate that he was born in Chia-ting;[1] others belive that he was born in Chiang-an;[2] and still others say that he was born in Kuang-an.[3] The third account is now known to be true.[4] Teng was a native of the Kuang-an county village of Hsieh-hsing, sixty miles

---

1. As recorded by Edgar Snow. Snow's contention is accepted by reference writers Howard Boorman and Winston L. Y. Yang. See Edgar Snow, *Red Star Over China* (N. Y.: Grove Press, Inc., 1961), p. 498; Howard Boorman, ed., *Biographical Dictionary of Republic of China*, Vol. III (N. Y.: Columbia Univ. Press, 1970), p. 252; Boorman, "Teng Shiao-p'ing: A Political Profile," p. 109; Winston L. Y. Yang, "Teng Shiao-p'ing," in *1978 Yearbook of the Encyclopedia Americana* (Danbury, Connecticut: Americana Corporation, 1978), p. 125.

2. See, for example, *Chung-kung Jen-ming-lu* (Who is Who in Communist China) (Taipei: Kuo-chi Kuan-hsi Yen-chiu-so 1967).

3. Refer to Li Huang, *Hsueh-tun-shih Hui-i-lu* (Memoirs from the Ignorant Student's Studio) (Taipei: Chuan-chi Wen-hsueh Ch'u-pan-she, 1973), p. 105; Donald W. Klein and Anne B. Clark, *Biographic Dictionary of Chinese Communism*, Vol. II (Cambridge: Harvard Univ. Press, 1970, p. 819; and *Chung-kung Jen-ming-lu*, 1978 edition, p. 942.

4. According to the September 14, 1920 edition of the Shanghai's *Shih-shih Hsin Pao* (The Current News), Teng was said to be a native of Kuang-an. In a recent publication, the above is confirmed. See Chang Yun-hou, et al., eds., *Liu Fa Ch'in-kung Chien-hseuh Yµn-tung* (The Study and Work Movement to

north of Chungking. Kuang-an is a famed tangerine-producing region in eastern Szechuan, located at the juncture of three Yangtze River tributaries — the Chia-ling, the P'ei, and the Ch'u.

At least four birthdates have been suggested for Teng: 1896, 1902, and 1904.[5] On his application for a visa to go to Japan in 1978, Teng disclosed that he was born on August 22, 1904.[6]

The question of Teng's real name has also caused some controversy. Much incorrect information seems to originate with Li Huan, a veteran of the Statist Chinese Youth Party. Li was a student in France during the twenties. As related in his memoirs, he welcomed Teng in Marseilles upon Teng's arrival from China as a member of the "Work and Study" group. According to Li, "Teng was not then called Teng Hsiao-p'ing; he was called Kan Tse-Kao. Those who came with him called him 'Hsiao Kan'; meaning 'Young Kan'. When I made a roll call, Teng answewered me as 'Kan Tse-kao'." Later in an overseas student meeting Teng was introduced to Li by Chou En-lai as "Teng Hsiao-p'ing." Li thus concluded that Teng was originally called "Kan Tse-kao," and "Teng Hsiao-p'ing" was the

France), Vol. I (Shanghai: Jen-min Ch'u-pan-she, 1980) p. 775. The pamphlets circulated by the Red Guards during the Cultural Revolution also maintained that Teng was born in Kuang-an. See "Chieh-k'ai Teng Hsiao-p'ing Te Fan-ko-ming Lao-ti" ("To Expose Teng Hsiao-p'ing's Counter-Revolutionary Past"), reprinted in Teng Hsiao-p'ing (Taipei: Kuo-li Cheng-chih Ta-hsueh Tung-ya Yen-chiu-so, 1978), p. 1; "Teng Hsiao-p'ing Yen-i Ti-i-Hui" ("The Romance of Teng Hsiao-p'ing, Chapter 1"), originally from a Red Guard pamphlet, reprinted in Chan-wang (Look, Hong Kong), June 16, 1975, p. 32; and "Teng Hsiao-p'ing Tsui-hsing Tiau-cha Pao-kao" ("A Report of the Crimes of Teng Hsia-p'ing"), reprinted in C. B. Kok ed., Teng Hsiao-p'ing (Hong Kong: Chung-kuo Wen-hua Chung-hsin, 1977), p. 25.

5. Consecutively: Edgar Snow, Random Notes on Red China 1936-1945 (Cambridge: Harvard Univ. Press, 1971), p. 137; Boorman, Biographical Dictionary, p. 252; Chung-kung Jen-ming-lu, 1978 edition, Snow, Red Star, p. 498 and Klein and Clark, Vol. II, p. 821.

6. See Hua-ch'iao Jih-pao (China Daily News, New York), October 11,1978. This was the first time the Chinese Government disclosed to the outside world Teng's birth date. The Red Guard pamphlets also used 1904 as the birth date of Teng. See "Chien-k'ai Teng Hsiao-p'ing Te Fan-ko-ming Lao-ti," p. 4.

name he used after he joined the Communist Party.[7]

Li's assertion that Teng's original name was "Kan Tse-kao" is the most popularly accepted version today.[8] But it is incorrect. During the Cultural Revolution Red Guard pamphlets published a detailed family history of Teng, asserting that all his relatives and ancestors used "Teng" as their family name.[9] While it is possible that Teng might have changed his entire name (both the family and the given name) in order to disguise himself, it is impossible that all those related to him would have changed their surname too. Moreover, Li's recollections are questionable. Li states that Teng came to Marsailles in July of 1920,[10] but Teng did not actually arrive until the end of October.[11] Li said that there were some 200 Chinese students on board the incoming ship but in reality only 89 Chinese students were on board the passenger ship in which Teng travelled.[12] Li said the group included students from the north and from Kwangtung. This contradicts the fact that all but four students were Szechuanese.[13]

Teng's original name was Teng Hsi-hsien.[14] His parents

---

7. Li Huang, *Hui-i-lu*, p. 106.

8. Consult Chi Hsin, *Teng Hsiao-p'ing*, (Hong Kong: Chung Hua Book Co., 1978), p. 3; *Chung-kung Jen-ming-lu*, 1968 edition; Chou Hsun, et al., *Teng Hsiao-p'ing* (Hong-kong: Kuang Chiao Ching Ch'u-pan-she, 1979), p. 65; Yen Ching-wen, "Chi-shang Chi-hsia Te Teng Hsiao-p'ing" ("The Ups and Downs of Teng Hsiao-p'ing"), *Ming Pao Yueh-k'an* (Ming Pao Monthly, Hong Kong), May 1974, p. 22; Chien Erh-ch'ing, "Pen-shi' Yu T'i-kao" ("Ability and Height"), *Ming Pao* (Hong Kong), February 13, 1979; *New York Times*, January 29, 1979; and *Time*, January 1, 1979, p. 22.

9. "Teng Hsiao-p'ing Yen-i Ti-i-hui;" "Teng Hsiao-p'ing Tsui-hsing Tiao-cha Pao-kao;" and "Chieh-k'ai Teng Hsiao-p'ing Te Fai-ko-ming Lao ti".

10. Li Huan, *Hui-i-lu*, p. 65.

11. Chang Yun-hou, et al., eds., p. 812; and *Shih-shih Hsin-pao*, September 14, 1920.

12. *Shih-shih Hsin-pao*, September 14, 1920.

13. Of the remaining four students one came from Hunan and three from Kiangsu. See *Min-kuo Jih-pao* (The Republic Daily News), September 11, 1920. The news was compiled in a text by Chang Yun-hou, et al., eds., Vol. I, p. 774.

14. See "Teng Hsiao-p'ing Tsui-hsing Tiao-cha Pao-kao," p. 25. Also, Chiang Tse-min, a schoolmate of Teng Hsiao-p'ing at the French Preparatory

called him "Hsi-hsien" hoping that he would become a sage someday. He continued to use this name when he left for France[15] but changed it to "Teng Hsiao-p'ing" when he later joined the Communist group. He preferred to call himself "hsiao" ("little") because the word also meant "young".[16] Later when he was organizing rebellion in Kwangsi he adopted the name "Teng Pin."[17] At that time it was common practice for the Communists to use different names to protect themselves from investigation.

After their conquest of China, the Manchus encouraged a large immigration to Szechuan which had been depopulated by wars with the Mings. The Teng family was said to come from Kwangtung.[18] They established their reputation during the reign of Ch'ien-lung when a Teng Shih-min earned the honorable title of Hanlin and was later promoted to Supervisor of the Judicial Department. Teng Hsiao-P'ing's father, Wen-ming, was a landlord who annually received some 26,000 kilograms of grain from his fields. Teng Wen-ming was a believer of the Wu Tzu Chiao, a local religious sect of Buddhism and Taoism, and

School, recalled that Teng was then called Teng Hsi-hsien. See *Fu Fa Ch'in-kung-chien-hsueh Yun-tung Shih-liao* (Historical Materials of the Study and Work Movement to France), Vol. III (Peking: Peking Ch'u-pan-she, 1981), p. 449.

15. In a list produced by the *Shih-shih Hsin-pao* on September 14, 1920, there appeared the name "Teng Hsi-hsien" among the students boarding the ship for France. The list was reprinted in Chang Yun-hou et al., eds., Vol. I, p. 775, and a footnote specified that "Teng Hsi-hsien" was "Teng Hsiao-p'ing".

16. Li Huang, *Hui-i-lu*, p. 106. Teng said he used this name when he engaged in underground activities during the turbulent period of warlordism. See *Hua-ch'iao Jih-pao*, February 9, 1979. Teng's remark matched what Li recollected in his memoir.

17. *Kuang-hsi Ko-ming Hui-i-lu* (Recollections of the Kwangsi Revolutions) (Nanning, Kwangsi: Jen-min Ch'u-pan-she, 1959), pp. 135-136. See also "Yu-chiang Shang-hsia Hung-ch'i Yang" ("Red Flags Fly Over the Right River"), in *Ko-ming Wen-wu* (Relics of Revolutions, Peking) September, 1978, p. 17. The article also reprinted a memorandum signed by "Teng Pin," who was the Political Commissar of the Kwangsi Red Army.

18. Chi Hsin, *Teng Hsiao-p'ing*, p. 3; *New York Times*, January 29, 1979.

had been a member of the clandestine *Ko Lau Hui* (Brother's Society). An influential man of the region, he established good relations with the Szechuan warlord, Lo Tse-chou. In 1928 he was made a regiment leader of Kwang-an, heading some six to seven hundred soldiers. In the following year he was appointed advisor to the district union of the neighboring eight counties. Teng Wen-ming died in 1938.[19]

Teng Wen-ming had been married four times. The full names of three of his wives — Chang, T'an, and Hsiao — cannot be traced. Only one, Hsia Po-ken, is known. Chang, T'an, and Hsiao died years ago, and whether Hsia is alive is uncertain. Chang bore no children but adopted a girl later called Teng Hsien-fu. Hsiao was survived by a son named Hsien-ch'ing, who worked as a financial administrator in the Chinese Communist Party (CCP) Southwestern Bureau after "liberation." Hsia, who was Hsiao-p'ing's senior by only two years, had two daughters: Hsien-jung, who died early, and Hsien-ch'un, who later worked in Tientsin. Hsiao-p'ing, the eldest son in the family, was the son of T'an. He had two brothers, Teng Ken and Teng Shu-p'ing, and an elder sister Teng Hsien-lieh.[20]

Like most eldest sons in Chinese families, Teng Hsiao-p'ing was the one most favored. When he became prominent Teng remained faithful to his family and treated his relatives well. For instance, he asked widow Hsia (his stepmother) to live with him in Chungking after liberation. Later when he was transferred to work in Peking, he took Hsia with him and treated her as his own mother.

---

19. "Teng Hsiao-p'ing Yen-i Ti-i-hui," p. 32; and "Chieh-k'ai Teng Hsiao-p'ing Te Fan-ko-ming Lao-ti," p. 1.

20. Wang Hsuan, *Kuan-yu Teng Hsiao-p'ing* (About Teng Hsiao-p'ing) (Taipei: Shih-chieh Fan-kung Lien-meng Chung-hua Min-kuo Fen-hui, 1978), pp. 13-14; and "Teng Hsiao-p'ing Te She-hui Kuan-hsi" ("The Social Relationship of Teng Hsiao-p'ing"), a Red Guard pamphlet, reprinted in *Teng Hsiao-p'ing*, p. 18; *Pei-mei Jih-pao* (The Peimei News, New York), January 29, 1979; and *Fu Fa Ch'in-kung-chien-hsueh Yun-tung Shih-liao*, Vol. III, p. 449.

Teng Ken, six years Teng's junior, had been a teacher in a Kuang-an girls' middle school, and had once edited a Kuomintang-owned newspaper. In 1941, Teng Ken went to Yenan at his brother's request and joined the staff of the *Hsinhua Daily News*. After 1949, Teng Ken quickly gained the position of Deputy Mayor of Chungking. In 1966, under the patronage of his brother, Teng Ken was transferred to Wuhan to assume the post of Vice-Mayor.[21]

The younger brother, Teng Shu-p'ing, was eight years younger than Teng. He inherited the family's properties after the father died. Shu-p'ing became the village headman and worked as the secretary of a Kuomintang local bureau. After liberation, in the fear that Shu-p'ing and his wife and other family members would be purged, Teng sent the couple to a cadre school and moved other family members to Chungking. Shu-p'ing stayed in a "revolutionary university" for about half a year and was later transferred to Kweichow to assume the post of Deputy County Magistrate. In the hard years after 1958, Teng frequently provided for his brother's daily needs. During the Cultural Revolution, Shu-p'ing was severely criticized and, unable to bear the harassment, killed himself on March 15, 1967.[22]

Teng Hsiao-p'ing was married three times. His wives were all Communists. He first married Chang Ch'ien-yuan in 1927 in Shanghai. Chang later died from a miscarriage.[23] The second wife was Chin Wei-ying, whom he married in 1932, in Kiangsi; they were later separated.[24] There were no children from his first two marriages.

21. "Teng Hsiao-p'ing Te She-hui kuan-hsi," p. 19; and "Teng Hsiao-p'ing Tsui-hsing Tiao-cha Pao-kao," pp. 30-32.

22. "Teng Hsiao-p'ing Tsui-hsing Tiao-cha Pao-kao," pp. 26-29; and "Teng Hsiao-p'ing Te She-hui Kuan-hsi," p. 19.

23. "Chieh-k'ai Teng Hsiao-p'ing Te Fan-ko-ming Lao'ti."

24. Ts'ai Hsiao-ch'ien, *Chiang-hsi Su-ch'u Hung-chun Hsi-ts'uan Hui-i-lu* (The Kiangsi Soviet and the Long march, A Memoir) (Hong Kong: Ta Chung-hua Chu-pan-she, 1970), p. 182.

Cho Lin, Teng's present wife, is twelve years younger than he. Born to a rich family in Hsuan-wei, Yunnan, she was originally called P'u Ch'iung-ying. Her father, P'u Tsai-ting, was a renowned ham maker. Cho Lin first encountered Marxism when she was in high school. She loved sports and was selected to represent her province in the national Olympics. Later she stayed in Peking and, after graduation from high school, was admitted to the Department of Physics at Peking University (Peita). It was during her college days that Cho was converted to Marxism. Before she could complete her education at Peita, the Sino-Japanese War broke out. She went to Yenan and enrolled in the Anti-Japanese Military and Political University. There she met Teng, who was then the Political Commissar of the 129th Division and they married in 1940. After their marriage, she changed her name to Pu Cho-lin and worked in the Women's Committee of the CCP North China Bureau. Cho Lin is the name she adopted in the seventies.[25] Cho since then has become the family name.

Cho Lin's father died in the early fifties, sometime before the land redistribution campaign began. The Cho family was denounced as counter revolutionary in those days. Cho's brother, P'u Te-san, the head of the family, was sentenced to a life term in prison. He was later released but subsequently imprisoned again during the Cultural Revolution. He suffered severe torture and soon died in prison.[26]

Cho and Teng have five childdren, two boys (Teng P'u-fang[27] and Teng Chih-fang[28]) and three girls (Teng Lin,[29] Teng

---

25. Chou Hsun et al., pp. 64-65; and the *Ch'ing-nien Chan'shih Pao* (Young Warrior Daily, Taipei), October 3, 1979; and *Teng Hsiao-p'ing* (Hong Kong: Ming-jen Tsung-kan She, 1978), pp. 23 and 25.

26. Chou Hsun, et al., p. 65.

27. Teng P'u-fang enrolled in the Department of Physics at Peking University not long before the onset of the Cultural Revolution. During the Cultural Revolution he was severely criticized. One day he fell from the stairs and wounded his spinal cord, thus paralyzing his lower body. The school authority accused him of trying to commit suicide, but P'u-fang asserted that he was pushed by someone. The accident crippled him permanently. In 1980 P'u-fang

Nan,[30] and Teng Jung[31]. The three girls are married and Teng Lin and Teng Nan each has a child, who reside occasionally with their grandfather.

Cho Lin has never been active in politics. She appeared in public only when Teng received foreign visitors. In recent years, she has accompanied Teng to the United States and Japan. In 1980 it was said that she worked as an advisor in the CCP's Military Commission.[32]

In 1905, when Teng was one year old, the civil examination

---

was sent to California and, in 1981, to Canada to receive medical treatment. It was said that Teng often listens to his advice. See Ying Lan, "Teng Hsiao-p'ing Te Erh-nu-men," ("Children of Teng Hsiao-p'ing"), in *Cheng Ming* (Debate, Hong Kong), February 1, 1979, p. 30; *Hua-ch'iao Jih-pao*, May 29, 1981; and Informant No. 2.

28. Chih-fang is the youngest of the five children. During the Cultural Revolution he was sent to the countryside. After Teng's comeback in 1973, he was admitted to Peking University. Following graduation, he worked in the Optics and Electronics Research Center in Peking. In 1976, when Teng was disgraced for the second time, Chih-fang was sent to a labor camp. He came to the United States in January 1980 and is studying for a doctorate in physics at the University of Rochester. See Ying La, "Erh-nu-men," pp. 30-31; *Chung-yang Jih-pao* (Central Daily, Taipei), June 20, 1979; *Newsweek*, September 15, 1980; and Jan Wang "China's Leap to American Campuses," *The New York Times Magazine*, November 15, 1981, p. 86.

29. Bearing a striking resemblance to her father, Teng Lin is small and round-faced. She graduated from the Central Art Insitute, majoring in Chinese painting. She is currently engaged in art work, and is regarded as one of the most promising artists in China today. Some of her pieces were recently exhibited in the New York Wally Findlay Gallery in December, 1981 along with other Chinese artists. See Yao Sheng-hui and Ts'ui Chiang, "Fang Ch'ing-nien Hua-chia Teng Hsiao-p'ing Nu-erh Teng Lin," ("An Interview with Teng Hsiao-p'ing's Daughter Teng Lin, the Young Artist") in *Ching Pao* (The Mirror, Hong Kong), September 9, 1980, p. 47; and *Shih-chieh Jih-pao* (World Journal, New York), January 5, 1982.

30. It is said that Teng Nan was the most beloved daughter of the Tengs. She frequently accompanied her father in public appearances. In 1964, she was admitted to the Department of Physics, Peking University. During the Cultural Revolution she was sent to the coutryside and was later married to a Kiangsi peasant. She has a daughter. See Ying Lan, "Ehr-nu-men," p. 31; and *Chung-yabg Jih-pao*, June 20, 1979.

31. Teng Jung was sent to a village in 1969. She later graduated from the Peking Medical School. See Ying Lan, "Ehr-nu-men," p. 31.

32. *Shih-chieh Jih-pao*, March 14, 1980.

system was abolished. A more Western-oriented education system was established to replace the traditional one and modern schools were built. After studying for a few years with a family tutor, Teng enrolled in one of these progressive schools.

As the old educational system waned, more and more students went abroad to study. The ancient empire was in decline, and patriotic students looked to western education as a way to help save their country. In 1912, a group of educators and politicians headed by Li Shih-tseng (who had spent many years in France) founded in Peking a "Society of Thrift-Study in France," with the specific purpose of sending Chinese students to France at modest expense. During and immediately after the First World War, France was short of laborers. Thus Li and his colleagues promoted the idea that students should go to France to exchange work for the opportunity to study. The program itself was known as "Diligent Work and Thrift Study" ("Ch'in-kung Chien-hsueh"). In 1916 and 1917, a Sino-French Educational Society was founded in both Peking and Paris to administer the program. The Society also established other branches in China to encourage as many students as possible to participate in the program. In order to prepare the students before going abroad, special schools were established in such large cities as Peking, Shanghai, Canton and Chungking. Students were required to take a one- or two-year course and were exempted from paying all school fees. Whoever graduated from the preparatory schools and could afford two hundred silver dollars for travel expenses could join the "Work-and-Study" program.[33]

The response was enthusiastic. During its heyday, from March 1919 until the end of 1920, tens of hundreds of students participated in the program. Most of the students were high-school age, although a few came from primary schools, colleges, and other walks of life. The oldest among them was 54.[34]

---

33. Chang Yun-hou, et al., eds., Vol. I, pp. 4-5; and Li Huang, *Hui-i-lu*, pp. 62 and 80.

34. She was Ko Chien-hao, mother of Ts'ai Ho-sen, a Communist veteran and close friend of Mao Tse-tung.

Twenty of them were under 15, and the youngest was only 10. In terms of ethnic composition, Szechuanese made up the majority of the student body, numbering some five hundred people. This was due to the publicity efforts of Wu Yu-chang, one of the organizers of the "Society of Thrift-Study" who was himself Szechuanese.[35]

In 1919, Teng graduated from middle school and enrolled in the Chungking preparatory school.[36] Considering that the 1911 Revolution broke out when Teng was still too young to understand its significance, we can say that the Revolution had little impact on him. However, the outbreak of the May Fourth Movement in 1919 did excite Teng and stir his awareness of politics and society. Years later, recalling his motive for going to France, he said: "We felt that China was weak and we wanted to make her strong. We thought the way to do it it was through modernization. So we went to the West to learn."[37]

The prep school used a modest temple in Chungking as a classroom. It was poorly equipped. The major subjects taught were French, Chinese, mathematics and a practical course in industrial arts. According to Chiang Tse-min, a schoolmate of Teng's, Teng was "energetic, quiet, and studied very hard."[38] The students participated in the nationwide protest against the Japanese during the May Fourth Movement. They called for the boycott of Japanese goods and the expulsion of "traitors" — those Chinese ministers deemed pro-Japanese. Teng's uncle, Teng Shao-sheng, studied in the same school and later went to France with his nephew.[39] According to Li Huang, Nieh Jung-chen (Teng's superior in the mid-1930's and later commander of North China Field Army) studied in the same school, in the

---

35. Chang Yun-hou, et al., eds., Vol. I, p. 2; and Li Huang, *Hui-i-lu*, p. 72.

36. "Chien-k'ai Teng Hsiao-p'ing Te Fan-ko-ming Lao-ti," p. 1; and "Teng Hsiao-p'ing Yen-i Ti-i-hui," p. 32.

37. *New York Times*, February 1, 1979.

38. *Fu Fa Ch'in-kung-chien-hsueh Yun-tung Shih-liao*, Vol. III, p. 448.

39. Ibid., p. 449.

same class with Teng.[40] That account is false. Nieh went to France in 1919 and Teng did not arrive until the next year.

Teng graduated from prep school in the summer of 1920. A public examination was held to select candidates who would be funded by grants (funds were collected from the enlightened gentry). Teng himself was not awarded a grant but his uncle was.[41] In September, Teng, together with other graduates from the same school, and accompanied by an officer of the Sino-French Educational Society, went to Shanghai. They stayed there for five days and then boarded a French passenger ship, the *André Lepon,* on the morning of September 11 heading for France.[42]

The "Work-and-Study" Plan attracted the attention of many people, and newspapers often printed stories about the students going abroad. Here again should be pointed out some of the inaccuracies of Li Huang's work, which, unfortunately, has been widely adopted by historians and biographers of modern Chinese history. Li claimed that Teng was the leader of the 89-student group,[43] but the actual leaders were three of the government grantees.[44] Li also contended that Ch'en I (formerly Foreign Minister of China, now deceased) was on the same passenger ship with Teng,[45] but Ch'en had already arrived in France a year before.[46]

Unlike Mao's adolescence, which was recorded by Edgar Snow,[47] there is little material available on Teng's childhood or early teens. Thus we are handicapped in attempting to pursue any detailed study of the effects of those formative years on

---

40. Li Huang, *Hui-i-lu,* p. 105

41. *Shih-shih Hsin-pao,* September 14, 1920.

42. *Min-kuo Jih-pao,* September 11, 1920; and *Fu Fa Chi'in-kung Chien-hsueh Yun-tung,* Vol. III, p. 449.

43. Li Huang, *Hui-i-lu,* p. 106-107.

44. *Min-kuo Jih-pao,* September 11, 1920. They were Wu (or Li) Yu-san, Yuan Wen-ch'ing and Wang Hsing-chih.

45. Li Huang, *Hui-i-lu,* pp. 65 and 105.

46. Chang Yun-hou, et al., eds. Vol. I, pp. 522-524.

47. Snow, *Red Star,* pp. 129-149.

Teng's psychological profile. Teng's childhood appeared to have been happy and he was loved and protected as indicated by his harmonious relationship with family members in later years. By contrast, Mao in his youth had cultivated a hatred for his father.[48] Not surprisingly, the adult Mao found himself at ease with the rebel's cause. Mao remained for his whole life an anti-authority advocate. Touting "to rebel is justified," the restless Mao, at the old age of 73, launched the violent Cultural Revolution. One of his aims was to encourage youth to challenge authority, to destroy the establishment, and smash the Party apparatus. Teng would never go to such an extreme. He observed discipline, respected his seniors, and frequently stood on the side of authority. If Mao was the unfaithful son who wanted to kill his "father" (the Party), Teng was the protected child who always found "home" (the Party, again) a shelter of warmth and safety. Liu Shao-ch'i also came from a background similar to Teng. He too experienced a caring and warm family life during his childhood. Thus he, like Teng, identified the Party with "home."

On the other hand, both Mao and Teng were the eldest sons in the family. In the traditional Chinese family system, the eldest son enjoys great authority. He holds an important position in the family which is perhaps next only to the father. When the father dies, he is the acknowledged inheritor of the family property along with the father's responsibilities: to guide the family and to provide the family with livelihood and shelter. He is respected not only by his siblings, but his mother as well. He cannot be challenged and his will must be observed. Very often the eldest son develops a strong and resolute character. Despite their many differences, both Mao and Teng shared this common "authoritativeness" in their character. They were difficult to sway. They were so sure and self-confident of themselves that they were intolerant of opposition. They had, in their political life, been forced to admit their "faults," but they would commit the same "mistakes" again when they were back in power. Chou

---

48. Ibid., pp. 132-133.

22

En-lai, by comparison, was always ready to compromise. Chou had to live in his uncle's house when he was still very young. There he learned how to be flexible in order to win the favor of others.[49]

Teng came from the interior of China, the Szechuan province, which is surrounded by mountains on all sides, was fairly self-sufficient, and until very recently constituted a separate entity in Chinese history. Thus the Szechuanese developed a character that other inlanders may share: sincere, practical, and hardworking but also conventional, stubborn and unimaginative. We can find these traits in Teng's personality too. In contrast, Chou En-lai grew up in the coastal trading cities of Shanghai and Tientsin.[50] He was more worldly, adaptive, imaginative, and sensitive.

We find Teng rather old-fashioned in many ways. In comparison to some of his colleagues, Teng seemed to observe the traditional moral codes. He treated his family members well, a responsibility that an eldest son is expected to assume. He married three times, but so far as we know was never an unfaithful husband. We have noted that his first wife died of a miscarriage. His second wife left him at a time when he experienced his first political setback. He married Cho Lin in 1940, and the couple remained loyal to each other even during the turbulent years of the Cultural Revolution when in many instances husband and wife would seek a divorce to avoid being purged. He took very good care of his children. He sent his elder son — who was crippled during the Cultural Revolution — abroad for better medical treatment. His second son is now studying physics in the U. S. A. and one of his daughters has been married to a Chinese diplomat stationed in the U. S. A.

Mao, on the other hand, was an unconventional figure. He married four times. Although he loved Yang K'ai-hui, Mao

---

49. Kai-yu Hsu, *Chou En-lai* (New York: Doubleday and Company, Inc., 1968), pp. 5-7.

50. Ibid., pp. 5, 10 and 15.

lived happily with Ho Chih-chen in Chingkangshan in the twenties, while Yang was left alone to care for the children under the trying reign of Ho Chien in Hunan. In Yenan, he abandoned Ho and fell in love with Chiang Ch'ing. Chou Enlai was another romantic at heart. His romance with a German maid (who is said to have given birth to a child for Chou) is still a mysterious love story that biographers of Chou are eager to know.

It is dangerous to rely too heavily on this kind of psychological analysis without additional material. The above observations are the most that can be suggested from what is known about Teng's upbringing.

Chapter 2

In France (1920-1926)

It took about 40 days for the passenger ship *André Lepon* to travel from Shanghai to Marseilles via Hong Kong, Saigon, Singapore, Colombo, and the Suez Canal. Teng's group arrived in Marseilles at the end of October, 1920.[1] Staff from the Sino-French Educational Society met them at the port and accompanied them to Paris.[2]

In theory the students from China were supposed to work and study at the same time. In reality this was not the case. An economic recession hit Europe in 1920 and the situation grew worse in the first half of 1921. The Chinese students had difficulty finding jobs. Of the 1,600 Chinese students in France at that time, nearly four-fifths were unemployed. Without a proper income they could not afford to study in schools. In addition, the Chinese students had to overcome a language handicap. Thus, not more than half of the students reported to schools.[3] In 1936, Teng told journalist Edgar Snow that he did not attend school in France but was forced to spend his five years there as a worker.[4]

1. Chang Yun-hou, et al.,eds., *Liu Fa Ch'in-kung Chien-hseuh Yun-tung,* Vol. I, p. 812.
2. *Fu Fa Ch'in-kung-chien-hsueh Yun-tung Shih-liao,* Vol. III, p. 451.
3. Chang Yun-hou, Vol. I, p. 14.
4. Snow, *Random Notes,* p. 137; and Snow, *Red Star,* p. 498.

Teng worked at the Schneider-Creusot Arms Factory. Other people who worked there and who later became Communist leaders were Chao Shih-yen, Li Li-san, Nieh Jung-chen and Fu Chung.[5] The factory employed some 30,000 workers of which one-third were Chinese and, of these, 150 were Chinese student workers. Teng was reported to have also worked in a rubber shoe factory in Montargis, a small town one hour south of Paris by train. He served as the cook for the Chinese student group living in the town.[6] As unskilled laborers, the Chinese students had no choice but to do heavy manual labor. It was a bitter experience for most of them, for they had been accustomed to an easy life at home. The five years of hard labor was a crucible for 16-year-old Teng, who had been raised comfortably in a well-to-do family.

Disappointed with the corrupt warlord politics at home and anxious to see their deteriorating country saved, patriotic students of the May Fourth generation were ready to engage themselves in politics. The Chinese students in France were equally eager to test their mettle. They were attracted to the French revolutionary tradition and were impressed by French political romanticism and the ideals of the 1789 Revolution. Since socialism was quite popular in France at that time and since the Chinese students had close contact with the French workers and shared their suffering and humiliation, they found Marxism appealing. Moreover, they were impressed with the success of the Bolshevik Revolution in Russia. They were grateful that the Bolsheviks renounced all the unequal treaties signed by the Tsarist government with China in the previous century which made Marxism still more attractive.

Radical groups of a strong political nature emerged. Ch'en Yen-nien, Chao Shih-yen, Ts'ai Ho-sen, Wang Jo-fei, and Chou En-lai were the most popular leftist student leaders of the time.[7]

---

5. *Fu Fa Ch'in-kung-chien-hsueh Yun-tung Shih-liao*, Vol. III, p. 452.

6. "Chieh-k'ai Teng Hsiao-p'ing Te Fan-ko-ming Lao-ti," p. 2.

7. Ch'en, Son of the founder and first General Secretary of the Chinese Communist Party, Ch'en Tu-hsiu, was executed by the KMT in 1927. Chao was

Li Li-san, Ch'en I, Nieh Jung-chen, Ts'ai Ch'ang, and Hsiang Ching-yu were notable activists.[8] Teng was, however, less active than others when he first arrived in France.

Three public disorders perpetrated by Chinese students in France broke out in the single year of 1921. The first one, the "February 28th Demonstration," was aimed at calling the attention of the Chinese Embassy to the problems of the students' livelihood and their difficulties in schools. The second demonstration, held on June 8th, was in protest against the secret negotiations of a French loan to China. The third one, a September protest in Lyons, objected to the admissions policy of the newly founded Franco-Chinese Institute in Lyons. The Institute was founded by Wu Chih-hui and Li Shih-tseng who also happened to be founders of the "Work and Study"program. Their policy refused top priority admittance to Chinese students who were already in France. Instead they tried to recruit new students from China. Some 104 of the 125 demonstrators in the latter protest, including Ts'ai Ho-sen, Ch'en I, Li Li-san, and Li Wei-han[9] were expelled from France.[10] There is no record that Teng had participated in any of the three demonstrations.[11] However, Teng did sign his name on a 242-signature petition to Ch'en Lu, the Chinese Ambassador to France, requesting that the

---

also executed in 1927. Ts'ai Mao's close friend, an important leader in Chinese Communism in the twenties, was executed in 1931. Wang, later a member of the CCP Politburo, was killed in an aircraft incident in 1946. Chou arrived in France in December 1920.

8. Li Li-san was leader of Chinese Communism in the second decade. Ts'ai, sister of Ts'ai Ho-sen, was wife of Li Fu-ch'un, and leader of the Chinese women's movement. She later became a member of the CCP Central Committee. Hsiang, wife of Ts'ai Ho-sen and leader of the Chinese women's movement in the 1920's, was executed in 1928. Cf. Li Huang, *Hui-i-lu*, p. 74.

9. Later director of the CCP United Front Work Department.

10. Chang Yun-ho, Vol. I, p. 13-27.

11. No record of Teng's participation in any of these events can be found in the memoirs of former Chinese students in France, including those of Li Wei-han, T'ang To, Hsu Te-heng, and Li Huang. See, for example, *Hui-i Ts'ai Ho-sen* (In Memory of Ts'ai Ho-sen) (Peking: Jen-min Ch'u-pan-she, 1980), pp. 28, 37-78, 107-109; and Li Huang, *Hui-i-lu*, pp. 83-85.

Franco-Chinese Institute be open to the Chinese students who were already in France so as to help solve their study problems.[12]

Communism was very popular in the French factories and many workers were Communists. Their ideology spread to the Chinese students working alongside them. Teng learned French from his factory colleagues and soon learnd about Marxism as well.[13] At that time, the Third International found the Chinese students studying in Europe a potential force for propagating revolutionary ideas. Since there existed no Chinese-oriented Communist organization then, the Third International established within the Communist parties in France, Germany, and Belgium a special bureau to accommodate the Chinese students.

Teng was admitted into the French Communist Party as a Chinese member.[14] Fellow students who joined the French Communist Party included Chou En-lai, Wang Jo-fei, Li Fu-ch'un, and Jen Cho-hsuan.[15] Chinese members were required to perform the same duties as the French members. They received Marxist instruction, were required to participate in strikes and demonstrations, and were taught to sing the "International."

Gradually, under the inspiration of the Young Communist International, the Chinese leftists in Europe decided to organize a Communist organization themselves.[16] At the end of June 1922, 18 delegates from France, Germany, and Belgium met in a suburb west of Paris.[17] They established the Young Communist

12. Chang Yun-ho, Vol. I, p. 22.

13. Chou Yu-jui, *Hung-ch'ao Jen-wu-chih* (Leaders of the Red Regime) (New York: Shih-chieh Jih-pao She, 1967), p. 188.

14. Snow, *Red Star*, pp. 498-499. Both Snow and the May 13, 1973 *Figaro* (Paris) maintained that Teng had joined the French Communist Party before joining the CCP.

15. Jen later defected to the Kuomintang.

16. The Young Communist International had once planned to establish in China a division of the Young Communist Party. See Wang Chang-ling, *Chung-kuo Kung-chan Chu-i Ch'ing-nien-t'uan Shih-lun* (A Critical History of the Chinese Communist League) (Taipei: Kuo-li Cheng-chih Ta-hsueh Tung-ya Yenn-chiu-so, 1973), p. 16.

17. Huai En, *Chou-tsung-li Te Ch'ing-shao-nien Shih-tai* (The Adolescent Days of Premier Chou-En-lai) (Szechuan: Ssu-chuan Jen-min Ch'u-pan-she,

Party (YCP) with Chou En-lai, Chao Shih-yen, and Li Wei-han elected to head its central executive committee. Chao was elected the General Secretary. Teng enrolled in the YCP in the same year.[18]

The student party soon contacted the Chinese Communists at home. In August 1922, the Central Committee of the CCP decided to create a CCP branch in Europe.[19] Chao Shih-yen was appointed Secretary of the branch and Chou En-lai, Ch'en Yen-nien, and Wang Jo-fei became executive members.[20] The YCP was renamed in February 1923 "The European Branch of the Chinese Communist Youth League," and was thus subordinated to the Socialist Youth League in China.[21] The original "central" executive committee was reorganized, with Chou En-lai as the Secretary.[22] The purpose of the League was to recruit and train future Communists as supervised by the CCP European branch. Chou En-lai later dominated the CCP European branch after Chao Shih-yen, Ch'en Yen-nien, and Wang Jo-fei left France in March 1923.[23] Teng became a CCP member in

1979), p. 168. Among the delegates were Chou En-lai, Chao Shih-yen, Ch'en Yen-nien, Li Fu-ch'un, Li Wei-han, Nieh Jung-chen, Liu Po-chien, Wang Jo-fei, Hsiao P'u-sheng, Fu Chung, Kao Feng, Mao Yu-shun and Jen Cho-hsuan.

18. "Chieh-k'ai Teng Hsiao-p'ing Te Fan-ko-ming Lao-ti," p. 2; *Le Monde*, May 13, 1975; and *Who's Who in Communist China* (Hong Kong: Union Research Institute, 1970), p. 610.

19. Huai En, *Shih-tai*, p. 169. Under the European Branch headquarters were three subdivisions: the French bureau, the German bureau and the Belgian bureau.

20. Ibid. Kai-yu- Hsu, *Chou En-lai*, pp. 31-32.

21. Huai En, ed., *Chou Tsung-li Ch'ing-Shao-nieh Shih-tai Shih-wen Shu-hsin Chi* (Selected Poems, Essays, and Letters of Premier Chou En-lai at Adolescence and Youth), Vol. II (Chengtu: Ssu-chuan Jen-min Ch'u-pan-she, 1980), p. 377; and Chang Yun-hou, et al., Vol. I, p. 36-37.

22. Haui En, ed., *Shih-wen Shu-hsin Chi*, Vol. II, p. 381; Chang Yun-ho, et al., Vol. I. p. 37. The committee was organized by five people: Chou En-lai, Jen Cho-hsuan, Yin K'uan, Wang Tse-k'ai, and Hsiao P'u-sheng. Under the executive committee were four sub-organs. They were the Society for Research of Communism, the Student Movement Committee, the Chinese Labor Movement Committee and the Publications Committee, to be headed by Jen, Yin, Wang, and Hsiao.

23. *Wu-ssu Yun-tung Hui-i-lu*, p. 512; and Huai En, *Shih-tai*, p. 170; and

1924.[24] Thus Chou became Teng's senior both in the League and in the Party.

The size of the Chinese Communist Party membership in France was small. With the departure of Chao Shih-yen and others, there remained no more than five members in Western Europe. The size of the League, however, was larger. When the Young Communist Party was first established in July 1922, it encompassed some 30 members. When in 1923 it was renamed the Communist Youth League, its number had increased to 72 and by early 1925 the number had grown into more than 300. The first official publication of the League was *The Youth* which was inaugurated in August, 1922 and edited by Ch'en Yen-nien.[25] Chou En-lai wrote many articles in this publication. The most boring job was mimeographing. Chao Shih-yen was first assigned to this job but he was so busy that he asked Teng to do it for him.[26] *The Youth* was edited and printed at 17 Rue Godefroy in south Paris.[27] It was a monthly journal for internal circulation only. Due to lack of funds and staff, only about a hundred copies were printed of each issue. For the most part the paper contained articles related to socialist doctrines and discussions of the inevitability of Chinese Communism.

A conference of the League was called on June 23, 1923. Teng was elected an executive member of the branch.[28] He now dressed like the average Frenchman and was the youngest of all

Kai-yu Hsu, *Chou En-lai*, p. 33.

24. *Le Monde* (Paris), May 13, 1975; Klein and Clark, *Biographic Dictionary*, Vol. II, p. 820; *Chung-kung Jen-ming-lu*, p. 943; and Teng Hsiao-ping, "Teng Hsiao-p'ing Tsai Chung-kung Chung-yang Shih-chieh San-chung-ch'uanhui Chung Te Chiang-hua Kai-yao" ("Outline of Teng Hsiao-p'ing's Speech at the Third Plenum of the Tenth Central Committee"), in *Ming Pao*, August 16 and 17, 1977.

25. Chang Yun-ho, *op. cit.*, Vol. I, p. 37.

26. Lin Huang, *Hui-i-lu*, p. 89.

27. Chang Yun-ho, et al., eds., Vol I. p. 38; and Huai En, *Shih-tai*, p. 170; *Wu-ssu Shih-chi Ch'i-k'an Chieh-shao* (An Introduction to the May Fourth Publications),Vol. II, Book 1 (Peking: San-lien Shu-tien, 1959), p. 39.

28. Huai En, *Shih-tai*, p. 177.

the members.[29] The conference decided to publish a semi monthly journal, *The Red Light,* to replace *The Youth.*[30] The first issue of *The Red Light* was printed on February 1, 1924 and was circulated jointly by the League and the CCP European Branch.[31] It was first edited by Chou En-lai, and later by Jen Cho-hsuan.[32] The mimeographing job again fell on Teng's shoulders. Teng's printing of the small Chinese characters was clear and readable, thus earning him the title of "Doctor of Mimeographing."[33] *The Red Light* was distributed to the public in the hope of extending its influence among the Chinese workers and students. The circulation increased gradually and the journal helped recruit more members. The journal also attracted readers at home and was praised highly by the CCP Central Committee.[34]

Besides the Communists, there were other political groups in France as well. The Kuomintang (the National Party) had its own followers as did the Statists. Because Kuomintang (KMT) policy at the time was one of cooperation with the Communists, members of the two parties co-existed rather peacefully in France. The Statists, however, bore no love for communism, nor did they approve of the collaborative policy of the KMT. In December 1923 they founded the Chinese Youth Party to compete with

---

29. Huai En, *Shih-tai,* p. 177; and *Wu-ssu Yun-tung Hui-i-lu,* Vol. II, p. 941.

30. Ibid.

31. See Chang Yun-ho, et al., eds., Vol. I, p. 42; and Huai En, ed., *Shih-wen Shu-hsin Chi,* Vol. II, p. 394. *The Red Light* had been issued in 33 numbers, the last of which was released on June 7, 1925. See I Ming, "Chou En-lai, Teng Hsiao-p'ing, Ch'ih-kuang" ("Chou En-lai, Teng Hsiao-p'ing and the Red Light"), in *Hua-ch'iao Jih-pao,* September 5, 1981.

32. I Ming, Li Tien-min, *Chou En-lai P'ing-chuan* (Biography of Chou En-lai) (Taipei: Li-ming Wen-hua Shih-yeh Kung-ssu, 1976), p. 27: Li Huang, *Hui-i-lu,* p. 89, and Cheng Hsueh-chia, *Chung-kung Hsing-wang Shih* (The Rise and Fall of the Chinese Communist Party), Vol. III (Taipei: Chung-hua Tsa-chih She, 1979), p. 112.

33. Li Huang, *Hui-i-lu,* p. 89; and Huai En, *Shih-tai,* p. 177.

34. *Chou En-lai Tsung-li Pa-shih Tan-ch'en Shih-wen-hsuan,* (Selected Essays and Poems in Memory of Premier Chou En-lai) (Peking: Jen-min Ch'u-pan-she, 1978), p. 174.

both the CCP and KMT. The Communists thereafter viewed the Chinese Youth Party as their most hostile enemy. Both sides engaged in heated debates, using their journals to attack each other. Teng also wrote articles in the party journal to attack the Statists.[35] More serious than the skirmishes in print, Communists and Statists actually engaged in fist fights. During meetings of the All Patriotic Associations Union (founded in July 1923), of which Teng was an executive member, followers of different orientations frequently fought with one another.[36] Later they even carried arms with them when attending these meetings.

In 1924, the KMT invited the Communists as individual members to join the KMT when many posts became vacant. The recruiting of Communists widened the intraparty conflict between rightwing and leftwing members of the KMT. In order to strengthen the position of the KMT leftists and to build their personal influence, more and more Communists left for China to take up posts in the KMT. Among those who departed was Chou En-lai, who left France in June 1924.

After Chou left, Li Fu-ch'un and Fu Chung[37] assumed the leadership,[38] and Teng also became more important. The Communists were now numerically weaker, but Li Huang of the opponent Chinese Youth Party warned his colleagues not to underestimate Teng.[39] On October 10, 1924, while the Chinese Youth Party was holding a National Day celebration party, Teng broke in with a group of leftists and roughed up the place. The angry intruders demanded a replacement of the flag used by the Pei-yang government with the flag of the revolutionary Canton government. The request was refused. Teng and his follow-

---

35. Chang Yun-ho et al., eds., Vol. I, p. 48. But the source did not specify the titles of the articles.

36. Li Huang, *Hui-i-lu*, p. 106

37. Later the Deputy Director of the army's General Political Department.

38. *Wu-ssu Yu-tung Hui-i-lu*, Vol. II, p. 942; Huai en, *Shih-tai*, p. 182. According to Huai, Li and Fu held the post of secretary of the CCP Europe Branch for the last two terms. See also p. 170.

39. Li Huang, *Hui-i-lu*, p. 106.

ers expressed their anger by shouting "Down with the Pei-yang running dogs" and then fled.[40]

The struggle soon widened in scope. In May 1925, to show solidarity with the May 30th demonstration at home, the Chinese Communists in France planned to stage a similar protest in Paris. Unable to get a permit, about a hundred Communists broke into the Chinese Embassy on June 21 and forced ambassador Chen Lu to sign a petition requesting France to give up her extra-territorial rights in China.

With more and more members returning home to engage in rebellions, the League's membership was reduced to approximately 100 people by the end of 1925. The main task of the League at this time was to mobilize its members to go back to China. Teng, along with Fu Chung, Li Cho-jan[41] and seventeen other leftists left for China, travelling via the USSR, on January 7, 1926.[42] A circular was issued the same day, stating:

> Twenty of our comrades going to Russia are scheduled to leave Paris tonight. . . . Soon they will return to China. Comrades! On seeing our fighters go to the front line one by one, we should always remember the slogan of "Going back to China at the earliest possible date!"[43]

On the second day after they left, the French police made an unexpected search of League headquarters. It was lucky for the Communists that Fu Chung and Teng had already departed.

Not until fifty years later did Teng return to France. In 1975 the Vice-Premier of China was received by the French president.[44] One wonders what feelings Teng might have had in

---

40. Ibid.

41. Li later became Deputy Propaganda Minister of the CCP.

42. Chang Yun-ho, Vol. I, p. 57. Some sources report wrongly that Teng returned to China in 1924. See for example, "Teng Hsiao-p'ing Yen-i Ti-i-hui," p. 32. Other sources say that Teng was deported in 1925, which is incorrect as well. See, for example, the *Pei-mei Jih-pao*, January 29, 1979.

43. Ibid.

44. Yuan Li, "Teng Hsiao-p'ing Te Fa-kuo Chih-hsing" ("Teng Hsiao-p'ing's French Trip") in *Chung-hua Yueh-pao* (China Monthly, Hong Kong), No. 719 (August 1975), pp. 41-42.

recalling his youthful days, which were mixed with toil, bitterness, and excitement.

It was in France that the landlord's son became a revolutionary. Hard work and political conflict had turned Teng into a determined, high minded young man. He was not the charismatic leader that Chou En-lai or Chao Shih-yen were, but his ability for organization was acknowledged.

From the very beginning Teng impressed people as a born careerist: he was ambitious, industrious, responsible, patient, and articulate. He accepted most assignments with eagerness and performed his duties well including such boring and mechanical tasks as mimeographing. But his mind for details enabled him, in later years, to rise above the average bureaucrats who were swallowed by the huge Party organization and turned into machine-like one-dimensional men.

It was also during his years in France that Teng came to believe in Marxism. The politically conscious Chinese of that time, the student intelligentsia in particular, were burdened with a humiliating inferiority complex stemming from decades of Chinese defeats since 1840. The Chinese attitude toward the West was ambivalent: on the one hand, they were anxious to build China into a rich and strong country after the Western model; on the other hand, they were resentful of the domination of Western civilization. Using Marxism as a political guide for repudiating what was judged to be a spiritually bankrupt Western civilization appealed to many Chinese. Although conceived in the West, Marxism was embraced as a kind of messianism that would save China from both feudal backwardness and imperialist oppression. Teng's understanding of Marxism at the time was very likely second-hand. Like other self-proclaimed socialists of the twenties, Teng probably did not have a deep understanding of the Marxist philosophy. It was the revolutionary strain in Marx that was most attractive to the radical Chinese intellectuals. The ideology was accepteed as a guide for class struggle. Marx the philosopher, the humanist, and the dialectician was never popular among the Chinese Communists. It

34

was Marx's call to arms and his iconoclasm that molded the character of most Chinese Communists, including Teng.

Teng stayed in France longer than most of the other CCP members, thus allowing his understanding of the West to be comparatively more comprehensive. This enabled Teng to distinguish himself in the coming years from the home-raised Communists who were ignorant of the outside world. The West's achievements in industry deeply impressed Teng. At a conference on education held in August 1977, Teng spoke with admiration of the French liner that took him to France half a century before.[45]

The early Chinese Communists could be grouped under three categories: those who were raised at home like Mao Tse-tung, Tung Pi-wu, and Li Hsien-nien; those who studied in the Soviet Union (the "Internationalists") like Wang Ming, Chang Wen-t'ien and Ch'in Pang-hsien; and those who returned from France. The last group had a broader understanding of the world than the domestic Communists and took a less orthodox approach to Marxism than the Internationalists. They were, as a whole, more like administrators than warriors. Constructive programs interested them more than battle. Thus the majority of the "Work and Study" group became pragmatic and proponents of modernization in later years. However, they did not establish a strong influence in the Party except during a brief period in the late 1920's, when Li Li-san dominated the Party line. Chou En-lai remained in the leadership for many years but was always overshadowed by others such as Wang Ming and Mao Tse-tung, because his group never consciously organized itself into a separate political entity. However, taking the back seat did not come without a blessing. Many of the French-returned Chinese Communists were able to survive repeated purges while moving ahead with their constructive projects and economic reform.

---

45. Chou Hsun, "Teng Hsiao-p'ing Yu Chung-kuo-shih Hsien-tai-hua" (Teng Hsiao-p'ing and the Chinese Model of Modernization), in *Kwang Chiao ching* (The Wide Angle, Hong Kong), No. 80 (May 16, 1979), p. 11.

Chapter 3

Returning Home From Moscow (1926-1929)

In the mid-twenties, it was customary for the Chinese Communists in Europe, before going home, to make a pilgrimage to Soviet Russia, the Mecca of the Communist revolution. Before Teng, Chao Shih-yen, Ch'en Yen-nien, Wang Jo-fei, Liu Po-chien, Nieh Jung-chen, Ts'ai Ch'ang and Jen Cho-hsuan had all visited Moscow for "further studies." Teng followed their path to Moscow and enrolled in the Sun Yat-sen University for Toilers of China (abbreviated in Russia as YTK).[1] This was the first and only time Teng pursued formal studies outside China. The Sun Yat-sen University, which admitted Chinese students only, was founded in the autumn of 1925 in memory of the late founder of the Chinese Republic. Sun was also esteemed as the initiator of the United Front Policy in China. The YTK was supposedly administered by the East Asian Bureau of the Third International, but was in reality run by the Soviet government. The school's funds came mainly from the Boxer indemnity returned by Russia. The YTK recruited students from

---

1. Yueh Sheng, *Sun Yat-sen University in Moscow and the Chinese Revolution* (Kansas: The University of Kansas Press, 1971), p. 1.

both the Kuomintang and the Chinese Communists for the purpose of training the cadres of both parties into possible leaders of a future revolution. Among the graduates who later became politically important were Chiang Ching-kuo, Ku Cheng-kang, Ku Chengting, Cheng Chieh-min, P'i I-shu — all from the KMT;[2] and the "Twenty Eight Bolsheviks," Ch'en Po-ta,[3] and Jen Cho-hsuan — all from the CCP.

Although officially dubbed a university, the YTK had only one department which admitted about three hundred students each year. It taught a two-year course and theoretically admitted only students who had already attended college for two years. In reality, however, the students came from different educational backgrounds and varied greatly in their academic ability. While some of the entrants had been college professors, some had never attended school before. Many students dropped out in the middle of the curriculum, but were still recognized as the YTK's graduates. All incoming students were given a Russian name and assigned to a class according to his or her linguistic capabilities. Each class was taught a range of subjects in one foreign language, such as French, English or Russian. Students were required to participate in discussions following lectures in their class's designated tongue. There were twelve classes in every academic year with 25 students in each class.[4]

Students could expect intensive study during their two years in Moscow. The curriculum included the history of the evolution of society, the histories of revolutions in the West, the East and Russia, economic geography, and political economy. Class

---

2. Chiang is now president of the Republic of China. Ku was a KMT veteran. His brother, Ku Chengting, served as a prominent member of the Legislative Yuan. Cheng was the head of the Nationalist Intelligence Agency while P'i was a woman leader of the KMT.

3. Mao's former secretary—who emerged as one of the leading figures during the early phase of the Cultural Revolution—was later purged.

4. Wang Chueh-yuan, *Liu-o Hui-i-lu* (The Moscow Days) (Taipei: San Min Shu-chu, 1969), pp. 11-12; Pai Yu, "Yu-kuan Liu-o Chung-shan Ta-hsueh" (The Moscow Sun Yat-sen University), in *Chuan-chi Wen hsueh* (Biographic Literature), No. 176 (January, 1977), p. 64; and Yueh Sheng, p. 68.

sessions were conducted as seminars. The lecturer would lead the discussion and students were encouraged to talk freely. The Russian language was taught six days a week, four hours a day. For an inspiring change of pace, leaders of the October Revolution were invited to give lectures. Among them the best known were Bukharin and Trotsky. Students received military training as well. On vacation days, they were organized to participate in field trips.[5]

Teng was among the first students to graduate. When Teng was admitted, he was assigned to Class Seven, a special class designed mainly for professional revolutionaries. Students were chosen for this class according to the number of years they engaged in revolutionary activities, not according to their language experience. Class Seven was known to other students as the Theoretical Class. Among Teng's classmates were Yu Hsui-sung (an early Chinese Communist leader), Shen Tse-min (one of the Twenty Eight Bolsheviks and brother of Mao Tun, the famed novelist), Ch'u Wu (the son-in-law of KMT veteran Yu Yu-jen), Chou T'ien-lu (later advisor to Hu Tsung-nan, the leading KMT general), Wang Pien (a woman, later director of the Shangtung Communist Youth League), Tso Ch'uan (Acting Chief-of-Staff of the Eighth Route Army during the second Sino-Japanese War), Hu Chung, and Li Chun-tse.[6] Supposedly, Teng acted as the interpreter in classes where French was the teaching medium.[7]

Communist students were very active at the YTK in helping to recruit new members whenever possible. Soon they dominated the University. Those who had been in France were the most active and took control of the CCP Russian Branch.[8] Teng, short but aggressive, was nicknamed by his fellow stu-

5. Pai Yu, p. 64; and interview with Pai Yu, in Taipei on February 9, 1980. Pai is a YTK graduate and presently a member of the Legislative Yuan.

6. Yueh Sheng, *Sun Yat-sen University*, p. 69.

7. Interview with Pai Yu.

8. Wang Chueh-yuan, *Liu-o Hui-i-lu*, pp. 74-80.

9. Yueh Sheng, *Sun Yat-sen University*, pp. 69-70.

dents the "little cannon."[9] He dressed like a Parisian and spent a lot of time in cafes with Teng Ming-ch'iu (brother of Teng Yen-ta, dean of the Whampoa Military Academy).[10]

While Teng was still in Moscow, Feng Yu-hsiang, the enlightened warlord from north China, visited the Soviet Union. After having secured the good will of the Kuomintang in 1923, the Soviets now turned their attention to north China in the hope of finding an ally. Feng was approached because he seemed more inclined to revolution than the other warlords. The Soviets promised to finance him if he would cooperate with the KMT and the CCP. Recently defeated by Chang Tso-lin and Wu Pei-fu, Feng was eager for ouside help to recover the territories he lost to them. When he arrived, he was welcomed by Russian officials and YTK students. On the second day after his arrival, he announced that he would join the KMT and pledge his support for the cause of national unification. Feng stayed in the Soviet Union for more than three months and spoke at the YTK for which he was given an honorary student ID card.[11] Moreover, Feng's daughter and son enrolled in the YTK.

It was agreed that advisors from the Soviet Union, the KMT, and the CCP would help to reorganize, and particularly to indoctrinate Feng's army. Teng was one of the CCP members assigned to work with Feng. In August 1926, when Feng started back to China, he was accompanied by Teng, Liu Po-chien, Shih K'o-hsuan, Chang Mu-t'ao, Hsiao Ming and 98 Russian advisors.[12] After an absence of six years, Teng returned to his country on September 16.[13]

---

10. Interview with Pai Yu.

11. James Sheridan, *Chinese Warlord: The Career of Feng Yu-hsiang* (Stanford, Calif.: Stanford University Press, 1966), p. 200.

12. Ssu-ma Lu, ed., *Chung-kung Tang-shih Chi Wen-hsien Hsuan-ts'ui* (The History of the Chinese Communist Party and Selected Documents), Vol. V (Hong Kong: Tzu-lien Ch'u-pan-she, 1977), p. 90; *Who Is Who In Communist China*, p. 610; and Kan Yu-lan, *Mao Tse-tung Chi Ch'i-tuan* (Mao Tse-tung and His Group) (Hong Kong: Tzu-yu Ch'u-pan-she, 1954), p. 150.

13. Wu Min and Hsiao Feng, eds., *Tsung Wu-ssu Tao Chung-hua Jen-min Kung-ho-kuo Te Tan-sheng* (From the May Fourth Movement to the Founding of the People's Republic) (Peking: Hsin-chao Shu-tien, 1951), p. 64.

The KMT was waiting for Feng. On September 17, Feng swore an oath in Wu-yuan, pledging his loyalty to the KMT and expressing his determination to overthrow the warlords and expel imperialism. At that time the KMT Northern Expeditionary Force was on the move. To match the KMT's efforts, Feng led his troops our of Suiyuan and captured Honan. Notably, Feng then had an army of some 200,000 soldiers, while the KMT had an enlistment of less than half of Feng's. Therefore, it was important for the Communists to win Feng's army over to their side, both for the sake of national unificaion and for the expansion of their own strength.

Feng reorganized his army. He set up a political department to carry out the tasks of education and propaganda. Not surprisingly, the Communists dominated the department. Liu Po-chien was appointed Director of the Political Department[14] with Teng as his deputy.[15] Wei Kung-chih (who later married Marshall Yeh Chien-ying) also worked in the same administration.[16] Because the department needed more staff members to facilitate its work, Feng built the Chung-shan Military Academy for the training of cadres in San-yuan on the outskirts of Sian. The academy was also controlled by the Communists. Many of the students were recruited from the Communist Youth organizations. The President was Shih K'o-hsuan.[17] Teng was appointed its Dean. Among the instructors was Liu Chih-tan, who later founded the Shensi-Kansu Soviet and was killed during a battle in 1936. The notable graduates from the academy were Kao Kang (later "Lord of Manchuria" in the early 1950's) and Hsi Chung-hsun (later Political Commissar of the First Field Army,

14. Tso-Kwang-yu, "Hui-i Ning-tu Ch'i-i" (Recollections of the Ningtu Uprising), in *Hung-ch'i P'iao-p'iao* (The Red Flags Fly), Vol. 19 (Peking: Chung-kuo Ch'ing-nien She, 1979), pp. 271-272; and Yueh Sheng, p. 139.

15. Chang Kuo-t'ao, *Wo Te Hui-i* (My Memoir), Vol. II (Hong-Kong: Mingpao Monthly Press, 1973), p. 660; Mark Sheldon, *The Yenan Way in Revolutionary China* (Cambridge, Mass.: Harvard University Press, 1971), p. 24.

16. Klein and Clark, *Biographic Dictionary*, Vol. II, p. 820.

17. Yueh Sheng, *Sun Yat-sen University*, p. 139. Shih was also the head of the Department of Political Defense (a GPU-like organ).

now a member of the CCP Politburo).[18] In addition, the Communists held many important posts in the municipal, educational, and mass organizations.

Teng and his colleagues employed different methods of appealing to the soldiers' consciousness. They spoke to them about the need to renounce unequal treaties, to overthrow imperialism, to help materialize Sun Yat-sen's Three People's Principles, and to serve the common people. Their goal was to train Feng's troops into a politically loyal and highly spirited fighting machine, an ideological army. At the same time, the Academy extended its teachings to peasants and students. Sian, where Feng's army was based, became one of the two revolutionary centers of the time. The other was located at Canton.[19]

However, the honeymoon between right and left elements of the KMT did not last long. A split between Nanking and Wuhan in early 1927 prompted leftists and rightists to try to win Feng to their side. After the April 12 coup, when the Communist elements in Shanghai were suddenly killed or arrested by Chiang Kai-shek, the Soviets planned to replace Chiang with Feng.[20] They even planned to build a base in the heart of Feng's area of control in the northwest.[21] But Feng dashed these hopes when he joined with Chiang. The two agreed after a two-day meeting in Hsuchou, on June 20 and 21, that Feng would help combat the Communists.

Feng's "betrayal" was not coincidental. In terms of military strength, Nanking under Chiang Kai-shek was superior to Wuhan, the left-wing stronghold of the KMT in league with the CCP. Moreover, Yen Hsi-shan, warlord of Shansi, declared his support for Chiang on June 26, thus further widening the gap

---

18. Sheldon, *The Yenan Way*, p. 21.

19. Yueh Sheng, *Sun Yat-sen University*, p. 138.

20. For details, see *The Tragedy of the Chinese Revolution* by Harold R. Isaacs (Stanford, Calif.: University Press, 1961).

21. Li Yun-han, *Tsung Jung-kung Tao Ch'ing-tang* (From Collaboration to Annihilation, A History of the First United Front) (Taipei: Chung-kuo hsueh-shu Chu-tso chiang-chu Wei-yuan-hui, 1966), p. 716.

in military strength between Nanking and Wuhan. Feng realized that even with his support Wuhan could not last long.

The Nanking government was more generous than Wuhan in supporting Feng financially. Furthermore, he was more inclined ideologically to Nanking. Feng always spoke as a revolutionary, but what he wanted was an "orderly revolution." He disapproved of radical revolutions of the Communist type, and felt uneasy about the growing Communist influence in his army. At first Feng accepted the Communists because he needed Russian help to expand his base of operations to the more prosperous areas south rather than remain in the underdeveloped northwest. But once he held Honan, "the heart of China," he felt no longer in need of Soviet assistance. He was ready to eliminate the Communist elements from his troops.

On July 8 more than 50 Communists, including Teng, were expelled from Feng's army and deported to Wuhan. The Russian advisors were told to return home.[22] Feng was rather moderate in ridding himself of the Communists because he did not want to break with Moscow and the CCP openly. However, after the bloody Canton Uprising, organized by the Communists in December 1927, Feng changed his attitude and adopted repressive measures against his enemies.[23]

In Wuhan Teng worked in the Party's Central Committee. He stayed with Li Wei-han, who was one of the five leading members og the CCP Politburo.[24]

On July 15, the Wuhan government shifted politically in favor of the KMT right wing and declared a split with the Communists. The KMT leftists were alarmed by the radical Communist land programs. Worse yet, they discovered evidence

22. "Chieh-k'ai Teng Hsiao-p'ing Te Fan-ko-ming Lao-ti," p. 3; Chi Hsin, *Teng Hsiao-ping*, pp. 12-13.

23. Wang Ch'i-chung and Lu Lu, Trans., *Su-lien Tsai Hua Chu-shih Ku-wen Hui-i-lu* (Recollections of the Russian Advisors to China) (Taipei: Kuo-fang-pu Ch'ing-pao-chu, 1976), p. 134; Sheridan, pp. 230-231, and p. 30.

24. "Chieh-k'ai Teng Hsiao-p'ing Te Fan-ko-ming Lao-ti," p. 3. Li had been to France in the early twenties and later became Director of the CCP United Front Department and is now advisor to the CCP United Front Department.

that the Communists were planning a coup. The purge of Communists in Wuhan dealt a heavy blow to the CCP. On August 7, an emergency conference was called at the house of a Russian official at Hankow (one of the three member cities forming the tri-city complex of Wuhan), which was attended primarily by members and alternate members of the CCP Central Committee. There were some twenty people present including Mao Tse-tung, T'sai Ho-sen, Ch'u Ch'iu-pai, Li Wei-han, and Jen Pi-shih. Lominadze of the Third International also attended the meeting as a strategical consultant. Teng jotted down the minutes.[25] The Party's General Secretary, Ch'en Tu-hsiu, was blamed for taking a rightist-opportunist course of action and accused of depending too much on the KMT. Ch'u Chi'u-pai was elected to replace Ch'en as head of the Party. The conference decided to end the united front policy and adopt an insurrectionary line. The meeting lasted for one day only because the hot weather and the KMT made its constituents uncomfortable. Business had to be concluded quickly or the Central Committee faced possible arrest by KMT agents.[26] At this historical "August 7th Conference" Teng met Mao for the first time.

The Party moved to Shanghai in the autumn of 1927 and conducted its activities underground. Teng moved with the Party. He took a boat to Shanghai and stayed there until the middle of 1929.[27]

In Shanghai, Teng mainly did office work. He was responsible for conveying orders and for preparing documents. At the Sixth Party Congress (held in July 1928), he was named the Deputy Secretary-General of the Party.[28] Teng surprised people with his ability to speak the Shanghai dialect without an accent after only a short stay in the province. His fluency enabled him

---

25. *Jen Pi-shih* (Changsha, Hunan: Jen-min Ch'u-pan-she, 1979), p. 67.
26. *Jen Pi-shih*, p. 68 .
27. Snow, *Random Notes*, p. 137.
28. "Chieh-k'ai Teng Hsiao-p'ing Te Fan-ko-ming Lao-ti," pp. 2-3.

to carry out his unerground duties with relative ease.[29]

Shortly after his arrival in Shanghai, Teng married Chang Ch'ien-yuan, secretary of a CCP county committee in Kiangsi. The couple rented a small flat in the concession area and lived a peaceful life for about a year and a half.[30]

If the French days had given Teng a "proletarian body," his Russian days seemed to foster within him a "proletarian mind." The five years he had spent in France enabled him to experience the hardships of the working class. Teng's brief stay in Russia put these experiences into the greater context of history and society from a Marxist perspective.

The Bolshevik style of organization impressed Teng. Lenin's principle of an elite and professional party founded on democratic centralism influenced Teng, in later years, to use discipline and rules as a means of achieving similar organization. When he first returned to China, he served under Feng Yu-hsiang whose army was known widely for its discipline. This again probably reinforced Teng's tendency for strict organization.

Often it is asked how extensively Teng's career was influenced by Western culture. During his five-year stay in France, Teng was preoccupied with physical labor and political activities. He never entered school and his contact with the outside world, apart from working, was almost certainly limited to his Chinese circle. The superiority of Western technology was plainly visible, a reality which Teng must surely have appreciated. But did he acquire sufficient knowledge to comprehand the complexities of the Western world? How far did he identify himself with Western culture? Even an outstanding scholar such as Liang Ch'i-ch'ao, the radical reformer who dreamed of duplicating Western constitutionalism in China, denounced Western civilization after a tour to Europe in the 1920's. Failure

29. Chou Yu-jui, *Hung-ch'ao Jen-wu-chih* (The Reds) (New York: Shih-chieh Jih-pao She, 1977), p. 189.

30. "Chieh-k'ai Teng Hsiao-p'ing Te Fan-ko-ming Lao-ti", p. 3.

to grasp the essence of Western culture has been the pitfall of all sincere Chinese advocates of "modernization" over the past one hundred years. These people have been amazed by Western material achievements. They have been eager to learn and to utilize the technology of the West. However, they have all stumbled on their ignorance of the more fundamental traditions which have made those technical achievements possible. Accordingly, it is still less likely that Teng, a student worker in his early twenties, was able to assimilate the underlying principles of the Western world into his personal credo. Despite his years abroad, Teng is not known to have undertaken any penetrating investigation into the foundations of Western culture. Like many Chinese students of the time, he accepted Marxism out of faith, without questioning it. Once he returned to China he was dragged into actual political struggles which allowed him no time for reflection on Marxist philosophy. This lack of vision constitutes one of Teng's weaknesses, to which we will return for further elaboration in the coming chapters.

We find few Western-like traits in Teng. In terms of manner, Teng never appears to people as a man who has studied abroad. Unlike the Internationalists, the students returned from Russia, who tried to impress people with their Russian mannerisms, or unlike Chou En-lai who charmed people as a sophisticated and westernized intellectual, Teng's character is thoroughly Chinese. He is not far removed from the Szechuanese peasantry.

Chapter 4

The Pai-Se Uprising (1929-1931)

At the Sixth Congress of the CCP held in Moscow in mid-1928, Ch'en Tu-hsiu's "opportunist" line and Ch'u Ch'iu-pai's "putschism" were both denounced. Ch'u was accused of provoking premature insurrections in the latter part of 1927 which almost ruined the Party.[1] He was removed from the post of General Secretary and the Politburo was reorganized. Of the seven newly elected Politburo members, two remained in the Soviet Union as CCP representatives. Three of the five Politburo members returning to China had studied in France. These were Li Li-san, who headed the Propaganda Department, Chou En-lai, who led the Oreganization Department and the Military Commission, and Ts'ai Ho-sen. Li and Chou, in particular, were influential to the point of nearly dominating the Politburo. The Sixth Congress gave CCP members who had studied in France unprecedented control of the Party.

---

1. They include the Nanchang Uprising, the Autumn Harvest Uprising (in Hupeh and Hunan) and Canton Uprising.

Defeats to the Party were attributed to lack of a consolidated base and military force. It was therefore decided to establish soviets in rural areas and to build a Red Army. The Communists gained time to reorganize themselves in 1928 when Chiang Kai-shek, wary from his Northern Expedition, was dragged into confrontations with dissident Kuomintang generals.

In June 1929, Teng was sent to Kwangsi Province as a Party representative to help promote and organize Communist activities there. His goal was to win Kwangsi soldiers over to the Communist side and eventually to build a Red Army base in that south-western province.[2]

Kwangsi was chosen because of its established reputation for revolt. The CCP had built their influence there during the years when Chang was occupied with the Northern Expedition. After the abortive Canton uprising, a number of Kwangtung Communists fled into Kwangsi, where they carried on their insurgent activities. Earlier, the Chuang ethnic minority had been organized by a Communist, Wei Pa-ch'un, and was very active politically.

Circumstances in the Kwangsi province became even more favorable for the Communists in 1929. Li Tsung-jen and Pai Chung-hsi, both military leaders of the province, openly revolted against Chiang. In the face of this, Chiang appealed to Yu Tso-po, a veteran Kwangsi general, to incite Li's troops to revolt. Yu succeeded in persuading his cousin, Li Ming-jui, who then commanded the 7th Army of the Kwangsi troops in the Wuhan front line, and Yang T'eng-hui, of the 57th Army, to reject the command of Li. The defection of two of their chief officers was a decisive blow to Li and Pai. The 7th and the 57th Armies marched back to Kwangsi and took the province. Yu was promoted by Chiang to governorship of the province and Li

---

2. Chi Hsin, *Teng Hsiao-ping*, p. 14; "Yu-chiang Shang-hsia Hung-ch'i Yang," p. 14.

Ming-jui was awarded its supreme military command. Yu and Li were both sympathetic to the Communist cause. Yu's brother, Yu Tso-yu, was himself a Communist. Althought Yu Tso-po and Li Ming-jui accepted Chiang's appointments, they were not whole-heartedly in support of him. Rather they wanted to build up their own stronghold and were therefore willing to invite the Communists to come to Kwangsi.[3] So came Teng.[4]

The main tasks of the Communists in Kwangsi were to establish influence in the military and the government organs, and to work with the activists in the Right River and Left River areas for the possible establishment of a revolutionary base. Teng appointed Ch'en Hao-jen as Yu Tso-po' secretary and named Hsu Kuan-ying as Li Ming-jui's general administrator. This arrangement enabled Teng to be informed at all times of events in both the Kwangsi goverment and army. Kung Ch'u and Feng Ta-fei were put in control of the Nanning Police Force; and Chang Yun-i, Yu Tso-Yu, Yuan Yeh-lieh, and Shih Shu-

---

3. Kung Ch'u, *Kung Ch'u Chiang-chun Hui-i-lu* (General Kung Ch'u's Memoirs), Vol. I (Hong Kong: Ming Pao Yueh-k'an She, 1978), pp. 245-246; and Wu Hsi, "Hui-i Lung-chou Ch'i-i Han Hung-pa-chun Chien-li Ch'ien-hou," (The Lungchow Uprising and the Fouding of the Red Eighth Army), in *Hung-ch'i P'iao-p'iao*, Vol. 19 (Peking: Chung-kuo Ching-nien She, 1980), p. 249.

4. Before and after Teng, other Communists journeyed to Kwangsi. Among those who worked under Teng were Ho Ch'ang, a Central Committee member of the CCP who died in March, 1934; Kung Ch'u, the Acting Chief of Staff of the Kwangsi Soviet in 1934 who later defected; Chang Yun-i, later a governor of Kwangsi; Ch'en Hao-jen, who left the CCP in 1931; Yuan Jen-yuan, later the vice governor of Hunan and presently the Deputy Secretary of the CCP Discipline Control Committee; Yeh Chi-chuang, later the Minister of Commerce; Li Ch'ien, the brother of Li Li-san who was originally called Li Lung-kwang; Hsu Kuan-ying, also known as Hsu K'ai-hsien, he later left the party; Yuan Yeh-lieh, later a Commander of the Third Field Army; Feng Tafei; Shih Ch'ih-feng; Li Kan-hui; Shih Shu-yuan; and Wan Tan-p'ing. Refer to Chang Yun-i, "Pai-se Ch'i-i Yu Hung-ch'i-chun Te Chien-li" ("The Pai-se Uprising and the Founding of the Seventh Red Army"), in *Teng Hsiao-p'ing Tzu-liao Hsuan-chi* (Selected Materials of Teng Hsiao-p'ing) (Hong Kong: Hsin Chung-kuo Tu-shu Kung-ssu, 1977), p. 9; Kung Chu, Vol. I., p. 168; and Wu Hsi, p. 249.

yuan were assigned to manage political work in the army. Lei Ching-t'ien,Yuan Jen-yuan and Li Kan-hui were sent to the Left River and the Right River to help consolidate Communist forces there.[5]

The political situation in Kwangsi was complicated. Both Chiang Kai-shek and the Communists wanted to win Yu Tso-po to their side, as did a new rival, Wang Ching-wei, leader of the Reorganization Clique inside the KMT. Wang's envoy came to Nanning as well, to try to bring Yu under his influence. As a result, the Communists faced a tough job of diplomacy. Teng and his appointees Kung Ch'u and Ho Ch'ang, held meetings in the Nanning Police Department every evening until late at night. Kung was head of the police then and found himself so busily engaged in Party work that his girl friend threatened to leave him. The couple interrupted meetings with heated quarrels but were eventually reconciled and married thanks to negotiations by Teng and Ho Ch'ang.[6]

A secret meeting place that Teng frequented was a small lantern repair shop in south Nanning.[7] The shop was situated in a two-storied building where Teng, Lei Ching-t'ien and other CCP members convened and forwarded Party directives.[8]

The CCP had done a successful job infiltrating the army. Chang Yun-i and Yu Tso-yu, for instance, each controlled a squad of security guards known as the Fourth and the Fifth Security Corps. Hsu Kuan-ying and Chang Yun-i secured the posts of leader and deputy leader of a Military Officer Training

---

5. Kung Ch'u, Vol. I, pp. 247-248; Chou Lo, "Kuang-hsi Tso-yu-chiang Su-ch'u Chih Hsing-ch'eng Han Pung-k'ui" (A History of the Left River and Right River Soviet Movement), in *Kung-tang Wen-t'i Yen-chiu* (Communist Problems Studies, Taipei), April, 1977, p. 74; and Chang Yun-i, p. 15.

6. Kung Chu, Vol. I, p. 248 and Vol. II, p. 503.

7. Located in #96, Chung-shan Pei Road, Nanning.

8. "Yu-chiang Shang-hsia Hung-ch'i Yang," p. 15.

Corps.[9] Through these important posts the Communists were able to install their own colleagues in army positions. Within a month, 300 members were absorbed into the military thereby giving the Communists control of the three corps in their command.[10] These forces later constituted the germ of the CCP Red Army in Kwangsi.

Three months after Teng arrived in Kwangsi, the political climate changed. Yu Tso-po and Li Ming-jui accepted the terms offered by Wang Ching-wei and pledged their support in opposing Chiang. The Communists advised them to wait patiently since they had not yet consolidated their foothold in the province. However, Yu and Li turned a deaf ear to this advice and fell prey to Chiang's designs. Chiang incited Yu's juniors to revolt, and Yu and Li were soon overthrovn. Before the ill-fated rebels had moved their army to the battle front, the Communists gave the excuse that the Fourth and the Fifth Security Corps and the Officer Training Corps were not sufficiently trained, thus convincing Yu and Li to leave these troops behind. After the Kwangsi army had departed, the Communists sent one division of the Fourth Corps to the Right River and one division of the Fifth Corps to the Left River to prepare a possible retreat. Chang Yun-i, who, besides heading the Police Department, was now the Garrison Commander and put in charge of the arsenal. When the news of Yu's defeat was received, Teng ordered CCP forces to withdraw to the Right River and Left River region.[11]

Teng transported the Party staff along with arms and ammunition by boat. Chang Yun-i led the army by foot to the Right River. The two rejoined in Pai-se in October. In the

9. Kung Ch'u, Vol. I., pp. 251-252. Mo Wen-hua, "Hung-ch'i-chun Te Tan-Sheng" ("The Birth of the Seventh Red Army"), in *Teng Hsiao-p'ing Tzu-liao Hsuan-chi*, p. 23.

10. "Yu-chiang Shang-hsia Hung-ch'i Yang," p. 15.

11. Chang Yun'i, pp. 12-13.

meantime, the Fifth Corps under Yu Tso-yu arrived in Lung-chow along the Left River in southwest Kwangsi, where the defeated forces of Yu Tso-po and Li Ming-jui had arrived earlier. Yu Tso-po and his men left for Shanghai some time later.[12]

The Left River and Right River are tributaries of the West River and are adjacent ot Kweichow, Yunan, and Vietnam. Along the river banks are mountain ranges occupied by the minority race of Chuang. Wei Pa-ch'un, the acknowledged leader of the Chuang minority, was also conveniently a Communist.

Pai-se, the major city along the Right River, had a population of less than 10,000. However, the city was both commercially and strategically important. Teng and Chang Yun-i resided in the Yueh-tung-hui-kuan, outside the South Gate.[13]

A meeting was called at which the following was agreed upon:

to reorganize the army and expel dissident members;

to set up soldiers' committees, uphold democracy and destroy warlordism;

to set equal terms between the officers and the soldiers and oppose mistreatment of soldiers and oppose corruption;

to organize and arm the masses to struggle against the landlords.

The resolutions, were still carried out under the banner of the KMT.[14]

Li Tsung-jen and Pai Chung-hsi returned to Kwangsi following the defeat of Yu and Li to resume their struggles against Chiang. Recognizing that the KMT was now preoccupied with internecine warfare, the CCP decided it was time to start a revolution in the province. In early November, Teng was ordered to

---

12. Chou Lo, p. 74.
13. "Yu-chiang Shang-hsia Hung-ch'i Yang," p. 15-16.
14. Chang Yun-i, p. 16; and Kung ch'u, Vol. I, pp. 255-256.

52

establish a revolutionary base in the Right River and Left River regions. The troops stationed in the Right River were renamed the Seventh Red Army while the troops stationed in the Left River region were called the Eighth Red Army. Teng convened a meeting to convey the Party directive. It was decided that on December 11th, the second anniversary of the Canton uprising, the Communists would set up a Soviet government in the Right River region.[15]

On the evening before the uprising, the Communists invited the local Pai-se leaders to a dinner. Here the locals were informed what would happen and were urged to cooperate with the new government. Though the local leaders knew that the take over was inevitable someday, they did not expect it so soon. Nevertheless, they reacted calmly and congratulated the Communists. Despite the good will, the Communists held them for two days to avoid unexpected betrayals.

On December 11th the uprising broke out as scheduled. Chief of Staff Kung Ch'u recalls the event in his memoir:

> In the morning of the eleventh, the weather was cool and cloudy, drizzling now and then. Before eight o'clock, the civilians and the army, assembled. . . . The flag was raised. Teng Hsiao-p'ing and Chang Yun-i each made a short speech. I then declared the founding of the Seventh Army and called out the names of the responsible leaders one by one. The gathering was then dismissed....[16]

Teng was appointed the Political Commissar and Chang Yun-i became the Military Commander of the Seventh Army. There were three divisions. The First Division, reorganized from the original Fourth security corps, was led by its former Deputy Commander, Li Ch'ien. The Second Division, which consisted

---

15. "Yu-chiang Shang-hsia Hung-ch'i Yang," p. 16; and Chang Yun-i, p.18.
16. Kung Ch'u, Vol. I, pp. 258-260.

of the local militia, was led by Hu Pin. The Third Division, led by Wei Pa-ch'un, was reorganized from the Chuang ethnic revolutionary force. Among the cadres was Wei's nephew, Wei Kuo-ch'ing, who later became Director of the General Political Department of the PLA, and an active supporter of Teng.

The student officers became cadres in each division. Those who later became famous were Yang Yung, now Deputy Chief of Staff and Li T'ien-yu. A division of the Seventh Army was equal to a regiment in equipment and number. The three divisions, comprising some 5,000 combatants, later were increased to 30,000 soldiers.[17]

The Seventh Army's headquarters were located in the Yueh-tung-hui-kuan, Teng's place of residence. Meanwhile, the Right River Government was set up and headquartered in En-lung. Lei Ching-t'ien was appointed its Chairman.[18]

Preparations were also under way in the Left River region. Teng went there personally with some of his colleagues to help facilitate the process. Finally, on February 1, 1930, the Eighth Army and the Left River Soviet government were inaugurated.[19] The Eighth Army comprised three divisions with an enlistment of about 3,000 under the leadership of Ho Shih-ch'ang.[20] Li Ming-jui, former Supreme Military Commander of Kwangsi, became the Chief Commander of the two armies.[21] Teng gain took the title of Political Commissar.

The Right River region included the following counties, all adjacent to Pai-se: T'ien-yang, En-lung, Tung-lan, Feng-shan, Kou-te, Ling-yun, Ssu-lin, En-yang, Hsiang-tu, and

17. Chang Yun-i, p. 19; Mo Wen-hua, p. 281; Kung Ch'u, Vol. I, p. 260; and Kung Ch'u, Vol. II, p. 358.

18. "Yu-Chiang Shang'hsia Hung-ch'i Yang," p. 16.

19. *Kuang-hsi Ko-ming Hui-i-lu*, pp. 125 and 135; and "Yu-chiang Shang-hsia Hung-ch'i Yang," p. 17.

20. *Kuang-hsi Ko-ming Hui-i-lu*, pp. 135-136.

21. "Yu-chiang Shang-hsia Hung-ch'i Yang," p. 17.

Chen-chieh. The Left River region, centered at Lung-chou, was composed of the counties of Shang-chin, Tsung-shan, Ming-chang, Ning-ming, and P'ing-hsiang. The Right and Left River Soviet — comprising both regions — was one of the relatively sizable territorial units then controlled by the CCP. However, the two regions never had the opportunity to link together.[22]

The relationship between the Left River Soviet and Vietnamese rebels in the south is worth noting. As Teng told Edgar Snow in 1936, the Lung-chou Soviet had connections with the Vietnamese rebels, who instugated wht worker-peasant rebellion in 1930.[23] The Vietnamese rebels were anti colonialist activists of the Vietnamese Nationalist Party. They launched an attack against the French colonists on February 9th. Considering themselves anti imperialist too, the Chinese Communists broke into the French embassy in Lung-chou the same day that the Left River Soviet was inaugurated. They confiscated embassy properties and expelled the French.[24] As a result, the Communists of the Left River Soviet had committed themselves to fighting a two-sided war: with the KMT on one side and the French colonists on the other. The Vietnamese revolution was soon crushed, causing many of the rebels to flee into China and join the Left River Soviet.[25] Teng remarked to Snow that French airplanes had bomed Lung-chou and that his forces retaliated by shooting down one of the attacking planes. Later, after the Left River Soviet was crushed, Vietnamese activists still kept in touch with the local underground Communists.[26]

Following the establishment of the Soviets Teng paid a visit to the Party Central in Shanghai to brief his comrades on the

22. Kung Ch'u, Vol. I., p. 303; and "Yu-chiang Shang-hsia Hung-ch'i Yang," p. 18.
23. Snow, *Random Notes*, p. 138.
24. *Kuang-hsi Ko-ming Hui-i-lu*, p. 127.
25. Klein and Clark, *Biographic Dictionary*,Vol. II., p. 821.
26. Snow, *Red Star*, p. 499.

work he had done in Kwangsi.[27] On his return he introduced a land reform after Mao's Kiangsi model. The experiment, however, was modest in character. It was carried out in only a few places such as Tung-lan and En-lung. Teng also worked with Wei Pa-ch'un in a collective farm experiment in Tung-lan, in which the communal members shared their lands, animals, and tools. Teng also gave lectures to cadres in nearby counties.[28]

From 1929 to 1930, the CCP succeeded in developing various bases despite numerous difficulies. On the other hand, the KMT had not been relieved of its internal wars. In May 1930, a large-scale war against Chiang was launched jointly by Yen Hsi-hsan, Feng Yu-hsiang, and Wang Ching-wei. Li Li-san, then the de facto head of the CCP, argued that the time was ripe for revolution. Thus in the middle of the year he ordered the Red Army to strike at some key cities. Li's final target was Wuhan. By capturing several provinces, he hoped to generate enough momentum to carry a national revolution. The Seventh and the Eighth Armies were ordered to mobilize in Kiangsi for ready action. Teng, possibly attending the National Conference of the Chinese Soviets in Shanghai,[29] was ordered to return to his province to prepare for war.

For security reasons, it took Teng two and a half months to return to Kwangsi.[30] By the time he arrived, the Eighth Army no longer existed. Kwangsi troops under Li Tsung-jen and Pai

---

27. "Yu-chiang Shang-hsia Hung-ch'i Yang," p. 20.

28. Ya Mei-ch'ang and Huang Chi-wen, "Chuang-chu Jen-min Te Cho-yueh Ko-ming Chan-shih" (The Brilliant Revolutionary Warrior of the Chuang People), in *Ko-ming Wen-wu*, July, 1979, p. 39; and "Yu-chiang Shang-hsia Hung-ch'i Yang," p. 21.

29. The purpose of calling the conference was to establish coordination among all soviets ready for insurrection. Forty-nine delegates representing the red armies and different soviets attended the meeting. See Wang Chien-min, Vol. III, 276-277.

30. Kung ch'u, Vol. I., p. 309.

Chung-hsi had invaded the Left River region in June, 1930, and crushed the Eighth Army. The Communist remnants, led by Li Ming-jui and Yuan Yeh-lieh, fled to the Right River and were combined into the Seventh Army.[31]

Upon arrival to his jurisdiction, Teng called a meeting. He conveyed the central directive that instructed the troops from his Soviet to march into Kiangsi and attack the cities on their way. A portion of the army would remain to defend the Right River region. However, Teng found Kung Ch'u, Wei Pai-ch'un, and Li Ming-jui strongly opposed to the central directive. The three argued that the Seventh Army would suffer severe losses if they were to make incursions east. They added that once the Seventh Army had withdrawn, the Right River region would be exposed to enemies. They proposed, instead, to turn north where the chances of being attacked were minimized. If Kweichow was captured, it could be linked with Kwangsi, thereby adding a vast area of land to Communist control. Teng, however, insisted on observing orders. He agreed that it would be safer to go north, but believed that capturing Kweichow would be insignificant compared with what might be achieved in the east. He therefore rejected the alternative strategy and ordered the army to Kiangsi, leaving 10,000 soldiers behind to protect the Right River Region. Wei Pai-ch'un was asked to stay behind because of his familiarity with the region.[32]

The withdrawal of the Seventh Army from the Right River region meant not only the death of the Right River Soviet, but a betrayal of the Chuang people as well. The Chuang minority

31. Ibid., pp. 306-307; Chang Yun-i, pp. 18-19; and *Kuang-hsi Ko-ming Hui-i-lu*, p. 140. Yu Tso-yu later escaped to Hongkong and after a while discreetly returned to Canton. He was captured by the KMT and executed. Ho Shih-ch'ang, the Political Commissar, helped lead the remnants of the Red Army to the Right River, but was killed on the way.

32. Kung Ch'u, Vol. I., pp. 309-311.

had long been disliked by the Kwangsi authorities. Having fought closely with the Communists since their arrival, the Chuang people were regarded as intolerable upstarts by the Kwangsi ruling class. Now that their Communist protectors were gone, the Chuangs were in no position to fight their enemies. Wei Pa-ch'un knew this well enough as he gravely watched the Seventh Army depart at the end of October 1930.

The Seventh Army moved along the frontier of south Hunan and north Kwangtung toward Kiangsi. They attacked cities on their way and engaged in armed conflict almost every day. Hunger and mountainous terrain were equally unrelenting. When winter set in many soldiers died from the cold. Severe losses forced the army to reorganize into two regiments, the 55th Regiment and the 58th Regiment. In January 1931, Communist Forces reached the Lo-ch'ang river, a strategic point held by the KMT. Teng ordered the army to cross the river. He and Li Ming-jui led the 55th Regiment ahead while Chang Yun-i followed with the 58th Regiment. However, the enemy's bombardment cut off communication between the two.[33] The 55th Regiment later arrived in Tsung-i, Kiangsi, and entrenched itself there.[34] Teng left the army and went to Shanghai, probably to report events to the Central Committee.[35]

---

33. Ibid., p. 327.

34. "Teng Hsiao-p'ing Yen-i Ti-i-hui," p. 33.

35. During the Cultural Revolution the Red Guards accused Teng of abandoning the army and escaping to Shanghai. They claimed that Teng was supposed to contact a Party representative somewhere near Tsung-i. At that time the CCP 55th Regiment in Tsung-i was engaged in a bitter fight with KMT troops. Teng supposedly heard the bombardment on his way, got frightened and ran away. He allegedly excused himself by saying that he got separated from the 55th Regiment and could do nothing but go to Shanghai to report to the Central Committee. See "T'ao-ping Teng Hsiao-p'ing (The Deserter Teng Hsiao-p'ing), a Red Guard pamphlet, reproduced in Chan-wang, November 1975, p. 29. Kung Ch'u also hinted that Teng was not a courageous person. "He would excuse himself at every battle," Kung said. See "Kung Ch'u ciang-chun Fang-wen Chi" ("An interview with General Kung Ch'u"), Ming Pao Yueh-kan, March, 1976, p. 12. However, if Teng did abandon his army and flee, he would

The two regiments later rejoined and arrived in Kiangsi in March. When they first set off from Kwangsi, they had 20,000 soldiers. Only 6,000 survived.[36] During the Cultural Revolution, the Red Guards criticized Teng for upholding the Li Li-san line and argued that he should have assumed full responsibility for the severe losses of the Seventh Army.[37]

The Right River Soviet was attacked by Kwangsi troops immediately after the departure of the Seventh Army. After a bitter struggle for half a year, the Soviet was crushed. The Kwangsi Soviet was the most short-lived and devastated of all the soviets that the CCP had established. Although Teng was only executing the Party's policy, he must have recalled the tragedy with regret when, in 1962[38] and 1975,[39] he inscribed monuments in honor of the late Wei Pa-ch'un and the headquarters of the Seventh Army in Kwangsi.

The Kwangsi days were the first time Teng was given full organizational responsibilities. Despite the backwardness of the province, its ethnic complexity, and many hardships, Teng tried his best to secure the province. Teng gained valuable experience from his "rehearsal days" in Kwangsi which enabled him, when serving as Political Commissar of the 129th Division and the Second Field Army in the following decades, to assume the more difficult jobs with confidence. He also learned from the Kwangsi experience how to establish a military base. This helped him greatly when, during the second Sino-Japanese War, he was assigned a similar job of building a Communist base in Japanese occupied areas.

surely have been punished by the Party, which would have affected his political future. However, there is no evidence to prove that Teng had been punished for this matter nor that such accusation was heard before the Cultural Revolution.

36. Kung Ch'u, Vol. I., p. 327. The Red Seventh Army was later incorporated into the Third Army Corps of P'eng Te-huai.

37. "Teng Hsiao-p'ing Yen-i Ti-i-hui," p. 33.

38. Ya and Huang, p. 41-42.

39. "Yu-chiang Shang-hsia Hung-ch'i Yang," p. 14.

Chapter 5

Becoming Mao's Man (1931-1935)

Li Li-san was too optimistic in his conviction that the time was ripe for revolution. His strategy of conquering individual cities as the first step toward a national revolution proved disastrous. Following the proven inadequacy of his policy, Li Li-san retired from leadership. A group of students who had recently returned from Russia led by Wang Ming and Po Ku, commonly known as the Twenty Eight Bolsheviks now dominated the Party. Chou En-lai, however, did not fall from power with his partner. He remained in the Politburo after making a critical review of himself and continued to head the Military Affairs Commission.

Teng assisted Chou in Shanghai[1] until his wife, Chang Ch'ien-yuan, died of a miscarriage. After recovering from his grief, Teng was sent to Kiangsi to work with Mao Tse-tung. When Teng first arrived in Kiangsi, he worked as Secretary of the District Party Committee of Juichin, "capital" of the Kiangsi soviet.[2] Later he was promoted to Secretary of the

---

1. *Ming Pao* (Hong Kong), November 1, 1978.
2. "Chieh-k'ai Teng Hsiao-p'ing Te Fan-ko-ming Lao-ti," p. 4.

Kiangsi Provincial Party Committee.[3] The position held great responsibility because Kiangsi was then the central soviet base of the Communists. Teng's appointment to the post was probably due to the recommendation of Chou En-lai, who arrived in Kiangsi in December 1931.

Before Teng came to Kiangsi, he was not very well acquainted with Mao. They had met in Wuhan in July 1927 and, as we have noted, both of them attended the August 7th Conference. It was in Kiangsi that the two became intimate friends. Teng was called one of Mao's "four warriors" along with three juniors: Mao Tse-t'an, Mao's third brother; Ku Po, Mao's secretary; and Hsieh Wei-chun—all of them members of the Provincial Committee of Kiangsi. The four were devoted to Mao and constituted an informal group defending Mao's name and position in the Party.[4]

Teng's devotion to Mao deserves attention. Unlike the other three, who had been Mao's followers for a considerable period of time, Teng was fresh from Shanghai. He had been working with Chou and was understandably a Party Central man. The relationship between the Party Central, based in Shanghai, and Mao was not a happy one. Although Mao acknowledged the Party Central's authority, he maintained his own style of doing things. The Party Central accused Mao of caring only to consolidate the Kiangsi base at the expense of winning more territories to communism. It regarded Mao's practice as "separatism." In April 1930, the Party twice ordered Mao to report to Shanghai; Mao disobeyed.[5] Mao responded indifferently to Li Li-san's tac-

3. Kuo Hua-lun, *Chung-kung Shih-lun* (An Analytical History of the Chinese Communist Party), Vol. II (Taipei: Chung-hua Min-kuo Kuo-chi Kuan-hsi Yen-Chiu-so, 1973), p. 383.

4. T'sai Hsiao-ch'ien, p. 91; and Kuo Hua-lun, Vol. II, p. 384.

5. Ssu-ma Ch'ang-feng, *Mao Tse-tung Yu Chou En-lai* (Mao Tse-tung and Chou En-lai) (Hong Kong: Nan-ching I-wen She, 1976), pp. 12-14.

tics of capturing cities as the first step for a nation-wide revolution. Aside from complaints, the Party Central could do nothing to Mao because he was protected by distance.

The situation changed at the end of 1931 when the Party Central decided to move from Shanghai to Kiangsi. Mao's position was immediately challenged. The men from Shanghai accused him of carrying out a bloody purge in which 20,000 men were killed. In addition, they severely criticized Mao's land program and military tactics. For Mao, the most important task during the time of consolidation was to win the support of the majority of the people. Thus his land redistribution policy was relatively mild. The Party Central, however, condemned Mao's approach as a denial of class struggle, and accused him of following a "rich peasant line." In regard to military strategy, Mao was a proponent of guerrilla warfare. He insisted that enemies should be "lured" into China's interior so that they could each be handled separately. Mao's ideas on guerrilla tactics were developed when he was in Chingkangshan where he had tested them successfully in combat with KMT troops. The Party Central, on the other hand, was in favor of open positional warfare. They maintained that it was too dangerous to allow the enemy to penetrate into the soviet base because this would threaten the very heart of the Communist regime. They argued, instead, that the Communists should take the initiative and attack the enemy directly. They denounced Mao's tactics as "escapist" and "rightist-opportunist".

Teng agreed with Mao's strategy.[6] He found Mao more practical and clear-minded than the idealistic Internationalist leaders. Thus he was drawn to Mao's side and became his active supporter. Mao obviously did not have the advantage in his conflict with the Party Central. In August 1932 he was removed from the post of Political Commissar of the Kiangsi Red Army.

---

6. Ibid, p. 44; and Kuo Hua-lun, Vol. II, p. 384.

The post was filled by Chou En-lai. Despite the setback, Teng remained a supporter of Mao. But he would pay for his loyalty.

In February 1933 the KMT launched its fourth encirclement campaign. The Party decided to try to halt the enemy beyond the border, an approach which Mao would never agree to. Lo Ming, a Maoist in Fukien, argued that the Communist army in the western Fukien province (including Shang-hang and Yung-ting) was not strong enough to hold the enemy. In addition, Lo believed the people there lacked the morale to fight. He suggested that the Party abandon the Fukien base and wait for a better time to retaliate. Lo Ming's advice was not taken well by the Party Central. In order to block the drift toward guerrilla warfare, a campaign was launched to denounce the "Lo Ming line." Lo was condemned for advocating "escapism" and discredited.

The anti-Lo Ming campaign was extended to Kiangsi. Whoever disagreed with the Party's military policy was purged. The anti-Lo Ming Line was, in fact, an extension of the Party's attack on Mao. The small Maoist group headed by Teng was singled out as representative of the Lo Ming Line in Kiangsi Province. They were accused of upholding the dangerous military tactic of "luring the enemy into the interior," instead of fighting the enemy in the "white area." They were also condemned for instituting a conciliatory program of "equal distribution of lands among peasants" thereby disregarding the class character of different peasants and for forming conspiratorial groups within the Party. Teng was replaced as the Secretary of the Provincial Party by Li Fu-ch'un. In addition, the "four warriors" were all given serious warning to mend their views.[7] The campaign against Mao's adherents, was fatal to the small group.

---

7. Ts'ao Po-i, *Chiang-hsi Su-wei-ai Te Chien-li Chi Ch'i Peng-kui* (The Rise and Fall of the Kiangsi Soviet) (Taipei: Kuo-li Cheng-chih Ta-hsueh Tung-ya Yen-chiu-so, 1969), pp. 494-495; and Ts'ai Hsiao-chien, *Chiang-si Su-ch'u, Hung-chun Hsi-t'suan Hui-i-lu*, p. 91.

Ku Po and Hsieh Wei-chun disappeared from the political scene and Mao Tse-t'an was ordered to stay behind in Kiangsi when the Party evacuated the base in 1934. He was later killed by the KMT in battle. Everywhere, those who were close to Mao, both in the government and the army, were criticized. Among them were Teng Tzu-hui, Ho Shu-heng, T'an Chen-lin, and Hsiao Chin-kuang.[8] This was the first of the three purges that Teng experienced in his political career.

In January 1934, at the Fifth Plenary Session of the Sixth Congress, the issue of the Lo Ming Line and the "Teng-Mao-Ku-Hsieh anti-Party group" was put on the agenda again. One participant argued during the session that Mao was the leader behind the conspiratorial group and should himself be punished. Tung Pi-wu presided over a follow-up investigation, but concluded that Mao could continue to hold certain political offices, there being insufficient evidence to prove his involvement with Teng's group. Thanks to Tung, Mao was saved from a possible purge.[9] Although Mao did not fall with the other followers of the Lo Ming Line, his position in the Party was weakened. Eventually, in August 1934, he was removed from all major responsibilities.

Chou En-lai's attitude at the time is worth noting here. Chou was strongly opposed to the Lo Ming Line and insisted that followers or sympathizers of Lo Ming be condemned.[10] He did nothing to protect Teng from the resulting purge. Given Chou's position in the Party at the time, had he so desired, he could have saved Teng from such severe disgrace. Chou and Teng had been close friends since their days in France. When Teng led the Pai-se uprising, he was responsible to Chou, who then headed the Military Affairs Department. Before Teng came to Kiangsi, he worked closely with Chou in Shanghai. But now

---

8. Ssu-ma Ch'ang-feng, *Mao Tse-tung Yu Chou En-lai*, pp. 47-48.
9. Kuo Hua-lun, Vol. II, pp. 434-435.
10. Kai-yu Hsu, p. 98.

Chou did nothing to protect his old comrade. Most probably, he was disappointed to see Teng, supposedly a Party Central man, become a follower of Mao. The Kiangsi days witnessed an extremely uneasy relationship between Teng and Chou.

On the other hand, the anti-Lo Ming attacks brought Teng and Mao even closer. After that time, Teng was acknowledged as Mao's man and his successes in the Party depended to a large extent on the ups and downs of Mao. Twelve years later the Lo Ming Line was reexamined. By that time Mao had emerged as the leader of the CCP. At the Seventh Plenary Session of the Sixth Party Congress, a document entitled "On the Resolutions of Certain Historical Issues" declared that the criticism of the Lo Ming Line made twelve years earlier had been a mistake.[11] Eventually, Teng was cleared.

Besides being attacked politically, Teng was further embittered by the split-up of his second marriage. When Teng first arrived in Kiangsi he met and wooed Chin Wei-ying (nicknamed "Ah Chin"). Chin, from Chekiang, had become a Communist in 1929 and thereafter served as a political tutor of the Red Army School in Kiangsi. Supposedly a pretty girl, easy going, disarming, and persuasive, she led a simple life before she met Teng.[12] She had earlier succeeded Teng as the Secretary of the Juichin District Party Committee.[13] Following their marriage, the two worked together in the Provincial Party Committee. When Teng was discredited in 1933, he faced a divorce at home as well. Chin was transferred to work in the CCP Organization Department. In January 1934, at the second National Soviet Congress, she was elected a member of the Presidium and

11. Ts'ao Po-i, p. 498.

12. *Chung Pao*, (Center Daily News, New York), March 10, 1982, and Ts'ai Hsiao-ch'ien, p. 176.

13. As told by Informant No. 2 in a personal interview conducted in Taipei, in January 1980. The interviewee was formerly a senior cadre of the CCP and later defected to the KMT.

a member of the Central Soviet Executive Committee, the highest executive organ of the Congress. Teng was excluded. Chin later married Li Wei-han, Teng's old friend in France and roommate in Wuhan. She was among the very few women who joined the Long March. In Yenan, Chin taught in the Anti-Japanese University. Later Li fell in love with a student and Chin, along with Mao's second wife, Ho Chih-chen, was sent to Moscow to recover her health. But the Soviets knew that they were unwanted. Chin died in Moscow soon after she arrived there.[14]

After Teng had been removed from all political responsibilities, he was assigned to teach at the Red Army Academy. The Academy, located in Juichin, was built in August 1933 for the purpose of training senior military cadres. Teng taught the caurse "Construction of the Party." Other teachers included Chou En-lai, Liu Po-ch'eng, Wang Chia-hsiang, Tung Pi-wu, Tso Ch'uan (Teng's classmate in the Sun Yat-sen University), Wu Hsiu-ch'uan, and Wei Kung-chih (Teng's colleague in Feng Yu-hsiang's army).[15] Among the students was Yang Te-chih, who is currently Chief-of-Staff of the People's Liberation Army. In 1934, Teng was transferred to work in the army's Political Department as editor of the "Red Star," a journal published every three days.[16] This was the least eventful period of his political career.

Open positional warfare restrained the KMT for a time only. In the next, and fifth, encirclement campaign, Chiang

---

14. Ts'ai Hsiao-ch'ien, pp. 175-186; *Chung Pao*, March 10, 1982; Chou Yu-jui, p. 190; and Wang Chien-min, *Chung-kuo Kung-chan-tang Shih-kao* (A Draft History of the Chinese Communist Party), Vol. II (Taipei: self-published, 1965), pp. 312-313.

15. James L. Price, *Cadres, Commanders and Commissars* (Boulder, Colo.: Westview Press, 1976). pp. 121-122; and Kung Ch'u, Vol. II, p. 504.

16. "Chieh-k'ai Teng Hsiao-p'ing Te Fan-ko-ming Lao-ti," p. 4; and Chi Hsin, *Teng Hsiao-ping*, p. 19.

Kai-shek employed "blockhouse tactics" to cut off all possible communication of the Communists with the outside world. The Kiangsi Soviet was now on the verge of collapsing. In October 1934, the Red Army decided to abandon the base and go North in order to survive. They retreated from Kiangsi and began a notorious year of suffering — the Long March. Many Maoists were left behind and most of them were later killed by the KMT. Luckily Teng departed with the army. He worked in the army's Propaganda Department and was said to have done his job well.[17] The Long March provided an opportunity for both Mao and Teng to make a comeback.

When the army reached Tsun-i, an enlarged Politburo meeting was called. Teng attended as an observer.[18] Mao took the floor and declared that the Party Central was responsible for the ignoble retreat that occurred before Chiang's army had even arrived in Kiangsi. He criticized the employment of harmful tactics in the face of a strong enemy. Supported by the military faction, Mao was empowered to lead the army in place of the Internationalists. Mao also supplanted Chou En-lai as head of the Military Commission although Chou was retained in the Commission as Mao's deputy. The Tsun-i Conference was a landmark event in the history of Chinese Communism, since Mao emerged as the supreme leader of the Party. Teng later recalled: "It was at this conference that the opportunist line was corrected. Comrade Mao, as the head of the Party, brought the Party onto the right path."[19]

---

17. Chou Yu-jui, p. 191.

18. According to a dispatch of China's official Hsinhua News Agency on January 9, 1980. This was the first time the CCP disclosed to the outside world the names of the attendants of the Tsun-i Conference. See *Ta Kung Pao* (Hong Kong), January 10, 1980. During the Cultural Revolution, the Red Guards accused Teng of falsely claiming to have attended the meeting. See "Teng Hsiao-p'ing Tsui-hsing Tiao-ch'a Pao-kao," pp. 36-38.

19. *Chung-kung Jen-ming-lu*, p. 942.

Following Mao's ascendency to power, Teng's position in the Party improved. In June 1935, when the First Front Army under Mao and the Fourth Front Army under Chang Kuo-t'ao met in Maukung, Szechuan, a rift occurred which caused CCP reorganization. The First Front Army was renamed the Left Army and was entrusted to the command of P'eng Te-huai and Lin Piao. Nieh Jung-chen and Teng became the Political Commissar and Deputy Political Commissar, respectively, of the Left Army's First Column. The Fourth Front Army was renamed the Right Army and given to the command of Hsu Hsiang-ch'ien, with Ch'en Ch'ang-hao appointed its Political Commissar.[20] Of all these appointments, Teng's return to favor was the most striking.

The Fourth Front Army, originally the chief military force from the O-Yu-Wan (Hupeh, Honan and Anhwei) Soviet, abandoned its base in 1933 and fled to northern Szechuan, where it founded a new base in 1934. When it heard that the First Front Army was on its way north, the Fourth Front Army went south to greet its comrade soldiers. Later, during the Second Sino-Japanese war, Teng developed a close tie with the Fourth Front Army when, as political Commissar of the 129th Division, he met many soldiers who had been drawn from the Fourth Front Army.[21]

The reunion of the two armies in Maukung was not a happy one. The Fourth Front Army boasted an enlistment 45,000 soldiers, while the First Front Army possessed a mere

20. Chang Kuo-t'ao, *Wo Te Hui-i* (My Memoirs), Vol. III (Hong Kong: Ming Pao Yueh-K'an She, 1973), p. 137.

21. The notable figures in the Fourth Front Army were Ch'en Hsi-lien, Ch'in Chi-wei, Li Te-sheng, Hsieh Fu-chih, Su Chen-hua, Ch'en Tsai-tao, Li Ch'eng-fang, Kuo Lin-hsiang, Chou Hsi-han, Tseng Shao-san, Wang Hsin-ting, Yu T'ai-chung, Wang Hung-k'un, Hsu Hsiang-ch'ien, Han Hsien-ch'u, Chang Ts'ai-ch'ien and Hsu Shih-yu (the last two were not later enlisted in the Second Field Army.)

10,000. Chang Kuo-t'ao was therefore unwilling to accept Mao's leadership. He challenged Mao's plan of marching northward and requested the recalling and re-election of the Party Central Committee. Chang proposed, instead, that the army head south and set up a soviet base in the border regions of Szechuan and Sikang.

Mao ignored Chang, and on September 2nd, he led his First Front Army northward without notifying his rival commander. He named his army the Shensi-Kansu Red Army, with P'eng Te-huai as the military commander and himself the Political Commissar.[22] Nieh Jung-chen and Teng Hsiao-p'ing were respectively appointed Political Commissar and Deputy Political Commissar of the Army's First Column.[23]

The Fourth Front Army, angry with Mao because he had left with his own army without any notification, went to the South to establish an independent government. The First Front Army continued its Long March, passing through eleven provinces and overcoming numerous hazardous mountains and rivers before finally reaching Shensi. For a while there existed two Party centers, each claiming legitimacy in what was the most serious split in CCP history.

Teng followed Li Li-san's orders when he was in Kwangsi. However, the disasters brought about by Li Li-san's strategy gave Teng the understanding that fanaticism would destroy the revolution. At that time Mao was a realist and disobeyed Li Li-san's directives. He believed that both Li Li-san and his successors, the Internationalists, were ignorant of Chinese realities. History proved that Mao was right. Teng shared Mao's vision of

---

22. The Shensi-Kansu Army consisted of three columns: The First Column, reorganized from the former First Army Corps, was led by Lin Piao; the Second Column, reorganized from the Third Army Corps, was led by P'eng; and the Third column, reorganized from a column directly serving the Military Commission, was led by Yeh Chien-ying.

23. Ssu-ma Ch'ang-feng, *Mao Tse-tung Yu Chou En-lai*, p. 91.

the future of the revolution and believed that his approach was the most practical to achieve a Communist state. Teng followed Mao closely at that time because he found Mao's realism attractive. Thirty years later he divided with Mao because he found Mao's idealism fanatical.

Mao and Teng cultivated a very special relationship during the Kiangsi days. Mao was Teng's senior by 11 years, but their relationship was not simply one between director and subordinate. Mao treated Teng as his younger brother and Teng looked upon Mao as a brother-teacher. Teng was also a good friend of Mao Tse-T'an, Mao's youngest brother. The two were only a year apart in age. When Mao remembered his deceased brother, he also probably associated Teng with him. This brotherly love between Mao and Teng helps explain why Teng would not go to extremes in opposing Mao and why Mao would not force Teng into oblivion during the Cultural Revolution when he was supposedly a leader of the opposition camp.

Chapter 6

The Wartime Years (1936-1949)

In the summer of 1936, Mao sent troops west to augment the recently defeated forces of the Second and the Fourth Front Armies in Szechuan. The Second Front Army, led by Ho Lung, had retreated earlier from its Hunan-Hupeh base to join Chang Kuo-t'ao in Szechuan.[1] The First Corps under Lin Piao halted at Hui-ning where they waited for the retreating forces of Ho Lung and Chang Kuo-t'ao. The Ho-Chang forces arrived at the Shensi stronghold in October.

Although settled in Shensi, the Reds were still exposed to frequent attacks by the KMT.[2] However, the dramatic Sian Incident brought the two opposing parties again into collaboration. The incident occurred in December 1936 when Chiang Kai-shek was arrested in Sian by Marshal Chang Hsueh-liang and his partner Yang Hu-ch'eng while Chiang was on an investigative trip there. Chang and Yang demanded that Chiang stop the internal war and turn his forces against the Japanese invad-

---

1. Li Feng-ming, ed., *Chung-hung Shou-yao Shih-lu Hui-pien* (A Chronology of Chinese Communist Leaders) (Taipei: Chung-kung Yen-chiu Tsa-chih She, 1969), p. 290.

2. On August 19th Teng received the U.S. correspondent Edgar Snow in Yu-wang-po, a town in Southern Ninghsia. Snow's interviews with Teng provide some of our most valuable insights in our pursuit of Teng's early career.

ers instead. The Japanese had indeed, by July 1937, launched an all-out war against China. The KMT and the CCP agreed to cooperate for a second time for the sake of the country.

The Communist army was incorporated into KMT forces, and was called the Eighth Route Army (later known as the 18th Route Army) with Chu Te and P'eng Te-huai as its Commander and Deputy Commander. Jen Pi-shih was appointed Director of the Political Department and Yeh Chien-ying the Chief-of-Staff. Teng worked under Jen as Deputy Director of the Political Department.[3] The Eighth Route Army consisted of three divisions: the 115th Division with Commander Lin Piao and Political Commissar Nieh Jung-chen; the 120th Division with Commander Ho Lung and Political Commissar Kuan Hsiang-ying; and the 129th Division with Commander Liu Po-ch'eng and Political Commissar Chang Hao. These divisions were reorganized mainly from the remnants of the original First, Second, and Fourth Front Armies with an infusion of new recruits. For example, the 129th Division consisted mostly of personnel from the Fourth Front Army, but it also included a number of officers and soldiers from the First Front Army. Similarly, some of the Fourth Front Army elements were incorporated into other divisions. The 115th Division led by Lin Piao was later divided into two forces: one led by Lo Jung-huan and the other led by Nieh Jung-chen. In addition, the CCP created a fifth force, the New Fourth Army, which was independent of the Eighth Route Army organization.

In the first few weeks following the outbreak of the Sino-Japanese War, Teng worked in the General Political Department in the Wutai area northeast of Shensi.[4] The Eighth Route Army was then under the command of the KMT warlord, Yen

---

3. Kuan Chien, "Wo Kan Teng Hsiao-p'ing" (My Views on Teng Hsiao-p'ing), *Tung-hsiang*, No. 6 (March, 1979), p. 46; and *Chung-kung Jen-ming-lu*, p. 942.

4. Klein and Clark, *Biographic Dictionary*, Vol. II, p. 821.

Hsi-shan, in defending northern Shansi. Before the Eighth Route Army set off to the front, Mao reminded the troops that their principal job was to strengthen Communist power. He commanded the Army to avoid direct combat with the Japanese so as to preserve their strength. Instead he told them to divide the Japanese forces by employing guerrilla tactics. He also ordered them to establish, if possible, soviet bases for staging guerrilla warfare in the rear of the Japanese controlled areas. In early September 1937, the Eighth Route Army crossed the Yellow River and moved towards Shansi. Teng crossed the river with army headquarters personnel and was on the same boat with Chu Te, Jen Pi-shih, and Tso Ch'uan, the acting Chief-of-Staff.[5]

The Eighth Route Army went into combat against the Japanese in Shansi. On November 9th, Taiyuan, the provincial capital, fell into Japanese hands. KMT troops retreated from the province to the west and south. The Eighth Route Army, however, was instructed by the CCP to remain there and fight independently. Thus the Communists did not withdraw with the KMT forces. They moved instead to the northeast, the northwest, and the southeast of the province to carry out guerrilla skirmishes. The Japanese, constrained by their modest numbers, could only hold the major cities of the province. The spacious rural areas were left open for the Communists to carry on their hit and run activities.

Soon, the 129th Division, with a strength of about 6,000 people, joined the local Communist organ in Shansi to establish a guerrilla base in the mountain areas of T'ai-hang and T'ai-yueh.[6] The mountains were strategically very important because they afforded access to the eastern plain. The wide and

---

5. From a photo taken while cross the river, reproduced in *Tung Hsi Fang* (The East and the West Monthly, Hong Kong), 1980.

6. The local Shansi organ was headed by Ch'ing-yu and Li Hsueh-feng and the student activists led by Po I-po (who later became China's Finance Minister and Vice Premier) and Jung Sheng-wu (who later became Deputy Finance Minister).

continuous ranges provided an ideal staging ground for guerrilla incursions and were readily defensible besides. Thus the 129th Division established its headquarters in the area of T'aihang mountain, as did the Eighth Route Army. The region soon developed into an important base held by the Communists during the war against the Japanese.

In January 1938, Teng replaced Chang Hao as Political Commissar of the 129th Division, partly because Mao wanted him to keep a close eye on the army.[7] The 129th Division had been reorganized from the former Fourth Front Army of Chang Kuo-t'ao. Because the Fourth Front Army had followed Chang for so long, Mao regarded it with suspicion.[8]

Moreover, Mao did not trust Liu Po-ch'eng, who now led the 129th Division. Liu, the one-eyed general, was a Szechuanese. Ten years older than Teng, Liu had studied military affairs in Russia for about two and a half years. He was one of the most brilliant military leaders in the CCP. Perhaps because of his formal training he disapproved of guerrilla tactics and believed that guerrilla warfare could be used only as a supplementary fighting strategy. During the anti-Lo Ming Line campaign, Liu had sided with the Party Central against Mao's tactics of guerrilla warfare.[9] In Maukung, when Mao suddenly led his First Army away to the north, Chu Te and Liu were left behind. They had no choice but to follow Chang Kuo-t'ao to the south. Liu, although a subordinate of Mao, seemed to work with Chang rather well. When Chang established a Party Central in the Szechuan-Kansu region, Liu was elected a Central Committee member. He was also appointed to head the army

7. "Chieh-k'ai Teng Hsiao-p'ing Te Fan-ko-ming Lao-ti," p. 7. But it is inaccurate, as stated in the same page, that Teng was transferred to the 129th Division because Chang died. In fact, Chang later went to Yenan and taught at the Anti-Japanese University. He died in 1942. See Li' T'ien-min, *Lin Piao P'ing-chuan* (A Critical Biography of Lin Piao) (Hong Kong: Ming Pao Yueh-k'an She, 1978), p. 2.

8. Chang Kuo-t'ao later defected to the KMT.

9. Ts'ao Po-i, pp. 480-481.

academy there. Chang thought so highly of Liu's military knowledge that he instructed his officers to learn from him.[10] Liu's ambivalent attitude toward Chang was viewed by Mao as a potential sign of disloyalty. Since Mao did not trust Liu, he found it necessary to send a confidant to watch over the army. Teng was chosen, among other reasons, because he was a Szechuanese who was acceptable to Liu.[11]

Over the next twelve years, despite several reorganizations of the 129th Division[12] Teng remained its Political Commissar. The force led by them was nicknamed the "Liu-Teng Army."[13] Before that, Teng had held different positions in the Party but it was not until his appointment as Political Commissar of the 129th Division that Teng genuinely became an important CCP leader.

From its base in the T'ai-hang-T'ai-Yueh mountain region, the 129th Division expanded to the east. They first moved to southern Hopeh, then northern Honan, and finally western Shantung, thereby gaining control of the Hopeh-Shangtung-Honan plain. The border region of the provinces of Shansi, Hopeh, Honan, and Shangtung (Chin-Chi-Lu-Yu) was especially fertile for Communist activity. The Division based its power there until 1945.[14] A unit of the 129th Division also pene-

---

10. Chang Kuo-t'ao, *Wo-te Hui-i*, Vol. III, p. 64; Kuo Hua-lun, Vol. III, p. 64; and William Witson, "The Field Army in Chinese Communist Military Politics," in *China Quarterly*, No. 37 (1969), p. 5.

11. In *Liu Shao-ch'i* (published by Institute of International Relations, Taipei, 1975), Li T'ien-min raised his point that Mao did not trust Liu Po-ch'eng. See Li, pp. 78-80.

12. In 1946, the 129th Division was reorganized as the Chin-Chi-Lu-Yu Liberation Army; in 1948, as the Central Plain Liberation Army; and in 1949, as the Second Field Army.

13. T'ang P'ing-chu, "Chuan-chan Chiang-Huai-Ho-Han" ("Fighting Up and Down, Back and Forth on the Yangtze, the Huai River, the Han River, and the Yellow River"), in *Teng Hsiao-p'ing Tzu-liao Hsuan-chi*, p. 47.

14. The area looked like a square box which joined the Tung-P'u railroad in the west and the Tsin-P'u railroad in the east. To the north was the Te-Shih highway and to the south was the Lung-Hai railway. The total area covered was some 690,000 square miles.

trated deeply into Shangtung. This branch was later developed into the East China Field Army led by Ch'en I.

In the work of expansion, Teng assumed a variety of responsibilities, not the least of which was planning military advances. Before actual military undertakings, however, he sent political cadres as "vanguard forces" to organize such projects as propaganda and mobilization of the masses. He also supervised the political organs founded in areas within the 129th Division's sphere of influence. Under Teng's leadership, four administrative districts were built in 1938. These were located in T'ai-hang, T'ai-yueh, southern Hopeh and the Hopeh-Shangtung-Honan border region. In 1940 he formed an office which incorporated the district administrative organs of southern Hopeh, T'ai-hang, and T'ai-yueh.[15] In the next year, Teng provided the impetus for the inauguration of the Chin-Chi-Lu-Yu Border Region Assembly and Government.[16] Teng was elected a member of both the Assembly and the Government.[17]

While Teng was in southern Hopeh he met Evans Carlson, a U.S. military ovserver who was travelling in northern China to investigate Japanese manuvers.[18] Carlson had a long talk with Teng and came away quite impressed. He described Teng as "short, chunky, and physically tough" with a mind "as keen as mustard." He was also astonished at Teng's knowledge of international affairs. Carlson was one of the very few interviewers of Teng during that period who kept a record.[19]

---

15. Ch'i Wu, *I-ko Ken-chu-ti Te Ch'eng-chang* (The Growth of a Base), (Peking: Jen-min Ch'u-pan-she, 1958), p. 50. The supervisor was Yang Hsiu-feng.

16. Chi Hsin, *Teng Hsiao-ping*, pp. 91-93; and *Chung-kung Jen-ming-lu*, p. 942. The Chairman of the Border Government was Yang Hsiu-feng and the Vice-Chairmen were Po I-po and Jung Sheng-wu.

17. Hsiao Hua, "Mao Tse-tung Te Pi-ch'en Teng Hsiao-p'ing" (Mao's Favorite, Teng Hsiao-p'ing), in *Chin-jih Ta-lu*, (China Today, Taipei), June 1963, p. 24.

18. Carlson, then a major in the U.S. Marine Corps, was later promoted to brigadier general.

19. Evans F. Carlson, *Twin Star of China* (New York: Dodd, Mead, 1940), p. 252. Carlson spelled Teng's name as "Tun Shao-pin."

As the leading bureaucrat on the war front Teng held many important positions. He was a member of the CCP North China Bureau, Director of the T'ai-hang Administrative District, Political Commissar of the T'ai-hang Military Region, and Secretary of the T'ai-hang Party Bureau the last being the highest authority of the Chin-Chi-Lu-Yu Border Region. He was, in fact, one of the most important policy makers and policy initiators of the war era.[20]

Teng wrote a number of articles during these years which were published in Communist journals such as the *Chieh-fang (The Liberation), Ch'ien-hsien (The Front Line),* and *Ch'un-chung (The Masses).* These articles gave detailed descriptions of the situation in Teng's border regions.[21] They called for the exploitation of every possible resource to strengthen Communist territories and to mobilize the masses. Many political societies were organized to educate the people and inspire their patriotic sentiments against the Japanese invaders. Government organs at different levels were organized in accordance with the tripartite system observed in Yenan. The system gave equal seats and votes to the CCP, the KMT, and the independent parties. A moderate land program, which included reduction of rent and taxes, with an accompanying increase of wages for tenant-farmers, was instituted. The program took the needs of rich peasants and landlords into consideration as well. A policy of self-sufficiency was promoted throughout the areas blockaded by the Japanese. Peasants were encouraged to cultivate virgin lands.

---

20. *Chung-kung Jen-ming-lu,* p. 942; Hsiao Hua, p. 24; Kuo Hua-lun, Vol. IV, p. 41; and "Chieh-k'ai Teng Hsiao-P'ing Te Fan-ko-ming Lao-ti," p. 8.

21. These articles include "Mobilizing New troops and Political Work Among New Troops" *Ch'ien-hsien* (Front Line, Yenan), Nos. 3 & 4 (Feb. 1938), "South Hopeh in Bitter Struggle," *Chieh-fang,* (Liberation, Yenan), No. 71 (May, 1939), "The Two Lines in the Enemy Rear," *Chieh-fang,* No. 72, (May 1939), "The Eighth Route Army Maintains the War of Resistance in North China," *Ch'un-chung* (The Masses, Chungking), Vol. III, No. 8 & 9 (July, 1939); and "Economic Reconstruction in the T'ai-hang Area," *Ch'un-chung,* Vol. IX, No. 1, (January, 1944).

Even army soldiers were sent to work the fields, with every soldier assigned one quarter acre of land to cultivate.[22] Small-scale industries were founded to manufacture weapons and other necessities. Guerrilla warfare was the rule, but under favorable conditions the Communists employed some mobile tactics. When, in 1941, the Japanese launched a large-scale attack on the border area, armed work teams were sent behind Japanese lines to disrupt the enemy's progress.[23]

Despite frequent Japanese attacks and even a few natural disasters, the Chin-Chi-Lu-Yu base survived. In mid 1942, the Japanese launched a massive offensive in the hope of crushing defenders of the Chin-Chi-Lu-Yu region. The war persisted for a year, but the Liu-Teng army managed to hold out with heroic sacrifices. After 1943, the Japanese experienced repeated setbacks in the Pacific, calling for more and more Japanese regulars to be transferred to the Pacific theater of war. For the time being North China was relieved of constant Japanese pressure. This gave the Communists a breathing spell to further their consolidation. On the eve of the Japanese surrender in 1945, the border base embraced some 15 million people in 197 counties.[24]

Most of the fighting undertaken by the Communists in northern China was on a minor scale and defensive in nature. The exception came in August 1940 when the Communists launched an attack on the enemy. In order to stop Japanese thrusts toward the northwest and southwest, the Communists in northern China sent a hundred regiments into the field to attack

---

22. Equivalent to 3 acres in the Chinese system.
23. Ting Ling, *I-erh-chiu-shih Yu Chin-Chi-Lu-Yu Pien-ch'u* (The 129th Division and the Shansi-Hopeh-Shantung-Honan Border Area) (Peking: Hsin Hua Shu-tien, 1950), pp. 35-49; Tseng Shao-san, "Ti-hou Wu-kung-tui," (Armed Work Teams Behind the Enemy's Line), in *Teng Hsiao-p'ing Tzu-liao Hsuan-chi*, p. 37; and the KMT Central Organization Department, ed., "Chin-Chi-Lu-Yu Pien-chu Shih-Cheng Fang-Chen" ("Policy Making in the Shansi-Hopeh-Shangtung-Honan Border Area"). (No date.)
24. James Harrison, *Long March to Power* (New York: Praeger Publishers, 1972), p. 302; and Wiliam Witson, p. 5.

the Japanese along the main communication lines there. Their aim was to sabotage Japanese communications. The most severe fighting occurred in the Chin-Chi-Lu-Yu Border Region, and the casualties of the Communists were enormous. Liu and Teng personally supervised the struggle which lasted for three months. Over 7,000 Communist soldiers were killed.[25] The Hundred Regiment Battle was the most famous offensive of the Liu-Teng army during the war to oust Japan. The battle began earlier than scheduled. Consequently it received no actual approval from the Party's Central Military Commission chaired by Mao. However, after the war, Mao sent a congratulatory telegram praising the swift stroke. He said "The battle of the Hundred Regiments excited the people. How about having another similar victory?"[26] However, during the Cultural Revolution, the battle was criticized for failing to observe Mao's directive to avoid direct conflict. The offensive brought a severe loss of manpower and was followed by furious retaliation on the part of the Japanese. Teng was accused by the Red Guards of having boasted of the event as a perfect victory.[27] It was in the same year the battle was fought, that Teng married Cho Lin.[28]

In 1942, when the Cheng-Feng Rectification campaign was launched, Teng returned to Yenan to take part in it. He did not stay there long, but was said to have had several long talks with Mao. On his return to the Chin-Chi-Lu-Yu base, Teng launched a similar movement to help restore order in the war-torn area. According to Chou En-lai, "Teng had sincerely cooperated with the Cheng-Feng movement and at the time was relatively free or completely free of mistakes."[29] Teng's performance in the campaign obviously won Mao's confidence and appreciation.[30]

---

25. Ting Ling, p. 26.

26. P'eng Te-huai, *P'eng Te-huai Tzu-shu* (Memoirs of P'eng Te-huai) (Peking: Jen-min ch'u-pan She), 1981, pp. 236 and 238.

27. "Chieh-k'ai Teng Hsiao-p'ing Te Fan-ko-ming Lao-ti," p. 8.

28. *Ch'ing-nien Chan-shih Pao*, October 3, 1979.

29, Harrison, *Long March to Power*, p. 344.

30. Chou Yu-jui, p. 194.

In 1943, Teng was called back to Yenan to assume the directorship of the General Political Department of the People's Revolutionary Military Council, the highest military establishment in the CCP. Teng was appointed to supervise the political duties of 570,000 Communist regulars and 2,500,000 militia. He stayed most of the time in Yenan but made regular trips to his old haunts in North China. Teng remained in this position until 1945. Within those three years, he trained a significant number of political cadres.[31]

At the Seventh Congress of the CCP, held in April 1945, Mao's popularity was at its zenith. The Congress elected a Central Committee which consisted of 44 members. In the new committee the Maoists dominated the Internationalists. Teng, who had been purged earlier by the Internationalists, was elected for the first time to the Central Committee. He ranked 28th in the Committee ahead of Yeh Chien-ying, Nieh Jung-chen, and P'eng Te-huai.[32] From then until the Cultural Revolution, Teng led a rather smooth and successful career.

The Second United Front between the KMT and the CCP actually fell apart in 1941 following the New Fourth Army Incident. After that, conflicts between the two parties continued incessantly. After the Japanese surrendered in August 1945, hostilities intensified. The Civil War broke out in mid-1946, almost immediately after an abortive U.S. attempt at reconciliation. Mao championed the overthrow of the KMT by force. Teng again found himself on the battlefield.[33]

The 129th Division was enlarged and reconstituted after the Sino-Japanese War and renamed the Chin-Chi-Lu-Yu People's

31. Snow, *Red Star*, p. 499; *Who's Who in Communist China*, p. 611; and Chou Yu-jui, p. 193.

32. Wang Chien-min, *Chung-kuo Kung-chan-tang Shih-kao* (A Draft History of the Chinese Communist Party), Vol. III (Taipei: Self published, 1960), p. 166.

33. Boorman, "Teng Hsiao-p'ing," p. 115.

Liberation Army (PLA). To veterans of the Japanese War it was still fondly known as the "Liu-Teng" army, for Teng was retained as its Political Commissar. The army consisted of twelve divisions with a number totalling 130,000, the largest of all the Communist armed forces of the time.[34] It specialized in guerrilla warfare and, according to a leading KMT general, was the swiftest and most disciplined army the Communists possessed.[35] The Liu-Teng army was instructed to fight in coordination with Ch'en I's New Fourth Army in eastern and central China. The Chin-Chi-Lu-Yu PLA was directed to gain control of the Peip'ing-Tientsin railroad while Ch'en I's army concentrated on either side of the Tientsin-P'uko railroad. The operation was intended to cut the KMT's communication line joining their forces in northern and southern China. In March 1947, Yenan was bombarded by Hu Tsung-nan, one of Chiang's top generals. In June, Ch'en I's army was held at bay by the KMT in the east. Mao therefore instructed the Chin-Chi-Lu-Yu PLA to push south to divert KMT troops from the Communist controlled areas. Teng was appointed Secretary of the CCP's Central China Bureau to lead the move.[36] After a month of preparation, Liu and Teng led seven divisions of 50,000 men across the Yellow River into the familiar battlefields of western Shangtung.[37]

On the second day after crossing the river, Liu and Teng addressed the assembled army. A cadre member recollected the event:

> I found military maps hanging on the walls marked with red and blue crosses. Commissar Teng appeared as usual — sincere, calm, and speaking with precision. He pointed to the map on the

---

34. Wang Chien-min, Vol. III, p. 567.

35. The remark was made by Huang Shao-hsiung. See Jerome Ch'en, *Mao and the Chinese Revolution* (New York: Oxford University Press, 1965), p. 254.

36. Chi Hsin, *Teng Hsiao-p'ing*, p. 27; and "Chieh-k'ai Teng Hsiao-p'ing Te Fan-ko-ming Lao-ti," p. 10.

37. Harrison, *Long March to Power*, p. 422.

wall and said, "The enemy is aiming at Shangtung and north Shensi.... Theirs are tactics of dumb-bells.

"They have concentrated their forces on both ends of our army and we are the handle in the middle. Our task is to break their lines and divert the warfare to the KMT-controlled areas.... We have to rush over the Ta-pieh Mountains, to liberate central China.... Our next move is to cross the Yangtze River and liberate the whole country.

"If we fail to break through, what will happen then? For sure we can destroy some of our enemies, but the resources of the liberated areas are not sufficient for a prolonged war. What Chiang Kai-shek wishes is to keep the wars in the liberated regions so that we will become exhausted. But we have to break through and smash the counter-revolutionary plans of Chiang".... [38]

On August 7th, the Liu-Teng Army marched southward at a speed of 30 miles per day. The army rolled across the central China plain and ran toward the Ta-pieh Mountains. To the KMT generals they appeared to be fleeing. The KMT believed the Communists' days were numbered because six or seven big rivers blocked their route to the mountains. They pursued the Reds leisurely. By the time the Nationalists realized their folly, it was too late to stop the Liu-Teng army from reaching the Ta-pieh Mountains on August 28. The Reds had succeeded in their mission of "racing a thousand miles" in less than two months. The Ta-pieh Mountains, bordering Honan, Anhwei, and Hupeh, were formerly the base of the O-Yu-Wan Soviet, the home of the Fourth Front Army. Many of Liu's officers were from this area. Since the KMT had placed its best army in northern China, the Communists did not find the KMT troops in central China too difficult to handle.

Within a few months Liu and Teng succeeded in developing the area into a Communist base. The movement of the Liu-Teng army was the first invasion the Communists directed

---

38. T'ang P'ing-chu, p. 47.

toward the south. The building of a base in the Ta-pieh Mountains constituted a threat to Wuhan and Nanking, the capital of the KMT regime. In the face of this, Chiang was forced to recall some of his troops from the north. As a result, The Communist headquarters in northern China were relieved of the immense pressure of the KMT army.

While Liu and Teng led their army to the Ta-pieh Mountains, Ch'en I's army marched into east Honan to fill the gap. In addition, a division of the Chin-Chi-Lu-Yu PLA comprising 20,000 soldiers led by Ch'en Keng and Hsieh Fu-chih moved into west Honan.[39] The three armies — Liu and Teng in the Ta-pieh Mountains, Ch'en I in east Honan, and Chen Keng in west Honan — formed a triangle ready to fight a decisive war with Chiang. Now the Communists had the upper hand, having turned from a defensive posture to an offensive one, while the KMT was forced to take the defensive.[40] Mao remarked that the move to the Ta-pieh Mountains was a historical turning point.[41] In order to control the central China plain, the CCP decided to enlarge and strengthen the Central China Bureau, of which Teng was the First, and Ch'en I the Second, and Teng Tzu-hui the Third Secretary.[42]

A land program was introduced in the Ta-pieh Mountain area. Since the principal enemy was no longer the Japanese imperialists but the feudal landlords, a more radical approach was adopted in order to win stronger peasant support. The new goal was to unite the poor peasants, to conciliate the middle peasants, and to purge the rich peasants. The war time policy of rent and tax reduction was replaced by a radical program of

---

39. Harrison, *Long March to Power*, p. 422.

40. See T'ang P'ing-chu, pp. 47-64; and Wang Chien-min, Vol. III., pp. 586-587.

41. Mao Tse-tung, *Mao Tse-tung Hsuan-chi* (Selected Works of Mao Tse-tung) (Peking: Jen-min Ch'u-pan-she, 1964), p. 1140.

42. Li Ta, "I Huai-Hai Chan-i" (Recollections of the Huai-Hai Battle), in *Hung-ch'i P'aio-P'iao*, Vol. 18 (Peking: Chung-kuo Ching-nien Ch'u-pan-she, 1979), p. 153.

land and property confiscation and redistribution. The poor peasants benefited most because they received the best land. Teng told his cadres that "some of our cadres have never come in close contact with the peasants. They isolate themselves from them. That is the landlord line. If you look down on the peasants you will also be looked down upon." He said that the majority line was sympathetic to the peasants.[43]

In September 1948, the CCP reorganized all its forces into five units: the Northwest Field Army, led by P'eng Te-huai; the East China Field Army, led by Ch'en I; the Northeast China Field Army, led by Lin Piao; the North China Field Army, led by Nieh Jung-chen; and the Central Plain Army, led by Liu and Teng. The Liu-Teng army was sent to defend central China. With 249,150 men, it was the largest of the five units.[44]

Three decisive battles enabled the Communists to take over China beginning in September 1948. These were the Battle of Liao-Shen (September 12, 1948 to November 2, 1948), the Battle of Huai-Hai (November 6, 1948 to January 10, 1949), and the Battle of P'ing-Tsin (November 14, 1948 to January 31, 1949). Victory in these battles helped the Communists to control most parts of China — the northeast, the north, and central China. The Huai-Hai battle in particular was the most important. The KMT's defeat following this 65 day struggle presaged its inevitable downfall.

The battlefield was centered near the city of Hsuchou, north of the Huai River. This location was the meeting point of the Tientsin-Nankin railway (from north to south) and the Sian-East Coast railroad (from west to east). Strategically it was so important that the KMT could not afford to lose it. The Communists sent 600,000 men, including seven divisions from the Central Plain Field Army and sixteen divisions from the

43. Teng Hsiao-p'ing, *Teng Hsiao-p'ing Tsai Erh-ti-wei-hui Shang Te Pao-kao* (Teng's Report to the Second Meeting of the District Party Committee), report published by the Party Committee of Hsin-hsien County, 1948.
44. Wang Chien-min, Vol. III, p. 570.

East China Field Army, to capture the city.[45] The KMT also set comparable manpower afield. It was the largest battle fought in the Civil War.

Since the two Communist armies were now combined into one, a new commanding structure was required to carry out the functions of strategic planning and policy implementation. Thus the CCP instituted a five-man "Front Committee" which included Liu Po-ch'eng, Ch'en I, Teng Hsiao-p'ing, Su Yu (second commander of the Third Field Army), and T'an Chen-lin (Deputy Political Commissar of the Third Field Army). Teng was appointed Secretary, the most responsible member of the Committee.[46]

Kuomintang troops were defeated mainly because they employed a strategy that ignored the geography of the central plain. The plains were best suited for mobile warfare. The KMT, however, adopted the strategy of garrisoning their troops. Nor did they garrison themselves in the south, thereby exploiting the natural barrier of the Huai River. Instead, they were stationed in the hostile north and exposed rather openly to onslaughts by the Communists. In addition, the KMT was recently defeated in the north in the Battle of Liao-Shen. This affected the morale of the KMT army defending the Huai river region. KMT generals were suspicious of one another and did not readily cooperate.

The Communists, on the other hand, adopted mobile army tactics. They cut the KMT off from their major lines of communication and isolated the enemy troops into separate units to be picked off one by one. Furthermore, they were able to mobilize the masses as food suppliers.

The KMT suffered great casualties in the Huai-Hai Battle. Spoils from the KMT camp included high-quality U. S. manufactured weapons that the Communists sorely needed. KMT

---

45. Each division consisted of 20,000 to 50,000 soldiers.
46. Li Ta, p. 161.

losses at Huai-Hai exposed Nanking and Shanghai to the Communists. Although Mao designed the blueprint of the battle, Teng, as the frontline commander, was responsible for last-minute decisions. In late January the Communists won the Pling-Tsin battle which opened the war for "liberation" in the south.

In February 1949, the Communist troops were given numerical designations which implied that they were ready for a national, not regional, war. The Northwest Field Army was called the First Field Army; the East China Field Army the Third Field Army; and the Northeast Field Army the Fourth Field Army. The North China Field Army was not given any designation. It was divided into five regiments which were subordinated to the PLA Headquarters.

The Second Field Army now consisted of three army corps. Each corps comprised three armies, with a total armed force of 300,000. Soon after the Huai-Hai Battle, the Second and the Third Field Armies were ordered to move from the Poyang Lake to the Yangtze River bank. When news spread of the breakdown of peace talks between the CCP and the KMT, the Communists crossed the Yangtze on April 21st. The chief command was once again awarded to Teng Hsiao-p'ing.[47] The Communists crossed the Yangtze with ease because KMT morale was low. Some KMT soldiers fled. Others either retreated or surrendered. On April 24th the combined forces of the Second and Third Field Armies took Nanking. A month later, Shanghai fell. A CCP East China Bureau was set up with Teng as its Secretary, the supreme authority in eastern China. With the fall of Shanghai, the KMT's doomsday arrived.[48]

---

47. Ho Ko-hsi, "Ta Kuo Ch'ang-chiang, Chieh-fang Nan-king" (Fight Across the Yangtze and Liberate Nanking) in *Teng Hsiao-p'ing Tzu-liao Hsuan-chi*, pp. 74-81; and Chi Hsin, *Teng Hsiao-p'ing*, p. 20.

48. *Who is Who in Communist China*, p. 611; "Chieh-k'ai Teng Hsiao-p'ing Te Fan-ko-ming Lao-ti," p. 11; and Wang Hsuan, *Teng Hsiao-p'ing*, p. 18.

In June, T'ang Tse, Teng's schoolmate in primary school, came across Teng unexpectedly in Shanghai at a banquet at the Yang Lo Restaurant. Yang Lo was a favorite gathering place for the Communists. T'ang discovered that the famous Communist was his former schoolmate. Teng told him about his good physical condition, rolling up his sleeve to show his muscular arm. Teng also told him that he was going to Hong Kong to meet the liberals there in preparation for the liberation of the southwest.[49]

On October 1, China was declared the People's Republic. Teng flew to Peking to attend the ceremony. He was elected a member of the Political Consultation Conference wich *which* served as a national representative body to legitimate and empower the new government. Teng was also elected to the Central People's Government Council and People's Revolutionary Military Council, two of the supreme organs of the state chaired by Mao. Also, Teng was appointed a member of the executive board of the Sino-Soviet Friendship Association.[50] Soon afterwards, Teng returned to the Army and continued the unfinished task of cleaning up the KMT.

The Second Field Army began an invasion of southwest China in early November. On November 15th Kweiyang fell. Fifteen days later, Chungking was occupied. Besides employing military tactics, Teng also considered every possible political strategy. He approached dissident KMT generals such as Lu Han (of Yunan) and Liu Wen-hui (of Sikang), persuading them to turn to the Communist side by rewarding them with titles similar to those that they then held.[51] In December, the two

---

49. According to Informant No. 1.

50. Klein and Clark, Vol. II, p. 822; and *Who is Who in Communist China*, p. 611.

51. It was agreed that Lu and Liu would maintain control over their territories and army. Later, however, they were transferred to other posts. Lu Han became Deputy Chairman of the National Commission of Physical Education and Sports, and Liu Wen-hui, a member of the People's Congress.

generals defected.[52] Without wasting a bullet, Teng and Liu were able to conquer two major provinces in the south.

Ho Lung and Li Ching-ch'uan, in the meantime, led their First Field Army and the 18th Regiment into the Szechuan province. On December 27th, Chengtu was taken. With the exception of Tibet, the southwest provinces were now all held by the Communists.

Teng's importance during the years of the war against Japan and the Civil War was considerable. These struggles were his most difficult challenges since joining the CCP. As Political Commissar of the 129th Division, Teng was responsible not only for propaganda work and mass mobilization, but he also had to participate in actual military operations. In reality, he held a more responsible and important position than Liu Po-ch'eng.[53]

Teng contributed greatly to the founding of the People's Republic. His pride is evident in the remark, "If [Lin Piao] had his Manchuria campaign, I had my Huai-Hai campaign; [Lin] had fought from northeast China to south China, I fought from Nanking to Chengtu."[54]

The war years left Teng with unforgettable memories. At the Eighth Party Congress (1956), when Teng recalled the days when "soldiers carried water for the people and officers covered the soldiers with blankets" he could not help weeping.[55]

It was during the wartime years that Teng established his close relationship with the army. It was easy for soldiers to cultivate a brotherly feeling toward each other during war time

---

52. Brian Crozier, *The Man Who Lost China* (New York: Charles Scribner's Sons, 1976), p. 345; Chou Yu-jui, pp. 193-194.

53. T'ang P'ing-chu, pp. 47-64.

54. Accordng to a Red Guard pamphlet, "Yang Ch'eng-wu Hen-p'i Teng Hsiao-p'ing" (Yang Ch'eng-wu Criticized Teng Hsiao-p'ing Severely), in *Teng Hsiao-p'ing*, p. 70. Yang Ch'eng-wu became the PLA Chief-of-Staff in 1966.

55. Dick Wilson, *Anatomy of China* (New York: The New American Library, Inc., 1969), p. 236.

because they shared the hardships and the fear of death. The Second Field Army became devoted to him. Teng also succeeded in cultivating a firm relationship with the Third Field Army. Some of the Third Field Army personnel — Chang Yun-I, Wei Kuo-ch'ing, and Yuan Yeh-lieh for example — had worked very closely with him during the Kwangsi revolutionary days. The Second Field Army and the Third Field Army had fought many battles together and had nourished a fraternal comradeship. During the Huai-Hai battle, Teng briefly commanded the Third Field Army. His ability to win the commitment of the army earned him strong support in the 1970s, when he had to face the political challenges of the ultra-radical groups.

Two decades of struggles with the KMT and the Japanese had transformed Teng into an able and experienced leader. As Political Commissar of the army, Teng cooperated with the military leaders in performing a variety of duties: administration, political tutelage, liaison, supervision, and military planning. Teng emerged as a civilian administrator as well as a military man. After the Civil War, he was one of the few "generalists" who was qualified to lead the nation. Some military men — Chu Te and Ho Lung, for example — lost their importance after 1949 and became more or less legendary heroes of the revolution. But Teng's flexibility was repeatedly acknowledged. He remained in the leadership and was given even greater responsibilities. The one-time revolutionary proved himself a capable statesman too. With the founding of the People's Republic, Teng's political career began a new chapter.

Chapter 7

From Chungking to Peking (1950-1956)

The five Field Armies remained in their occupied areas following the conclusion of the Civil War. From 1949 to 1954, China was divided into six administrative regions, each under the authority of a Field Army.[1] These regional administrations functioned as an intermediary between the central government and local governments. The commanders of the field armies automatically became head of the regional government.

The Southwest Region included the provinces of Szechuan, Yunnan, Kweichow, and Sikang. The region was administered by three leading organizations: the CCP Southwest Bureau, the Southwest Military and Administrative Committee (SWMAC), and the Southwest Military Regional Authority. These organizations were led by Teng, Liu Po-ch'eng, and Ho Lung respectively.

---

1. The administrative regions were:

The North China Region, led by the former North China Field Army;
the Northeast Region, led by the Fourth Field Army;
the Northwest Region, led by the First Field Army;
the East China Region, led by the Third Field Army;
the Southwest Region, led by the Second Field Army;
the Central-South China Region, led by the Fourth Field Army.

Teng was the Party's First Secretary in the Southwest; Liu Po-ch'eng was the Second Secretary. Teng's other positions included Vice Chairman of the SWMAC, Chairman of the Finance and Economic Committee, and Political Commissar of the Southwest Military Region.[2] Teng also administered Chungking as its mayor.[3] In 1951, when Liu Po-ch'eng was transferred from the region, Teng assumed most of his duties.[4] Although Liu still held the chairmanship of SWMAC, he was no longer politically important in that region.

After not seeing his home province for thirty years, Teng now returned with pride and prestige. He stayed in the Southwest Region for about two and a half years and was the most powerful man there. During the Cultural Revolution he was labeled by the Red Guards as "Emperor of the Southwest."[5]

Liu Po-ch'eng was obviously less esteemed by the Party Central than Teng. Unlike other military commanders such as Lin Piao and P'eng Te-huai, Liu did not assume full party, governmental, and military power in his region. He was only allowed to head the governmental structure of SWMAC. The Party was controlled by Teng and the army was led by Ho Lung. In 1951 Liu was transferred to Nanking to lead the PLA Military Academy. In 1954, he also assumed directorship of the PLA General Training Department. Within four years, however, he had resigned from both posts. After 1958 Liu held no more important posts. Evidently, Mao would not allow him to settle in any place for fear that he might establish his influence.

There were many tasks to be accomplished in the Southwest regions, which was one of the least-developed areas in China. The priorities of that region were consequently different from those of other regions. Economically, prices were stabilized,

---

2. Dorothy J. Solinger, *Regional Government and Political Integration in Southwest China, 1945-1954* (Berkeley, Cal.: University of California Press, 1977), p. 91; and Klein and Clark, *Biographical Dictionary*, Vol. II, p. 822.

3. "Teng Hsiao-p'ing Tsui-hsing Tiao-ch'a Pao-kao," p. 25.

4. Solinger, *Regional Government,* p. 148.

5. "Chieh-k'ai Teng Hsiao-p'ing Te Fan-ko-ming Lao-ti," p. 12.

unemployment was checked, and the circulation of goods between cities and villages increased. Construction for the Chengtu-Chungking railroad also got under way. Some 400,000 ex-KMT soldiers were retrained and joined the ranks of the Red Army. Remnants of the Kuomintang that had organized guerrilla activities in the Southwest Region were more or less uprooted by 1950. In the cities, workers, students, and women were organized into teams to promote public works. Before the war, opium was cultivated extensively in the region and many local people were opium addicts. Now the cultivation and sale of opium was prohibited; dens were closed and addicts were healed. A political campaign was launched to fight bureaucracy and power play among the Party cadres. Students, workers and peasants were trained to work in the Party organization and government. Because the southwest was an ethnically diversified region, autonomy was now given to the minority groups. The government helped them develop their economy, but did not interfere with their habits and customs.[6] The conquest of Tibet began in October 1950. In May 1951 a treaty was signed between the Chinese government and Tibet to conclude the "peaceful liberation" of the province.

In order to implement a successful land reform, Teng first had to fight the landlords and the bandits. He called for a campaign to eliminate the bandits, overthrow the landlords, reduce land rents, and return bonds to the peasants — actions which

6. Teng Hsiao-p'ing, "Kai Kuo I-nien Tsai Hsi-nan" ("One Year in the Southwest after Liberation"), in *Hsin Hua Yueh-pao* (New China Monthly), Vol. II, No. 6 (1950), pp. 12-32; Teng Hsiao-p'ing, "Kuan-yu Si-nan Kung-tso Ch'ing-kuang Te Pao-kao" (Report on the Progress of Works in the Southwest), in *Hua-tung, Chung-nan, Hsi-pei, Hsi-nan Ssu-ta Hsing-cheng-ch'u Kung-tso Ch'ing-k'uang chi Kung-tso Jen-wu* (Work Conditions and Tasks of the Four Great Administrative Regions — East China, Central-South China, Northwest China, and Southwest China) (Shang-hai: Hsin-hua Shu-tien, 1950), pp. 57-60; and Liu Po-ch'eng, "Hsi-nan-ch'u Te Kung-tso Jen-wu" ("Working Aims in the Southwest Region"), in *Hsin Hua Yueh-pao*, Vol. II, No. 5 (1950), pp. 996-999.

were highly praised by the central government and adopted by Peking as a model to be introduced to other areas as well.[7] In April 1950 and February 1951 Teng went to Peking to report on the progress of his construction projects.[8]

Teng refused to rest on his laurels and soon set new priorities for future works. Speaking at the Second and the Third Military and Administrative Committee Plenums, Teng called for the speeding up of land reform, the strengthening of cultural and educational work, and the promotion of ideological reform. In addition, he urged the people of the region to support their country in resisting the U. S. imperialists in Korea.[9] The nationwide campaign of San-fan and Wu-fan (The Three Anti's and Five Anti's) was also observed in the region to fight corruption and waste. Teng promoted a cooperative movement between villages of providing mutual assistance. Before long the Southwest matched the level of development in other regions and took an equal hand in building the nation.

Political regionalism was on the rise. Regional leaders, who had fought arm in arm with the soldiers for many years and who shared their hopes and frustrations, readily cultivated a group of devotees from among the army. The central government was therefore anxious to centralize its power. From 1952 on, regional power gradually declined. Many senior regional officials were transferred to Peking. In 1952, Teng was called to Peking and his position as the First Party Secretary in the region was taken over by Ho Lung. Although in January 1953 he was selected for a second term as Vice Chairman of the SWMAC, he spent most of his time in Peking while the actual administrative duties fell to Ho Lung.

Teng's rapid ascendency was due not only to his ability,

---

7. Liu Po-ch'eng, pp. 996-999; Hsiao Hua, "Mao Tse-tung Te Pi-ch'en Teng Hsiao-p'ing" (Mao Tse-tung's Favorite — Teng Hsiao-p'ing), in *Chin-jih Ta-lu* (Mainland China Today, Taipei), June 1963, p. 24.

8. Klein and Clark, *Biographical Dictionary*, Vol. II, p. 822.

9. Solinger, *Regional Government*, pp. 98-99.

but to his good relationship with Mao. In August 1952 Teng became Vice Premier of the State Administrative Council. When this cabinet-like Council came into being in 1949, it had four Vice Premiers: Ch'en Yun, Tung Pi-wu, Kuo Mo-jo, and Huang Yen-p'ei. Until 1954 when the central government was reorganized, Teng was the only official to be added to the Vice Premiership in the State Administrative Council. In February 1953 he was elected to the Standing Committee of the First Chinese Political Consultation Conference National Committee.[10]

While he was in Peking, Teng became involved in the conduct of foreign affairs. In November 1953 he joined a delegation to North Korea to negotiate a loan from China. When Khruschev visited China in September 1954, Teng participated in the talks. It was agreed at these meetings that Russia would assist China economically, that the Soviet army would withdraw from Port Arthur, and that the Soviet government would dissolve all its shares in any Sino-Soviet joint-stock companies in Sinkiang. These agreements demonstrated to the outside world that China was an independent country with a status equal to that of the Soviet Union. Teng also became the spokesman for Chou En-lai in the State Administration Council. In the past, before Teng was appointed to the Council, Tung Pi-wu had assumed the job of spokesman when Chou went abroad.[11]

Teng became one of the important planners of economic and financial development, for he had gained valuable experience while working in the southwest. In November 1952, the State Planning Committee was set up to direct and supervise the First Five Year Plan. Kao Kang was its chairman and Teng was one of the 15 members appointed to the committee. Teng held this job until 1954. In September 1953, he replaced Po I-po as China's second finance minister and at the same time was

10. Klein and Clark, *Biographical Dictionary*, Vol. II, pp. 822-823; and Solinger, *Regional Government*, p. 148. In 1954, Teng was re-elected to the Second CPPCC Standing Committee.

11. Boorman, "Teng Hsiao-p'ing — A Political Profile," p. 117.

appointed Vice Chairman of the Central Government Finance and Economic Committee. After making invaluable contributions, Teng resigned from both posts nine months later.[12]

Teng also played an important role in planning the reorganization of the government. The three committees formed to facilitate this work were:

the Committee for the Drafting of the Constitution, headed by Mao Tse-tung;

the Committee for the Drafting of the Electoral Law, headed by Chou En-lai; and

the Central Election Committee (whose function was to survey the election of the National People's Congress), headed by Liu Shao-ch'i.

Teng was the only official who served on all three committees. He was the Secretary-General of the Central Election Committee and was responsible for drafting the report on the program of elections. He was also asked to prepare the details of the Election Law for the Committee for the Drafting of the Electoral Law.[13]

In September 1954, the government was reorganized. Teng became a Vice Premier of the State Council and a Vice Chairman of the National Defense Council. The National Defense Council, which consisted of 15 vice-chairmen, held no significant power.[14] With the adoption of a new constitution and the reorganization of the government, the early regional administrations were abolished. The provinces were now directly under the central government's control. Although Teng no longer held any title in the Southwest Region, his influence remained strong there because of his long-term relationship with the

---

12. Klein and Clark, *Biographic Dictionary*, Vol. II, pp. 822-823. After Teng's resignation, Li Hsien-nien was named head of the Finance Ministry.

13. *Kung-fei Chung-yao Tzu-liao Hui-pien* (Collection of Important Materials on the Communists) (Taipei: Chung-yang Wen-wu Kung-ying She), Part II, Vol. IV, pp. 55, 67; and Klein and Clark, Vol. II, p. 823.

14. Klein and Clark, *Biographic Dictionary*, Vol. II, p. 823. Teng was re-elected to the National Defense Council in 1959 and 1965.

Second Field Army.

Teng's rapid rise in the Party bureaucracy is noteworthy. In May 1954, he became the Secretary-General of the CCP. Under him were T'an Chen-lin, Sung Jen-chi'iung, Liu Lan-t'ao, and Yan Shang-k'un.[15] The function of the Secretary-General was mainly to link Party with practice. In the late 1920's, when Teng was in Shanghai, he was said to perform a similar job there. The post was abolished in the 1940's but with its reinstatement in 1954 the Secretary-General was given the power to head all the departments under the Party's Central Committee. In this position Teng was assigned to handle the "Kao-Jao case," the first notable purge conducted by the CCP since 1949.

Kao Kang had been Teng's student at the Chung-shan Military Academy in Shensi in the 1920's and later participated in the founding of the Shensi-Kansu Soviet. After the Civil War, Kao became the most powerful man in the northeast for which he gained a seat in the CCP Politburo. He had a close rapport with Stalin and was inclined to work with the Soviet dictator to "particularize" the region. Mao, of course, could not tolerate Kao's relatively independent opertion in Manchuria. In 1952 he transferred Kao to Peking to assume the Chairmanship of the State Planning Committee. But Kao's influence in Manchuria remained strong and he kept all the titles he had held previously in northeast China.

Jao Shu-shih was an important figure in east China. In 1952 he was transferred to Peking to assume the post of Director of the CCP Organization Department. Jao grew attached to Kao, for the two shared a discontent for the leaders in the central government. They were not, for example, pleased with Mao's economic policies. The believed that economically developed Manchuria and east China should be given more resource allocations and receive special treatment to maintain their leading positions. Mao, on the other hand, maintained that a balanced economic strategy would give all regions an equal opportunity

15. *Ming Pao* (Hong Kong), December 14, 1978.

for development.

More serious than the quarrel over economic policy were the complexities of a power struggle. Kao insisted that there were two "CCPs": the CCP of the red base and the CCP of the white base, in the KMT-controlled areas. He said that the "red base" party had a tougher job during the war and made greater contributions to the founding of the state than had the "white base" party. He considered himself a typical red-base man and considered Liu Shao-ch'i and Chou En-lai typical of the white base Thus he demanded that Liu and Chou resign from their posts and that he be appointed to the Vice Chairmanship. Kao was unafraid of challenging authority because he knew Stalin backed him. Unfortunately for him, Stalin died in 1953. This proved fatal to Kao's ambitions.

In February 1954, Liu Shao-ch'i hinted at the Fourth Plenary Session of the Seventh Party Congress that Kao and Jao would be purged, although he only alluded to their names. After the plenum Chou and Teng each presided at a forum to expose the "Anti-party crimes" of Kao and Jao. Chou's forum discussed mainly the "crimes" of Kao Kang while Teng discussed those of Jao.[16] It is likely that Teng was appointed Secretary-General at this time. In August, he succeeded Jao Shu-shih as head of the CCP Organization Department.[17] The posts Teng now held required him to watch closely the discipline of the Party members. Not surprisingly, he took a leading position in denouncing both Kao and Jao.

The denunciation campaign lasted one year. At the end of March 1955, a National Delegates Conference was called where Teng spoke on the anti-Party crimes of Kao and Jao.[18] The con-

---

16. Mo I-te, "Jao Shu-shih Hai Ho-jo Ma?" (Is Jao Shu-shih still Alive?), *Tung-hsiang* (The Trends, Hong Kong), April 1980, p. 8.

17. *Fei-wei Jen-wu-chih* (Biographies of the Reds), p. 5240.

18. Yao Mung-hsiuan, ed., *Fei-tang Nei-pu Tou-cheng Wen-ti Lun-chi* (Commentary Essays on Power Struggle in the CCP) (Taipei: Kuo-chi Kuan-hsi Yen-chiu-so, 1975), p. 207. The full report has not been published. The published resolution on the "Anti-party bloc" should be the summation of the report.

ference, after hearing Teng's report, concluded that Kao had attempted to establish an independent kingdom in Manchuria and that he and Jao had planned conspiratorially to overthrow the government. Both were removed from Party membership. Kao killed himself, while Jao disappeared from public view and was reportedly still alive in 1967.[19]

The Kao-Jao case was the first major power struggle in the CCP since the founding of the People's Republic. Teng's efforts to safeguard the central leadership won the appreciation of Mao, Liu, and Chou. At the Fifth Plenum, he was rewarded by election to the 12-member Politburo.[20] Also elected to the Politburo was Lin Piao. Lin's election, however, had little to do with the Kao-Jao case. Most probably, Mao hoped that Lin and Teng would balance the strength of Chu Te and P'eng Te-huai in the Politburo.

Teng frequently played the role of a diplomat. Since the mid-1950's more and more foreign leaders were paying visits to China. Teng often acted as host to these foreign visitors and held talks with them. In February 1956, the 20th Congress of the Communist Party of the Soviet Union (CPSU) was opened in Moscow. A Chinese delegation led by Chu Te and Teng Hsiao-p'ing attended the event.[21] At the congress, Khruschev openly denounced Stalin and his one-man-rule and personality cult. The resolution that was finally adopted at the 20th Congress had immense impact on Soviet relations with China, which is analyzed in detail in the following chapter.

In retrospect, Teng enjoyed the most peaceful and satisfactory part of his political career during the years 1950 to 1956: the revolution was accomplished, national construction was in progress, and China's international position was acknowledged

19. Mo I-te, "Jao Shu-shih," p. 8.

20. Franklin W. Houn, *A Short History of Chinese Communism* (Englewood Cliffs, N.J.: Prentice-Hall, Inc., 1967), p. 90. The other twelve Politburo members were: Mao, Liu, Chu Te, Chou, Ch'en Yun, Chang Wen-t'ien, K'ang Sheng, Lin Po-ch'u, Tung Pi-wu, P'eng Chen, P'eng Te-huai, and Lin Piao.

21. Klein and Clark, *Biographic Dictionary*, Vol. II, p. 824.

after the Korean War. Teng was in his forties, in good heatlh, and rising rapidly in the Party.

The years of working in the southwest were Teng's glorious days. He returned to his native province with great prestige. In the Southwest Region he worked with a fair degree of independence from Peking and was thus able to be inventive in formulating new policies. His work won appreciation from the central government and his relationship with Mao was excellent. He regarded himself as a Sung Chiang-like figure and even called his subordinates after the nicknames of the followers of Sung Chiang.[22] Many of the cadres working with him in the Southwest Region later became his loyal supporters in Peking, for example, Hu Yao-pang, Wan Li, and Sung Jen-ch'iung.

Teng's rapid ascendency after his transfer to the central government was without comparison at that time. He was on such good terms with Mao, Liu, and Chou En-lai that he became the rising star of the Party. By the mid fifties Teng had emerged as one of the most influential figures in Peking.

In the years ahead he climbed even higher to become the third most influential man in the party next to Mao and Liu. But with greater responsibility came greater pressures. The country's economy was entering a new and unpredictable stage. He began to find areas of friction between his views and Mao's. The year 1956 concluded the peaceful political life of Teng. After that, he was dragged into more complicated political issues which required a keen adaptability in addition to his role as the competent administrator and bureaucrat.

---

22. *Jen-min Jih-pao*, June 2, 1976. Sung Chiang was the righteous outlaw of the Sung Dynasty. The Robin Hood-like character had 108 blood brothers.

Chapter 8

The General Secretary (1956-1965)

The Eighth Party Congress was held in September 1956, eleven years after the last Congress was called. This was the first time a party congress met after the founding of the People's Republic. As Secretary-General of the Party, Teng was responsible for preparing the agenda.[1] On the first day of the meeting, Teng was elected to the 13-member presidium. People often associate Teng with the Eighth Party Congress because it was he who, in addition to speaking at the conference denouncing personality cults, was elected to the position of General Secretary of the CCP.

The Congress endorsed China's support for the Soviet denunciation of personality cult, deemphasized Mao's supremacy, and introduced the concept of collective leadership. Since 1949 China had pursued a policy of leaning completely on the side of the Soviet Union. Economically and technologically, China depended greatly on Russia; thus, the Chinese Communists often followed the example of their Russian comrades. At the 20th CPSU Congress, Khrushchev denounced Stalin and advocated collective leadership. The Chinese followed suit. Mao,

---

1. Klein and Clark, *Biographic Dictionary*, Vol. II, p. 820.

Stalin's counterpart in China, soon found his authority being challenged.

Liu Shao-ch'i and Teng each delivered a report to the Congress. Liu's involved political work and Teng's proposed a number of revisions to the Party Constitution.[2] Unlike the reports made at the Seventh Party Congress, these reports referred less to the greatness of Mao and more to the principle of collective leadership.[3] The new Constitution deleted two articles from the previous one — "Mao Tse-tung's Thought is the Guideline of the Party's Work" and "To Learn Mao Tse-tung's Thought is the duty of every CCP member."[4]

Teng made a report denouncing leadership by charisma rather than constitution. He referred to the example of the 20th CPSU Congress in rejecting personality cults and said that the correctiveness of collective leadership should produce an impact on other Communist states as well. He added that one could not deny the existence of a personality cult in China. He also said:

> Loyalty to a leader is essentially a matter of showing attachment to the interests of the Party, to the interests of the class, to the interests of the people, and not of making a myth out of the individual concerned. One important contribution made by the Twentieth Congress of the Soviet Communist Party was to emphasize the fact that the personality cult can lead to all kinds of disastrous consequences.[5]

---

2. Teng's report is an important reference for the understanding of the then internal operation of the CCP.

3. Liu Shao-ch'i, for example, referred to Mao's name only four times at the Eighth Party Congress. In the 1945 Party Congress, however, he made reference to Mao as many as 105 times.

4. It was P'eng Te-huai who proposed to delete the line of "Mao Tse-tung Thought" from the Constitution. Peng's motion was seconded by Liu. See "P'eng Te-huai Te Tzu-kung Tse" ("Self Appraisal of P'eng Te-huai"), in *Chung-kung Chi-mi Wen-chien Hui-pien*, p. 178.

5. Teng Hsiao-p'ing, *Kuan-yu Hsiu Kai Tang-chang Te Pao-kao* (Report on the Revision of the Party Constitution) (Peking: Jen-min Ch'u-pan-she, 1956), pp. 47, 52-53.

Mao, however, was still considered the leading proponent of the collective leadership in China. Teng reported:

> Our Party, in its evolution, has established a tradition of collective leadership.... The Central Committee adopted a resolution in September 1948 to strengthen the Committee system [to decide all important issues] which helped greatly to promote the idea of collective leadership.[6]

Teng stated that this decision was made by Mao.[7] He added:

> Our Party disapproves of personality cults. On the eve of national victory, the Party adopted Comrade Mao Tse-tung's proposal. . . that birthday celebrations for Party leaders and the use of party leaders' names to designate places, streets, and enterprises should be prohibited. This decision has had a wholesome effect in checking the glorification and exaltation of individuals.[8]

In addition, Teng emphasized the following:

> Marxism never denies the importance of the individual's role in history. . . nor does it deny the leader's role in the Party.... According to Lenin, a leader is a symbol of authority, experience, and unity. Whoever possesses these qualities will be a great asset to any Party. From our many year's experience of struggles, we agree that Lenen's view is correct.[9]

It is probably safe to say that Teng's report was really more of a defense than an attack on Mao. However, it gave his opponents a good excuse to attack him during the Cultural Revolution. The Red Guards, for example, claimed, "[Teng had been] parroting Khrushchev and in the name of opposing personal cult [directed] the spearhead straight at Mao."[10] Chiang Ch'ing,

---

6. Ibid., p. 47.

7. Mao Tse-tung, *Mao Tse-tung Hsuan-chi* (Selected Works of Mao Tse-tung) (Peking: Jen-min Ch'u-pan'she, 1964), pp. 1234-1235.

8. Teng Hsiao-p'ing, *Hsiu-kai Tang-chang*, p. 53.

9. Ibid., p. 52.

10. See Richard Solomon, *Mao's Revolution and the Chinese Political Culture* (Berkeley, Cal.: University of California Press, 1974), p. 275.

the wife of Mao, later attacked Teng for accepting Khrushchev's speech uncritically. She said that Teng had ignored Mao's contribution and leadership in the Chinese Revolution and had disparaged the people's love for Mao.[11] The report he made at the Eighth Party Congress was to be labelled a "poisonous weed."[12] Ch'en Yun, presently a member of Politburo's Standing Committee, allegedly admitted in an April 1979 speech that one of the reasons Teng was purged in the mid-sixties was for having delivered the speech he did in 1956.[13]

In the election of Central Committee members at the Eighth Party Congress, Teng's rise was prominent. He gained the fourth majority vote while Chou En-lai was only sixth in position. The Conference also introduced structural changes to the Party. First, a new post, the General Secretary, (assumed by Teng) was created to replace the Chairman of the Central Secretariat, the post formerly held by Mao. Second, a number of vice chairmanships were created in the Central Committee, filled by Vice-Chairmen of the Politburo. Liu Shao-ch'i, Chou En-lai, Chu Te, and Ch'en Yun were appointed to the new slots. Third, a Standing Committee consisting of the Chairman, the Vice-Chairmen, and the General Secretary, was created as the power core of the Politburo. Fourth, the Politburo was enlarged from 13 members to 17 members.[14] These posts were to be elected by the Central Committee. A motion to install an

11. Chiang Ch'ing, "Tsai Hung-wei-ping Ta-hui Shang K'ung-su Teng Hsiao-p'ing Shih Ta Tsui-chuang" ("Exposing Teng Hsiao-p'ing's Ten Major Crimes at the Red Guard Rally"), reproduced in Kuo Chih-ping, ed., p. 21.

12. "Ch-e P'i-p'an Fan-ko-ming Hsiu-cheng-chu-i Kang-ling 'Kuan-yu Hsiu-kai Tang Te Chang-ch'eng Te Pao-kao'" ("To criticize Thoroughly the Anti-Revolutionary Revisionist Guidelines: 'The Report on the Revision of Party Articles'"), a Red Guard pamphlet reproduced in *Teng Hsiao-p'ing*, p. 36.

13. Ch'en Yun, "Lun Chieh-chueh Tang-ch'ien K'un-ching Chih Tao" ("On Solution to the Present Dilemma"), reproduced in *Ch'i-shih Nien-tai* (The Seventies, Hong Kong), April 1980, p. 74. However, the New China News Agency denied on April 13, 1980 that the so-called Ch'en Yun Speech was genuine.

14. They were Mao Tse-tung, Liu Shao-ch'i, Chou En-lai, Chu Te, Ch'en Yun, Teng Hsiao-p'ing, P'eng Te-huai, Lin Piao, Lin Po-ch'u, Tung

Honorary Chairman was accepted. Certainly, this post was reserved for Mao after his retirement.[15]

The reorganization of the Party structure indicated a move toward collective leadership. Mao's power was somewhat decreased and a semblance of intraparty democracy was established.

As General Secretary, Teng's job was to supervise the administration of Party affairs. Formerly, when Mao chaired the Secretariat, the Secretariat controlled such functions as decision-making and the operation of the Party. Now, the Standing Committee of the Politburo took over the decision-making function and the Secretariat was reduced to an administrative organ. According to the 1956 Party Constitution, the Secretariat was to "attend to the daily work of the Central Committee under the direction of the Politburo and its Standing Committee."[16] The title "General Secretary" had been used after 1925 when the Fourth Congress of the CCP was convened. Until 1938, when it was temporarily abolished, the position was the most supreme in the Party. The position Teng now held was less powerful than that of his predecessors and subordinate to the now supreme Chairman of the Central Committee. But it still possessed highly important functions. The General Seretary was to supervise the implementation of policy, to conduct organizational matters, and to train and appoint cadres. He was the top executive in the Party and controlled the operation of Party affairs; thus, the success or failure of implementing the Party's policies depended solely on the Secretariat. As General Secretary, Teng acquired a better and more comprehensive knowledge of Party affairs. Accordingly, he had more authority in the Party.

From the composition of the Secretariat, one can understand the importance of the position of General Secretary.[17]

Pi-wu, P'eng Chen, Lo Jung-huan, Ch'en Yi, Li Fu-ch'un, Liu Po-ch'eng, Ho Lung, and Li Hsien-nien. The last six were elected to the Politburo in 1956.

15. See *Chung-kuo Kung-ch'an-tang Chang-ch'eng* (Constitution of the Chinese Communist Party) (Peking: Jen-min Ch'u-pan-she, 1956), Article 37.

16. Article 37.

17 Under Teng, the 1956 Secretariat included P'eng, Chen (Deputy General

Besides Teng, five of the Secretaries serving the 1962 Secretariat were Politburo members, and two were alternate members. In a sense, Teng's Secretariat was like a super cabinet: it consisted of a number of secretaries, each specializing in a line of work such as agriculture and legislation. Under these different departments was a network that relayed the Party's directives to the related government ministries and then monitored how orders were carried out on the provincial and local levels. In other words, the provincial Party structure or the local Party structure would pass on the CCP's directives to the related provincial government department or local government department in the same way the departments under the CCP Secretariat dealt with the departments of the State Council. Although Teng held the sixth position in the Standing Committee, he possessed greater power than Chu Te, Ch'en Yun, and even Chou En-lai (all three were Vice Chairmen of the Politburo). Thus in terms of power, Teng's importance in the Party was next only to Mao and Liu. He had emerged as one of the few actual rulers of China.

In response to the Soviet denunciation of Stalin, Mao launched the Hundred Flowers Campaign in 1956. He urged the intellectuals of different orientations to voice whatever grievances they had. To Mao's mind, the Campaign would show the outside world that China was not an autocratic state and that China was more democratric than the Soviet Union. Besides,

Secretary), Wang Chia-hsiang, T'an Chen-lin, Li Hsueh-feng, T'ang Cheng, and Huang K'o-ch'eng. Its composition varied from time to time. In 1958, Li Fu-ch'un and Li Hsien-nien were appointed members. In 1962, T'ang Cheng and Huang Ko-ch'eng were removed from the Secretariat because of their involvement in the P'eng Te-huai case. Lu Ting-i, K'ang Sheng, and Lo Jui-ch'ing were the new appointees. In 1966, Yeh Chien-ying, T'ao Chu, and Liu Ning-i were included. Other important figures were Liu Lan-t'ao, Yang Shang-k'un and Hu Ch'iao-mu. See Peter Moody, Jr., *The Politics of the Eighth Central Committee of the Communist Party of China* (Hamden, Conn.: The Shoe String Press, Inc., 1973), pp. 36-37; and Ssu-ma ch'ang-feng, *Wen-ko Shih-mo* (The Beginning and the End of the Cultural Revolution) (Hong Kong: Pai Yeh Shu-wu, 1976), p. 121. Except for K'ang Sheng and Li Hsien-nien, all others were purged during the Cultural Revolution. Li Fu-ch'un and Li Hsueh-feng, however, retained their posts.

after six years of Communist rule, the intellectuals seemed quiescent. Mao hoped that a liberal climate would enhance the intellectuals' willingness to serve the Communist cause. In addition, criticisms from the intellectuals would help to expose and correct whatever mistakes the Party had made.

Mao's idea was supported by Chou En-lai and Lu Ting-i (then Director of the Party's Propaganda Department), but was opposed by such organization men as Liu and Teng. The latter believed that a mass movement without the Party's lead would be undisciplined and perhaps uncontrollable. They also disapproved of permitting the involvement of non-Party elements in the Party's rectification process. This would discredit the Party, they argued.[18] Thus Liu Shao-ch'i did not mention the term of "Hundred Flowers Campaign" (which was launched four months before the Congress) in his report to the Eighth Party Congress. When he referred to the rectification campaign, he said nothing about the need for "supervision by the democratic parties."[19] Teng, on the other hand, stated at the Congress that if the Party had made any mistakes, the Party would correct them itself. He said:

> In order to help the comrades overcome their shortcomings, and correct their mistakes, it is necessary to develope *intra-party criticism* and self-criticism.[20]

Teng has consistently insisted that Party rectification should be an internal affair. In January 1980, he reaffirmed this belief. He said: "Our Party has committed serious mistakes in the past, but these mistakes were corrected by *ourselves*, not by any external force."[21] The difference of opinion regarding the issue of

---

18. See Harrison, *Long March to Power*, p. 473.

19. *Eighth Party Congress of the Communist Party of China* (Peking: Foreign Language Press, 1956), Vol. I, pp. 76-77.

20. Teng Hsiao-p'ing, *Hsiu-kai Tang-chang*, p. 58. Author's emphasis.

21. Teng Hsiao-p'ing, "Kuan-yu Mu-ch'ien Hsing-shih Han Jen-wu Te Pao-kao" (On the Present Situation and Tasks, A Report), *Cheng-ming*, March 1980, p. 21. Author's emphasis.

whether or not the Party should always play the leading role in movements of reform became even more obvious between Liu and Teng on the one hand, and Mao on the other in the coming Socialist Education Campaign and Cultural Revolution.

Protests demanding liberalization broke out in Poland and Hungary in the fall of 1956, organized by the discontented elements in both countries. In order to prevent a similar uprising in China, Mao believed that the intellectuals should be encouraged to speak up. The issue was discussed many times in Party meetings; but nothing decisive was settled.[22] Thus Mao decided to bypass the Party and have the government apparatus launch the campaign instead. In February 1957, as Chairman of the People's Republic, Mao called an enlarged session of the Supreme State Conference. At the conference he opened everything up to criticism, even Marxism. (Apparently due to the opposition in the Party, Mao's speech to the Conference was not published until June and only in a revised version.) In May, at a gathering of intellectuals and propagandists, Mao expressed his sincere hope that the Hundred Flowers Campaign would bring constructive criticism. The intellectuals, however, were hesitant to speak out because previous crackdowns had frightened them. Nevertheless, after considerable urging, they began to express their opinions. Their frankness surprised Mao, who thought the intellectuals were generally contented with Communist rule. If there were any complaints, he believed they would simply be grievances against administrative deficiencies and the incompetence of some junior bureaucrats. Mao did not foresee that the intellectuals, particularly the former democrats, would be so discontented with Communist rule that some would even demand the end of it. Rallies and strikes were held to oppose the government. These developments proved that Mao had mis-

---

22. For instance, the Second Plenum of the Eighth Central Committee held in November 1956, the Enlarged Political Bureau meeting held in late December 1956, and Conference of the Provincial Party Secretaries, held in January 1957. See Harrison, *Long March to Power*, p. 472.

judged and that the organization men were right.

On June 18, a revised version of Mao's speech to the February Supreme State Conference was published. The revision included six articles which emphasized self-discipline and self-control. The speech stressed that criticism was welcome if it was beneficial to the socialist cause and to the strengthening of the Communist rule.

All non-Party intellectuals who had criticized the Party were now labelled as rightists and were purged. Almost overnight, the liberal Hundred Flowers Campaign was turned into an oppressive Party-led Anti-Rightist Movement. The leading role of the CCP was reasserted.

In his report on the campaign to reform the Party (presented at the September 1957 Third Plenary Session), Teng stated that the intellectuals should be reorientated and "proletarianized." He said:

> Don't belittle the meaning of the present anti-rightist campaign. This is a socialist revolution brought into the political and intellectual world...[it] helps lay to rest such issues as...whether we should follow the socialist path, whether we need the guidance of the Communist Party, whether we need proletariat dictatorship, and whether we want democratic centralism.... They [the bourgeoisie] cursed socialism and hated Communist rule. They had guidelines, organizations and plans. Their aim was to restore capitalism and reactionary rule. ...
>
> The leadership of the CCP, the principles of the proletariat dictatorship, and democratic centralism should never be questioned.[23]

Although two decades later Teng removed the "rightist" label against the liberals, he insisted that the Anti-Rightist Campaign had progressed properly and regretted only that the campaign had been carried to extremes.[24] The movement also

---

23. Teng Hsiao-p'ing, *Kuan-yu Cheng-feng Yun-tung Te Pao-kao* (Report on the Rectification Campaign) (Peking: Jan-min Ch'u-pan-she, 1957), pp. 1-3, 6.

24. Teng Hsiao-p'ing, *Hsing-shih Han Jun-wu*, p. 13.

touched Party members. Teng asserted in his report that the rightist elements in the Party should be exposed and purged with the same diligence as the non-Party rightists.[25] From late 1957 through 1958, almost one million Communists fell into disgrace.

The same report also revived Mao's radical Twelve-year Program on national agricultural development.[26] For many years there existed two groups of opinions inside the Party over the issue of agricultural collectivism. Mao and his minority group (which included people like Ch'en Po-ta) believed that China lacked sufficient capital to increase agricultural production by any means other than by mobilizing the masses; thus this group favored immediate collectivization. A more moderate group believed that collectivization should be postponed until rural mechanization had been introduced. This group included Liu Shao-ch'i, Chou En-lai, Ch'en Yun, Teng Tzu-hui (Vice Premier and Director of the CCP Rural Work Department), Li Fu-ch'un (Vice Premier and Minister of Finance), and Po I-po (Vice Premier and Chairman of the State Economic Commission). Teng also belonged to the moderates.[27]

A semi-socialist model using cooperatives was introduced as early as 1953. Called the Agricultural Producers Cooperative (APC), the concept was very unpopular with the peasants. Co-op members were forced to pool their instruments, labor, and land despite assurances that they still had individual ownership. The moderates met in May 1955 at a Central Work Conference to discuss ways to remedy the problem. It was decided that the number of the APC's would be cut. Within the next two months

25. Teng Hsiao-p'ing, *Cheng-feng Yun-tung*, p. 28.

26. Ibid., p. 17.

27. "Teng Hsiao-p'ing Shih Tzu-ch'an-chieh-chi Te Tsung Tai-piao" (Teng Hsiao-p'ing is the Major Representative of Bourgeois), in C. B. Kok, ed., p. 145; "Kao Fan-an Te Tzou-Tzu-p'ai Shih-fen Ku-li" (The Capitalist-Roader who Reverses the Verdict is Very Isolated), in C. B. Kok, ed., p. 89; and Byung-joon Ahn, *Chinese Politics and the Cultural Revolution* (Seattle: University of Washington Press, 1976), p. 16.

about 200,000 cooperatives were dissolved.[28] This, of course, contradicted Mao's will. Mao made an extensive tour among the provinces to secure the support of the local leaders for the cooperative program and, in July, called an unprecedented conference of provincial Party secretaries. Mao, in his report to the conference, described the moderates as "tottering along like a woman with bound feet, always complaining that the others are going too fast."[29] He requested that the present form of APC be further developed into more collectivized types of cooperatives. Finally, the moderates yielded. By appealing to the provinces for their support, Mao developed a favorite tactic that he used again and again in the coming years.

As a result, the Party adopted in January 1956 a radical agricultural plan drafted by Mao — "The 12-Year Draft Outline for Agricultural Development." According to this Outline, advanced cooperatives were to be organized all over the country. Although the draft needed the approval of the Central Committee, its actual operation had already begun and was promoted everywhere. The advanced cooperatives were fully socialized, resembling the Soviet collective farms. Lands were owned collectively by cooperative members. The size of the cooperative was enlarged: it now consisted of 100 households instead of just 20 to 30.

However, the plan did not work out as expected. The peasants were unenthusiastic about collectivization. Mismanagement and faulty planning worsened their morale and efficiency. Once again, the moderates' views were upheld. Beginning in April 1956 the application of the 12-year plan was slowed down. The previous moderate and gradualist line was restored in place of reckless advance. In a speech given in the next year, Teng said:

---

28. Teng's involvement in this matter subjected him to criticism in later years. See "Kao Fan-an Te Tzo-tzu-p'ai Shih-feng Ku-li," p. 89 and Parris Chang, *Power and Policy*, pp. 13-14.

29. *Mao Tse-tung Hsuan-chi*, Vol. V., p. 168.

In China our mules are slow, but this has its good side. Cars are fast, but if you lose control, you get killed. If the mule goes slowly, at least it goes securely.[30]

But political and economic developments since July 1957 reversed the situation once more. Because of the Anti-Rightist Movement, people would not dare say "no" to a radical approach toward agricultural development. Thus, some of the moderates began to change their attitudes, including Liu Shao-ch'i, P'eng Chen, and Teng Hsiao-p'ing.[31] At the Third Plenary Session, Teng became Mao's spokesman. Although Ch'en Yun, Chou En-lai, and Teng Tzu-hui each made a report at the conference, only Teng Hsiao-p'ing's report was published in full.[32] Teng explained the 12-year Draft Outline in his report on rectification. He spoke highly of the plan and urged the conference to adopt it in its revised form. Teng even hinted that he would fight against any inclination toward conservatism.[33] To guarantee its adoption, Mao had, before the meeting, toured the country again to win local support.

The successful launching of Sputnik by the Soviets also helped the 12-Year Plan gain approval. Chinese radicals probably appealed to the people by referring to the Soviet example: only a revolutionary approach to the economy would bring achievements equal to those of their Soviet counterparts.

Soon after the Third Plenary Session, Teng followed Mao on a second trip to the Soviet Union in November 1957. The trip was made for three reasons. First, it was the 40th anniversary of the October Revolution and China was invited to attend the celebration in Moscow. Second, a summit meeting of all Communist countries would be held at the same time. Third and most important, China hoped to gain further Soviet assist-

---

30. "Jen-min Kung-she Ten Sheng-li Han 'Ch'ao-yueh le Chieh-tuan' lun Te P'o-ch'an," *Jen-min Jih-pao*, February 4, 1968.

31. Dittmer, *Liu Shao-ch'i*, p. 39.

32. *Jen-min Jih-pao*, October 19, 1957.

33. Teng Hsiao-p'ing, *Cheng-feng Yun-tung*, p. 17.

ance because the earlier Soviet economic aid program had expired.

The summit meeting seemed very successful. Teng stated in a summary report made after returning to China that the conference witnessed the solidarity of Communist countries. In reality, however, the Chinese and the Soviets found they could not agree on a number of issues. In the relationship between the Communist states and the capitalist states the Chinese leaned more in favor of war than coexistence. Regarding the style of Communist activities in the third world the Soviets advocated gradualism over revolution.

During his two-week stay in Moscow, Mao tried to be cooperative and patient in order to gain Soviet aid. When the Soviets disappointed him, they affected not only the relationship between the two giant Communist states, but the internal politics of China as well. Mao decided that China should rely more on herself than on others. He was prepared to launch a radical economic program which would stress self-reliance and mass mobilization.

In his memoirs, Khrushchev said that while Mao was in Moscow, Mao had confided to him that he had no admiration for such people as Liu Shao-ch'i, Chou En-lai, and Chu Te. Kao Kang, in particular, was hated the most by Mao. Teng was the only one who received Mao's compliment. Mao told Khrushchev, "See that little man there? He's highly intelligent and has a great future ahead of him."[34] Obviously Teng was Mao's favorite at the time. It was conceivable that Mao saw Teng as his successor. The two, evidently, had a very intimate friendship at that time.

Two weeks after his return from Moscow, Mao launched the Great Leap Forward. He fancied that China would catch up with and overtake the per capita productivity of Great Britain's

---

34. Nikita Khrushchev, *Khrushchev Remembers* (Boston: Little, Brown and Company, 1974), pp. 252-253.

heavy industry within 15 years. In May 1958, he passed the General Line for Building Socialism which called for "faster, better, and more economical" production. In August, he introduced the People's Commune. The slogan of the time was to uphold the "Three Red Banners" — the Great Leap Forward, Building of Socialism, and People's Communes. Mao emphasized that industry and agriculture should be given equal treatment, that both foreign and Chinese methods should be used, and that an equilibrium should be maintained between the heavy and the light industries. Mao thought that China would overcome the problem of a lack of capital by working hard. He hoped that by inspiring the revolutionary sentiment of the masses, material incentives could be down played. On Mao's command hundreds of thousands of furnaces were built across the country. Even primitive methods of refining steel were employed. The advanced Agricultural Producers Cooperatives were now incorporated into the People's Commune. Communal members were told to observe the principle "from each according to his ability, to each according to his needs." In Maoist ideology, the commune was not only a production unit but also a political, military, and educational structure. Mao and the Maoists believed that the People's Commune would be a short-cut to a socialist society.

At that time, many Party members believed that mass mobilization was the only way to industrialize China without Soviet aid. At the Fifth Plenary Session, held in May 1958, there were changes in personnel. Lin Piao was elected to the Politburo Standing Committee and was appointed the fifth Vice Chairman of the CCP. In addition, T'an Chen-lin (member of the CCP Central Secretariat), Li Ching-ch'uan (Party Secretary in Szechuan, Teng's man), and Ko Ch'ing-shih (Party Secretary in Shanghai) were also elected to the Politburo.[35] At that time, Lin, T'an, Li and Ko were all Maoists. Needless to say, their

---

35. Jurgen Dome, *The Internal Politics of China, 1949-1972* (London: C. Hurst & Company, 1973), p. 91.

promotion strengthened Mao's influence in the Party. Liu Shao-ch'i and Teng also pledged their support for Mao's new course by saying that it would help "speed up the economy."[36] With the support of such powerful men as Liu and Teng, Mao's program was secure. Twenty years later, when commenting on the Great Leap Forward, Teng said: "Chairman Mao was the main person responsible." But "it wouldn't be fair to blame Chairman Mao only... we veterans shared a good deal of the blame."[37]

It did not take the Great Leap Forward long to reveal its inadequacies. Steel refined from the primitive backyard furnaces was of low quality and unsuitable for industrial purposes. The People's Commune did not seem to stand up any better. The peasants were in the mood for resistance because the working hours were long, material rewards were scanty, and regimentation was intense.

In November 1958, the Sixth Plenum was convened in Wuhan to make adjustments. Peasants were allowed private ownership of houses, vegetable gardens and livestock. The working hours were rescheduled not to exceed eight hours a day. Communes in the cities were dissolved. A comprehensive investigation of the existing program was conducted.[38]

The most surprising outcome of the Wuhan Plenum was the acceptance of Mao's resignation from State Chairmanship. In April 1959, Liu Shao-ch'i succeeded Mao to the post. According to official statements, it was Mao's idea to withdraw from daily administration so that he could concentrate on "questions of the direction, policy, and line" of the Party and the state.[39] Mao said that to allow other leaders to assume administrative responsibilities would gradually build up their standing so that they could succeed him without any dispute when he died.[40] In

---

36. Falaci's interview with Teng.
37. Ibid.,
38. Dome, *Internal Politics*, p. 107.
39. Parris Chang, *Power and Policy*, p. 103.
40. Mao said this on December 12, 1958. See *Mao Tse-tung Ssu-hsiang*

other words, Mao would be more concerned with ideological leadership and the building of the Party line while Liu and Teng would concern themselves with operational leadership and daily administration. But Mao's resignation came at the time when his economic policy had become bankrupt. It was an act of admitting errors which, Mao hoped, would help pacify the opposition. With Mao's quasi retirement, Liu and Teng became more important. Since Teng's appointment to lead the Secretariat, he had frequent contacts with Liu Shao-ch'i. The two now assumed the first-line responsibilities and a more intimate relationship began to develop.

Criticisms of the Great Leap Forward and of Mao's errors increased day by day. The most severe attack came from P'eng Te-huai, the Defense Minister. P'eng's attack on Mao was straightforward and sharp. The antagonism reached its climax at the Eighth Plenary Session held in Lushan, in August 1959. Mao's response to P'eng's challenge was hysterical. He said that if the Party sided with P'eng he would go to the mountains and fight a guerrilla war all over again. The Party yielded to Mao. P'eng along with his supporters — Deputy Foreign Minister Chang Wen-t'ien, PLA Chief of Staff Huang Ko-ch'eng, and First Party Secretary of Hunan Chou Hsiao-chou — were purged. A widespread purge was launched against anyone who shared P'eng Te-huai's views.

The moderates gave way to Mao in order not to split with him. P'eng's criticism, however, had challenged Mao's prestige sorely. The most reward Mao got from this Congress was the replacement of P'eng as Defense Minister with Lin Piao. In later Pyears, Mao used Lin and the CCP Military Commission to challenge the civilian Party bureaucrats. Mao knew that the control of the army usually counted decisively in a power struggle.

Teng did not attend the Lushan conference because of an

Wan-sui (Long Live the Mao Tse-tung Thought) (reprinted in Hong Kong, 1969), p. 257.

injured foot.[41] But he stood on Mao's side in opposition to P'eng. In an article written by Teng to celebrate the tenth anniversary of the People's Republic, Teng attempted to defend Mao and the Great Leap Forward. Teng argued that although in practice the Great Leap Forward made mistakes, the policy was fundamentally correct. Without mentioning any names, Teng criticized P'eng and his group:

> Some of the rightist elements in our Party did not see the remarkable achievement of the Greap Leap Forward.... They exaggerated faults made in the progress of the movement, which the masses had already corrected, and used these as excuses to attack the Party line. They 1958 movement positively promoted our country's economy. But the rightist ignored this aspect and maintained instead that the movement was disastrous. The People's Communes worked well. But the rightists accused the commune movement of being an economic regression. They said that only by the dissolution of the communes would the people's livlihood be improved. The masses, however, believed that we had made great advancement. It was good, the masses said. It was bad, the rightists said. The rightist opportunism was obviously a reflection of the bourgeois fear of the mass movement in our Party.[42]

Despite Teng's harsh criticisms of P'eng, the consquences of the Great Leap Forward were serious enough to prove P'eng correct. The situation grew worse in the next couple of years because of natural disasters. The economic crisis became widespread. The period from 1960 to 1962 was generally referred to by the CCP as the "three bitter years." With the withdrawal of the Soviet experts from China in 1960, the situation deteriorated. Liu and Teng were forced to try new approaches to combating

---

41. Wang Hsuan,
42. Teng Hsiao-p'ing, "Chung-kuo Jen-min Ta T'uan-chieh Han Shih-chieh Jen-min Ta T'uan-chieh" (The Great Unity of the Chinese People and the Great Unity of the Peoples of the World), in *Jen-min Jih-pao* (Peking), October 2, 1959. The article was published in *Pravda*, October 1, 1959 and was reprinted in *Jen-min Jih-pao* on the second day.

the decline.[43] Beginning in 1961, a series of regulating programs were introduced to restore economic normalcy. In order to get a clearer picture of the situation, Teng went to the Sun-i county of Hopeh province in the spring of 1961 and stayed there two weeks for "squatting" and investigating.[44] Teng concentrated on developing a new strategy to incite the people to action.

Under his leadership, the Secretariat prepared in March 1961 the "Sixty Articles on Agriculture."[45] These articles forbade coercive measures, discontinued industrial enterprises in the countryside except during slack seasons, and prevented the interference of communal authorities in a family's sideline occupations. Larger sized communes were subdivided, increasing, in 1962, the number of People's Communes from 24,000 to 74,000. This indicated a return to the earlier model of the advanced APC's. The maxim "from each according to his ability, to each according to his needs" fell into disuse. A three-level system consisting of communes, brigades (equivalent to a higher level APC) and teams (equivalent to a lower level APC) was introduced. Teams were given land, cattle, farm implements, and their work was recorded in a separate accounting unit. They were also given some power in managing production affairs.

Also implemented was the *San-tzu-i-pao*, the Three Freedoms and One Guarantee. Peasants were allowed to own private

---

43. Besides Liu and Teng, other important figures at the time who participated in the reconstruction program were Ch'en Yun, Teng Tzu-hui, Li Fu-ch'un, Po I-po, and Li Hsien-nien.

44. "Chieh-k'ai Teng Hsiao-p'ing Kao 'P'ei-to-fei' Chu-lo-pu Te Hei-mu" ("Uncover the Black Mask of Teng Hsiao-p'ing's 'Petofi Club'"), a Red Guard pamphlet reproduced in *Teng Hsiao-p'ing*, p. 25; and "Ch'ang-kuan-lo Fan-ko-ming Shih-chien Te Ch'ien-ch'ien Hou-hou" ("Before and After the Counter-Revolutionary Incident of Ch'ang-Kuan-lo"), a Red Guard pamphlet reproduced in Ting Wang, ed., *Chung-kung Wen-hua-ta-ko-ming Tzu-liao Hui-pien* (Collected Materials of the Chinese Cultural Revolution), Vol. V (Hong Kong: Ming Pao Yueh-kan She, 1970), p. 229.

45. Chalmers Johnson, ed., *Ideology and Politics in Contemporary China* (Seattle: University of Washington Press), p. 271.

plots, to run small private enterprises and to sell their produce to the free markets. In addition, each household was responsible for certain output quotas on the public land assigned to it (*Pao-chan-tao-hu*). In some cases, collective lands were divided among peasants on a long-term basis (*Fen-tien-tao-hu*). The peasants were also allowed to carry on private farming (*Tankan*).

According to Chiang Ch'ing, the two most liberal measures — *Pao-chan-tao-hu* and *Fen-tien-tao-hu* — were ideas of Teng.[46] Teng said that because of regional differences, each area would be allowed to have its own style of readjustment. "Whatever style the masses want, adopt that style. What may be illegal, make it legal."[47] He also said: "The present major concern is to produce more foodstuffs. So long as it raises output, private farming is permissible. White or black, so long as cats can catch mice, they are good cats."[48] The "white or black cat" reference has become a favorite quotation since then. People would sometimes refer to Teng's working style as "catism." The implementation of these programs in reality destroyed the existence of "big" and "public" communes.

The Secretariat also formulated "Seventy Articles on Industry" in September 1961. The foreman-responsibility system (coupled with Party leadership) was implemented; workers were paid according to the quality of work done; and bonuses were permitted.[49] Wages increased while at the same time production of consumer goods received higher priority. Profit making became the first consideration in operating a business. Unprofita-

---

46. Chiang Ch'ing, "Teng Hsiao-p'ing Shih Ta Tsui-chuang," p. 22.

47. "Teng hsiao-p'ing Tsen-yang Fan-tui San-mien Hung-ch'i" ("How Teng Hsiao-p'ing Opposed the Three Red Flags"), a Red Guard pamphlet reproduced in *Teng Hsiao-p'ing*, p. 93.

48. See "Ch'e-ti Ch'ing-suan Teng Hsiao-p'ing Fan Tang Fan She-hui-chu-i Fan Mao Tse-tung Ssu-hsiang Te T'ao-t'ien Tsui-hsing" (To expose thoroughly Teng Hsiao-p'ing's Anti-Party, Anti-Socialism, and Anti-Mao Tse-tung Thought Crimes), a Red Guard pamphlet reproduced in *Teng Fei Hsiao-p'ing Tzu-liao Chuan-chi*, p. 103.

49. Teng Hsiao-p'ing, *Wen-hsuan*, pp. 259 and 375; and Johnson, pp. 275-276.

ble businesses were closed. Encouragement was given to industries related to agriculture. Expertise became an important asset.

The Liu-Teng pragmatism replaced the radicalism of the Great Leap Forward and the People's Republic took the road toward economic recovery.[50] The situation seemed to improve after 1962. Although some of the recuperative measures gained Mao's approval, Mao did not share the Liu-Teng rationale. To Liu and Teng, the success of these programs was a guide to future planning. To Mao they were temporary measures only. Once the economic crisis was over, they were to be removed. Mao never believed that the Great Leap Forward was a mistake. He admitted that errors were made in actual practice, but he insisted that the principles were unshakeable. The Great Leap Forward model was Mao's guarantee that China would not follow the path of the revisionist Communist states. Therefore, when the economic situation was normalized in 1962, Mao requested that these liberal measures be stopped. The request was made at the Tenth Plenary Session, September 1962.

The intimate relationship which had held Mao and Teng together for several decades began to change. After 1960, Teng seemed more inclined toward Liu and less devoted to Mao. Teng found himself sharing many of Liu's views on domestic policies. The two worked together in the central administration which necessitated a frequent meeting of the minds. On the other hand, Mao became less agreeable to Teng. Teng was not pleased with Mao's autocratic style of leadership.[51] Because Mao had gone into quasi retirement, Teng contacted him less. In March 1961, Mao chaired a Central Work Conference in Canton to review the Sixty Articles. He found that Teng had already made decisions on some items. Mao reproached him thus: "Which emperor has decided these?"[52] Mao expressed a similar dissatisfaction a few years later, claiming that Teng had built

---

50. Parris Chang, *Power and Policy*, p. 131.
51. Fallaci's interview with Teng.
52. Chiang Ch'ing, "Teng Hsiao-p'ing Shih Ta Tsui-chuang," p. 21.

up an "independent kingdom" himself.[53] "They were treating me like a dead ancestor," Mao complained of Liu and Teng. They would nod to Mao at conferences, but then sit on the other side in order not to be too close to him. When Mao spoke, they applauded; but they did not seriously implement Mao's directives.[54]

Both Liu and Teng had endorsed Mao's radical economic plan earlier, but their attitudes were modified by experience. A circle of "new rightists" gathered around them which included P'eng Chen, Li Hsien-nien, Li Fu-ch'un, Li Ching-ch'uan, T'an Chen-lin, Lu Ting-i, and Ulanfu. The new rightists followed the example of the old rightists in denouncing the Great Leap Forward as impractical and unrealistic. Like P'eng Te-huai, Ch'en Yun, and Teng Tzu-hui before them, the new rightists even criticized Mao. Many of them were formerly Mao's supporters. Mao found himself almost alone in the Party.

In re-examining the Great Leap Forward, Teng said that the Communists had done foolish things. "Not only will the people blame us," he declared, "we should also blame ourselves." He said that the People's Commune had been introduced too hastily because it was against the wishes of the people. He concluded that it was human miscalculation rather than natural disasters that accounted for the economic crisis. "The lesson we learned is a serious and unforgettable one," Teng confessed.[55] He cast aspersions at Mao when he said, "if in practice [the "Three Red Banners" policy] cannot be done, we have to make corrections. I do not care who initiated it. We did wrong and it's useless to cover it up."[56]

Mao's prestige had never sunk so low as now. Even the intellectuals began to defy him. Satirical articles were published

53. Teng Hsiao-p'ing, "Tsai Chung-kung Chung-yang Kung-tso Hui-i Shang Te Chien-t'ao" ("An Examination at the CCP Central Work Conference"), in *Teng Hsiao-p'ing*, p. 293.

54. Ross Terrill, *Mao* (New York: Harper and Row, 1980), p. 29.

55. "Teng Hsiao-p'ing Tsen-yang Fan-tui San-mien Hung-ch'i," p. 90; and *Jen-min Jih-pao*, April 10, 1967.

56. Chiang Ch'ing, "Teng Hsiao-p'ing Shih Ta Tsui-chuang," p. 22.

in large numbers. The most well known example was the historical drama, *Hai Jui Dismissed from Office*, written by Wu Han, a Deputy Mayor of Peking and a former university professor. Hai Jui, the principal character of the play, was an honest official of the Ming Dynasty who was dismissed from office because he spoke courageously for the people. Audiences would easily relate him with P'eng Te-huai. In addition, Teng To, a Secretary of the Peking Municipal Party Committee and close friend of Teng Hsiao-p'ing, also wrote many sarcastic essays against Mao in two of his newspaper columns, "Evening Chats at Yenshan" and "Notes from the Three Family Village."[57]

In the cultural field, the Liu-Teng group also held a different view from Mao. Mao launched an offensive at the September 1962 Tenth Plenum against the critics of his cultural policy. He said, "Using novels to carry out anti-Party activities is a big invention. In order to overthrow a regime, it is always necessary to prepare public opinion and carry out ideological work in advance. This is true of the revolutionary class as well as of the counter-revolutionary class."[58] Mao said that although the bourgeoisie had been overthrown in China, remnants of the reactionary class would use the old ideas, old culture, old customs and old habits to revive the capitalist rule. He called for a revolution in the cultural world.

Although Liu, Teng and the leaders of Chinese culture did not oppose Mao openly, they did not take his words seriously. Mao claimed that those who opposed him and his policies were representatives of the bourgeois and that a cultural revolution would be another form of class struggle. Liu and Teng, however, agreed with Chou Yang, the leading official in charge of cultural affairs. Chou said that even though it was true some of the artists and writers failed to understand Marxism, the "cultural workers" should not be construed as enemies of the people.

---

57. The "Notes" column was written in rotation with Teng T'o, Wu Han, and Liao Mo-sha, Director of the United Front Department in the Peking Municipal Party Committee.

58. Mao Tse-tung, *Wan-sui*, pp. 435-436.

Teng added that it was normal to have different viewpoints in the academic world.[59] To pacify Mao, articles directed at him were restrained for the time being, but people like Wu Han and Teng T'o remained unaffected. In Mao's eyes, Wu Han (who identified P'eng Te-huai with Hai Jui) was an harassment. But Wu was protected by P'eng Chen, his superior in the Peking Municipal Government, and Teng Hsiao-p'ing, his long-time bridge game partner.[60]

Teng once complained that repeated political pressure on the media only alarmed people. Some journalists were too scared to write anything. "The New China News agency receives only two stories a day!" Teng grumbled. "Motion pictures show only troops and fighting while this film is not permitted to be shown, and that film is not permitted to be shown."[61]

Beginning in 1962, Chiang Ch'ing took the lead in reforming the Peking opera. Teng openly attacked Chiang's scheduled performances: "I support wholeheartedly the idea that the Peking opea should be reformed. But I just do not feel like watching these plays!" He said that there were only a few plays performed and all of them were related to revolutions or military struggles. "Maybe someday the old plays will be performed again, who knows!" Teng exclaimed.[62] It was said that Chiang Ch'ing once told Teng's wife Cho Lin that she would like to discuss with Teng the problems existing in the cultural field. She complained that for years Mao's directives on cultural reform had not been executed. But Teng just ignored her.[63]

---

59. "Teng Hsiao-p'ing Fan Mao Yu-lu" (Quotations from Teng Hsiao-p'ing's Anti-Maoist Sayings), a Red Guard pamphlet reproduced in *Teng Hsiao-p'ing*, pp. 72-73.

60. "Chieh-k'ai Teng Hsiao-p'ing Kao 'Pei-to-fei' Chu-lo-pu Te Hei-mu," pp. 27-28.

61. Chiang Ch'ing, "Teng Hsiao-p'ing Shih Ta Tsui-chuang," p. 23.

62. Ibid., pp. 72-73.

63. "Pa Teng Hsiao-p'ing Tsung Hei-wo Li Wa-ch'u-lai Shih-chung" ("Taking Teng Hsiao-p'ing Out of his Black Hole to Expose Him to the Public"), a Red Guard pamphlet reproduced in *Teng Fei Hsiao-p'ing Tzu-liao Chuan-chi* (A Collection of Materials on Teng Hsiao-p'ing) (Taipei: Kuo-fang-pu Tsung-cheng-chan-pu, 1978), p. 23.

Teng also expressed his dislike of the prolonged campaign against the academicians. He said that certain people would seek any chance to attack others just to build their fame. These people, he argued, might not have any learning, but would nevertheless exaggerate the faults of others. In a Secretariat meeting held in March 1965, Teng expressed his concern about the slurs against scholars.[64] After that, most of the newspapers and periodicals stopped criticism of the so-called "bourgeois writers" and "reactionary academic authorities."[65]

Education was another field where Teng contradicted Mao's view. Mao believed that the chief aim of education was to indoctrinate students politically and to set them up as workers in labor crews. In other words, Mao emphasized more the students' "redness" than their "expertise." Teng, however, believed that students should be encouraged to engage in academic research and that expertise always came first. He said, "Labor work should be assigned. . . but it should not be too excessive.... Laboring should not affect the proper learning in schools." Teng reminded officials that the function of university education was to advance sciences to a higher level by continued research and experimentation. In August 1961, he introduced the Sixty Articles on Higher Education which stressed the "three fundamentals," theory, knowledge, technique, and professional leadership in academic institutions. Teng disagreed with Mao about shortening the school term and forcing students to work and study simultaneously. Furthermore, Teng supported the traditional degree system which Mao disliked the most.[66]

In January 1962, an Enlarged Conference of the Central Committee was called. Seven thousand cadres from the central governments and the provinces met to discuss and examine the

64. "Teng Hsiao-p'ing Fan Mao Yu-lu," p. 72.

65. Parris Chang, *Power and Policy*, p. 162.

66. Chiang Ch'ing, "Teng Hsiao-p'ing Shih Ta Tsui-chuang," p. 22; and "Teng Hsiao-p'ing Te Chiao-yu Lu-hsien," (Teng Hsiao-p'ing's Education Line), a Red Guard pamphlet reproduced in *Chan-wang*, October 1, 1975, pp. 30-31.

policies of the last three years. Teng delivered a summary report at the conference, and made many unfavorable comments about Mao. Shortly before this conference, Mao had downplayed the effects brought by the Great Leap Forward as not that serious. He said that the present situation was "extremely favorable." But Teng gave a different message at the Conference: "It was the political situation which the Chairman found extremely favorable... Not only could you not describe the economic situation as being favorable, you could call it extremely unfavorable."[67] In addition, Teng remarked, "The dictatorial trend [in the Party] is very serious... We have introduced campaign after campaign. It appears as though this is the only way we can mobilize the masses. It is no good to carry out a new campaign every day." Liu Shao-ch'i stated in his report that man-made mistakes accounted for seventy percent of the economic disasters.[68] Mao, on the other hand defended his excuse that natural disasters were beyond man's control. Only Lin Piao and Chou En-lai took Mao's side. Liu Shao-ch'i proposed that a chance be given to reinstate those who had been purged because of their opposition to the radical Great Leap.[69] The 1962 Conference was the beginning of the open split between Mao on the one hand and Liu and Teng on the other.

In February 1962, Teng requested that those who were falsely charged during the Anti-Rightist Campaign of 1959 be reinstated. He said that eighty percent of the cadres were wrongly convicted.[70] Although there were a limited number of cadres being pardoned, Teng's call was enough to make Mao angry.

---

67. *Nihon Keizai*, August 8, 1967; and "Chang-kuan-lo Fan-ko-ming Shih-chien Ten Ch'ien-ch'ien Hou-hou," p. 229.

68. *Nihon Keizai*, August 8, 1967.

69. Fan Yung-jen, "Chung-kung Cheng-ch'uan Erh-shih Nien" ("Twenty Years of the People's Republic of China"), in *Ming Pao Yueh-kan* (Hong Kong), November 1969, p. 36; and Ch'an-kuan-lo Fan-ko-ming Shih-chien Te Chien-ch'ien Hou-hou," p. 229.

70. Johnson, *Ideology and Politics*, pp. 381-382. During the Cultural Revolution, the Maoists called Teng's act "reverse wind."

In September 1962, at the Tenth Plenary Session, Mao fought back. He stressed again and again the importance of class strugge.[71] A resolution to his liking was adopted which was aimed at halting the further decentralization of the People's Commune. A Red Flag commentary which appeared in November 1966 said:

> Comrade Mao Tse-tung had analyzed the situation and contradictions of the time at the Tenth Plenary Session of the Eighth Party Congress. He made a critique against the bourgeois tendency in the Party and helped to correct the rightist orientation held by some of our Party members.[72]

Chiang Ch'ing, Mao's wife, said years later:

> The prelude of the Great Cultural Revolution started with Chairman Mao's call issued at the Tenth Plenary Session of the Eighth Central Committee of the CCP in 1962.[73]

After years of inactivity, Mao's comeback did not gain him much. Although Mao seemed to win his cause at the 1962 Plenum, his victory was superficial. The Party apparatus was firmly held by Liu and Teng. In reality, they executed Mao's directives whatever way they liked, emphasizing their own pragmatic principles.

Mao urged at the same meeting that another rectification campaign be launched. The Socialist Education Campaign (SEC), or the *Ssu-ch'ing* (Four Cleans Movement), was extended to correct "mistakes" of a political, ideological, organizational, or economic nature. Mao's aim was to try to arrest the revisionist tendency. But in the eyes of the powerholders, the moderate policy as practiced since 1960 had saved the country from economic collapse. They feared that another political campaign

---

71. Mao Tse-tung, *Wan-sui*, p. 431.
72. "Tsai Mao Tse-tung Ssu-hsiang Te Sheng-li Tao-lu Shang Ch'ien-ch'in" ("To March on the Victory Path of the Mao Tse-tung Thought"), *Hung Ch'i* (Red Flag, Peking), November, 1966.
73. Roxane Witke, *Comrade Chiang Ch'ing*, p. 297.

would only alienate the peasantry. Although they were unwilling to cooperate, they adopted, at Mao's request, the "Draft Resolution of the Central Committee of the CCP on Some Problems in Current Rural Work," commonly known as the First Ten Points. The draft, Mao's first directive on the SEC, emphasized class struggle.

Four months later, however, the Party adopted another resolution. The so-called Second Ten Points ("Some Concrete Policy Formulations of the Central Committee of the CCP in the Rural Socialist Education Movement") was prepared by Teng as a supplement to Mao's draft.[74] Teng's draft borrowed much of the phraseology from the First Ten Points and mentioned here and there the importance of carrying on class struggle. But the new draft was a pragmatic guideline. The combatant spirit of Mao's draft was minimized. Because many cadres spent too much time on political matters, production was on the decline. The Second Ten Points thus emphasized that the rectification campaign go hand in hand with production work and that "at no stage of the movement should production be affected." To prevent the movement from going to extremes, the Second Ten Points set forth guidelines to direct its course. Teng's draft drew a distinction between profiteering and speculation, and described the proper conduct of family businesses. As criteria for judging the merit of the SEC, people were urged to use the Sixty Articles on the People's Commune, which permitted private plots, sideline occupations, and free markets. It said that if a cadre was found guilty of non-antagonistic wrong doing he was to be treated with leniency. Radical measures were to be avoided.[75]

---

74. "Chung-kuo Nung-t'sun Liang-t'iao Tao-lu Te Tou-cheng" ("Struggle between the Two Roads in China's Countryside"), *Jen-min Jih-pao*, November 23, 1967. Another article credited the Second Ten Points to Teng and P'eng Chen. See "Teng Hsiao-p'ing Fan Mao Tse-tung Ssu-hsiang Yen-lun I-pai Li" (On Teng Hsiao-p'ing's Anti-Mao Tse-tung Thought Speeches: One Hundred Examples), a Red Guard pamphlet reproduced in *Teng Fei Hsiao-p'ing Tzu-liao Chuan-chi,* p. 143.

75. Parris Chang, *Power and Policy,* pp. 150-151.

Mao's draft and Teng's draft also differed on the issue of who should take the leading role in the SEC movement. The First Ten Points put the poor and lower middle peasant associations in charge of the campaign, but the Second Ten Points stressed the leadership of the Party.[76] Mao wanted to use an extra-Party force to carry out the campaign, as in 1956 and 1957. This time, however, the organization men insisted that the Party should maintain order. Liu and Teng sent out many work teams to control the movement.

In summary, the Second Ten Points was moderate in tone and conciliatory in nature. The Maoists later described Teng's draft as "removing the burning brands from the boiling cauldron" to "negate the essential content of the struggle between the two classes and between the two roads, completely discarding the line, principles and policies" of the SEC as formulated by Mao.[77]

Mao introduced his Twenty-three Points ("Some Problems Currently Arising in the Course of the Rural Socialist Education Movement") at the January 1965 Central Work Conference, warning the Party not to get involved in the Campaign. He accused the moderates of pretending to be Marxists. Mao's new document stressed that the key point of the SEC was to "correct those people in positions of authority within the Party who take the capitalist road."[78] This quotation was repeated time and again during the Cultural Revolution. At that time, Mao had already decided to remove Liu and Ten. His first task was to regain practical control of the Party by terminating the division of responsibility he himself had instituted. For the time being, however, the Party aparatus was held firmly by the Liu-Teng group which ignored most of Mao's instructions and went its own way. The war in southeast Asia forced Mao to wait to regain power. Fighting in Vietnam had intensified since Febru-

---

76. Harrison, *Long March to Power*, p. 487.
77. "Chung-kuo Nung-t'sun Liang-t'iao Tao-lu Te Tou-cheng."
78. Teng Hsiao-p'ing, *Wen-hsuan*, p. 389.

ary and the fear that it would spread to China diverted attention away from the intraparty struggle.

As General Secretary of the Party, Teng also managed foreign affairs. He had visited the Soviet Union three times, North Korea once, and Rumania once. When China openly reproached Soviet revisionalism, Teng engaged in the Sino-Soviet debate and became an outstanding theoretician-spokesman. In general, Teng agreed with Mao in the promotion of international Communism and the opposition to Soviet expansionism despite their differences on many domestic issues.

Four years after his last visit, Teng joined Liu Shao-ch'i on a third trip to Moscow in November 1960. Teng was the deputy leader of the Chinese delegation sent to attend the World Communist Summit Conference and the 43rd anniversary celebration of the October Revolution. The conference, which included delegates from 81 communist parties, was one of the most important meetings ever held in Moscow.[79]

The Sino-Soviet split started as early as 1957 and widened in subsequent years. The Chinese claimed that the People's Commune was a short-cut to Communism and believed that they had set an example of economic development for the Third world. This angered the Soviets, but for their part the Soviets infuriated the Chinese. They refused to help the Chinese Communists during the Taiwan Strait crisis; Khruschev flew to the United States to hold talks with Eisenhower at Camp David; and they withdrew all their technicians and advisors from China in 1960 without prior notification. To compete with Soviet Russia for leadership in the Third World, China started building an anti-Soviet bloc. Finally, tension between the two giant Communist states came to a head during the 1960 Summit Conference.

The two countries engaged in heated debates over what policy to pursue toward the capitalist states and what kind of revolution to promote in Third World nations. The Soviet Union held the view that the time was not ripe for going to war with

---

79. Klein and Clark, *Biographic Dictionary*, Vol. II, p. 825.

the capitalist countries because the communists were militarily
not strong enough. In order to prevent the outbreak of a nuclear
war, the tactic of peaceful coexistence was the best way to buy
time for building strength. The Soviets believed that socialism
would eventually overtake capitalism through peaceful competition. The Soviets also discouraged local wars in the Third
World because they could lead to large scale wars involving the
Western countries. They advocated instead a peaceful transition
to socialism. Democratic reformist tactics were encouraged.

The Chinese, on the other hand, maintained that the Communists should not negotiate with the capitalist countries. In
fact, they belived that negotiation was impossible. Armed struggle as a means to power had always been a basic Chinese belief.
Chinese Communists were eager to support revolutions in the
Third World because they held that this was the only way to
gain power.

Teng was China's major spokesman at the conference.[80] He
conducted heated arguments with Mikhail Suslov, the Russian
delegate and party ideologist.[81] The French Communists, in a
pamphlet circulated later, attacked Teng as espousing a "leftist"
and "erroneous" line.

The conference brought to the surface hostile undercurrents
between China and the Soviet Union. Instead of generating
goodwill, the two-week meeting served only to excite competition between the two countries. A declaration was published at
the end of the conference which endorsed the Soviet policy
toward the capitalist nations. But China did not lose ground
either. The declaration approved a more radical approach to
revolutions in the Third World. The compromise indicated that
the Soviet Union could no longer count on complete domination of the international Communist movement.

---

80. Harold Hinton, *An Introduction to Chinese Politics* (New York:
Praeger Publishers, 1973), p. 134.

81. Suyin Han, *Wind in the Tower* (Boston: Little, Brown and Company,
1976), p. 250.

132

In July 1961, Teng held a talk with North Korean Premier Kim Il-sung which gave rise to a Sino-Korean Treaty of Friendship, Cooperation, and Mutual Assistance. China hoped to win North Korea to her side in opposition to the Soviet hegemony. In September Teng led a Chinese delegation to North Korea to attend the Fourth Congress of the Korean Workers Party. The Chinese reaffirmed their support of the Korean cause of national liberation. The Chinese also emphasized the necessity of using force to achieve this aim. On the other hand, the Russians appeared more reserved and less militant than the Chinese. In referring to the newly released Soviet Draft of the Party Program, Teng stressed its hidden self-interest. He said that the program "outlines the gigantic plan of the *Soviet* people."[82] In saying so, Teng denied the "universal character" of the draft as claimed by the Soviet satellite states. Teng's meaning, as understood by everyone, was that China would not be bound by the draft.

The relationship between the two countries deteriorated further in 1962 and 1963. China condemned the Soviet Union for weak action in the Cuban missile crisis. She denounced Soviet support of India in the 1962 Sino-Indian Border War. Starting in January 1963, China began to attack Khrushchev by name.

The Soviets invited the Chinese to hold talks in Moscow on February 27. On March 7, Teng notified the Soviet ambassador to China that the People's Republic was amenable to holding talks "on important questions concerning the international Communist movement."[83] Chou En-lai informed the Soviet Union that Teng would lead a Chinese delegation to Moscow. In preparation, Teng drafted a paper on China's attitudes toward international Communist movements. According to Teng, the paper was later published under the title "A Proposal

---

82. Donald S. Zagoria, *The Sino-Soviet Conflict, 1956-1961* (New York: Atheneum, 1973), p. 372. Author's emphasis.

83. Klein and Clark, *Biographic Dictionary*, Vol. II, p. 825.

Concerning the General Line of the International Communist Movement," commonly known as the Twenty-five Points. But Ch'en Po-ta remarked later that Teng's original draft was not acceptable to Mao. Mao wrote another piece which became the published version of the Twenty-five Points.[84] The document was included in an open letter to the Russian people published on June 14.[85]

The Chinese delegation included, in addition to Teng, P'eng Chen, the Mayor of Peking, K'ang Sheng, a member of the CCP Central Secretariat, Yang Shang-k'un, the Office Secretary of the CCP, Liu Ning-i, a member of the Central Committee, and P'an Tzu-li, the Chinese ambassador to the Soviet Union.[86] Except for P'an Tzu-li, the delegates were all experienced negotiators who had been involved in previous Sino-Soviet debates. When Teng left Peking almost all the senior leaders came to see him off.

The talks were doomed to failure even before the delegation arrived in Moscow on July 5. The open letter was worded like an ultimatum and served only to anger the Soviets. A few days before the talks, the Soviets expelled five Chinese activists who were caught distributing the Russian translation of the letter on Soviet soil. Just one day before the talks, the Soviets published an official statement, which declared that the Chinese had no intention of reconciling their differences — possibly a fair assessment. When Teng and the Chinese delegates arrived in Moscow they were delayed for several hours at the airport. The Soviets were concurrently holding talks with the British and the Americans on limiting nuclear testing, a treaty the Chinese strongly opposed. All these incidents indicated that neither side was in the mood for making concessions.[87]

---

84. "Yang Ch'eng-wu Hen P'i Teng Hsiao-p'ing," p. 71.

85. The letter is featured in *Chung-su Lun-chan Wen-hsien*, pp. 1-58.

86. Klein and Clark, *Biographic Dictionary*, Vol. II, p. 825.

87. Edmund Clubb, *China and Russia* (New York: Columbia University Press, 1971), pp. 461-462; and Robert S. Elegant, *The Center of the World*, (New York: Funk & Wagnalls, 1968), p. 398.

Surprisingly, the talks lasted two weeks. The Chinese proposed that a world conference of all Communist Parties be called to resolve the differences. They also proposed that if a conference were called, the voting procedure be amended. The Chinese suggested that the voting power of a country be calculated according to the size of its Communist Party and the population it served. The Soviets of course could not accept this —China had the largest Communist Party in the world and she had 700 million people.[88]

Upon his return home, Teng received a grand welcome. Even Chiang Ch'ing, who rarely appeared in public, welcomed Teng at the airport. On the other hand, after the departure of the Chinese delegation, *Pravda* published an open letter to the Communist world accusing the Chinese of trying to usurp the international Communist leadership and of propagating a disastrous nuclear war. The Russians signed a treaty with the United States and the United Kingdom for a partial moratorium on atomic testing.[89] The relationship between the two countries was virtually destroyed.

Teng played a leading role in the Moscow talks and was very proud of having stood up to the Soviets. During the Cultural Revolution a big caricature poster appeared of Teng boasting that his two greatest achievements in life were the Huai-Hai Battle and the Anti-Soviet campaign.[90]

In retrospect the gap separating Teng and Mao emerged in the mid-1950's when the two became engaged in different affairs and found they could not always agree. Mao's chief interest lay in the principles and direction of the Party, while Teng involved himself in daily administration. The theoretician found the practitioner too ready to surrender his ideals and compromise with reality. On the other hand, the practitioner found the theoretician too idealistic and unable to understand the difficul-

---

88. Clubb, *China and Russia*, p. 462.
89. Elegant, *Mao's Great Resolution*, p. 398.
90. "Yabg Cheng-wu Hen Pi Teng Hsiao-p'ing," pp. 70-71.

ties of putting theory into practice. The two were still on excellent terms in the fifties because Teng was not yet a "rightist" like Ch'en Yun and P'eng Te-huai. But developments after 1959 proved that the moderates were correct. Without hesitation Teng cast his lot with them.

It was more a quarrel over approaches than aims that brought Mao and Teng into conflict in later years. Both Mao and Teng believed that tomorrow's China would be a socialist country where people would be free from hunger, suffering, and exploitation. With the founding of the People's Republic, the Communists faced new challenges. As revolutionaries, their job was to fight. As statesmen, their job was to build. While Mao stuck to the radical tradition, Teng was transformed into a bureaucrat.

Mao was a fighter, not a manager. He found it boring to sit in the office and establish procedures for the proper conducting of business. He believed in deeds, not paperwork. Mao saw the building of socialism as another form of revolution. He asked people to sacrifice themselves totally in work and forget their individualtiy. He wanted to implement a new ethic which would turn all the Chinese into sacred heroes, advancing society with the voluntary participation of every individual. In Mao's view a socialist man was the one who would deny any self-interest, who would work day and night for the common good, and who would accept any excessive work as glory. Mao believed that a "poor and blank" country like China would rise to splendor if the "six hundred million Chinese were Yao or Shun."[91]

Teng did not share Mao's dreams of quick glory. In Teng's mind, China's backwardness was the major obstacle to its progress. The mobilization of the masses was essential, but not necessarily the determining factor. With the overwhelming percentage of the population illiterate, the masses were far from easy to rally around ideology. Mao's hopes of surpassing British

---

91. Yao and Shun were legendary emperors of China's Golden Age.

industrial capacity within 15 years were recognized by Teng, in the sixties, as a ludicrous fantasy. Teng perceived that a highly spirited, but untrained Communist could not accomplish more than a profit-minded skilled worker. He believed that only when people were economically sufficient could one talk to them about socialism. Teng's priority was therefore to increase the wealth of the country. Modernization was essential to increasing productivity. In other words, Teng considered the economic means (material incentive) more important than the political means (moral incentive) in exciting the enthusiasm of people. And it was ultimately over the issue of modernization that Teng found himself differing with Mao.

Many aspects of modernization were disliked by Mao, such as specialization, standardization, professionalism, and elitism. Mao shared Marx's view that a socialist man should be a "total man." Standardization and specialization only turned people into machines, alienating them from society and other individuals. To overcome alienation required the insights gained by sharing the experiences of others. This required one to be a generalist. At the same time a peasant could be a soldier, doctor, and a writer. Participation — to go to the masses and to learn from the masses — was a Maoist theme of dealienation. Elitism was another concept hated by Mao. An uncorrupted commoner would always be more politically conscious than those at the top because the latter were separated from the masses and failed to understand them.

On the other hand, Teng as the organization man was more concerned with efficiency. He felt that standardization and routinization were monotonous, but that they saved unnecessary cumbersomeness and minimized inefficiency. A standardized system was calculable while human favor was difficult to count on.

Mao resembled the young Marx in many ways. The author of the 1844 *Paris Manuscript* was a humanist whose concern was the individual. The central premise of the *Paris Manuscript* presented man as a social being. Man's alienation from society and other individuals was due to the capitalist mode of production, a condition that could be relieved only by revolution aimed at overthrowing the capitalist state. We understand from the *Paris Manuscript* that Marx was in many ways a voluntarist who believed that people could push history forward and that political activism could overcome economic constraints. Hegelian as well, the young Marx held to the principle of dialectics, maintaining that history evolved and progressed permanently. The founding of a socialist state was only a beginning, not the end. Mao shared Marx's emphasis of political mobilization over economic development and denied that class struggle would cease after a socialist state was founded.

Teng believed that history was lineal in development and that a great leap from feudalism to socialism, while bypassing capitalism, was impractical and unMarxist. Although Teng did not say anything to abolish Communist rule and return to capitalism, he did believe that economic progress would determine everything. When productivity was low, when people's incomes were barely enough to keep them from hunger, and when the majority of the population was illiterate, how could one expect the masses to act saintly for the sake of a distant utopia? Only in heavily industrialized countries where alienation was rampant would conditions be favorable for building socialism. By Marx's prediction, a socialist revolution was most likely to break out in Germany or Great Britain because the two countries were the most industrialized at that time. But history failed Marx. Teng, however, admitted no fault in Marx's teachings. He pronounced any denial of "economism" as "great but empty talk."

If Mao was the Marx of the *Paris Manuscript*, Teng was the Marx of *The Capital*. While Mao inspired the radical youth of the Western world to challenge the establishment, Teng Hsiao-p'ing's brand of Communism was more acceptable to leaders of Western governments. Mao was a romantic revolutionary; Teng was a practical realist.

Chapter 9

The Cultural Revolution
(1966-1973)

At a joint meeting of the Politburo and regional Party Secretariats held from September to October 1965, Mao requested that the education system be reformed and that the full-time study program be changed to a part-work and part-study program. His request was turned down by Teng.[1] Mao's more immediate concern, however, was to carry on the rectification campaign in the cultural world, and to continue criticizing the "bourgeois thought" in academic circles. In particular, he insisted that Wu Han, the historian-playwright who wrote *Hai Jui Dismissed from Office* be reprehended. Again, few took his words seriously and Teng still invited Wu Han to his bridge parties.[2] This was the last formal request Mao made before the Cultural Revolution.

When Mao realized that he could no longer maintain con-

---

1. Bridgham, "Mao's Cultural Revolution: Origin and Development," p. 16; and Stephen Uhalley, Jr., *Mao Tse-Tung* (New York: New Viewpoint, 1975), p. 148; and Stanley Karnow, *Mao and China* (New York: The Viking Press, 1972).

2. "Chieh-k'ai Teng Hsiao-p'ing Kao 'Pei-to-fei' Chu-lo-pu Te Hei-mu," p. 27.

trol of the Peking Party machine, he went to Shanghai, the base of the radicals. He commissioned Yao Wen-yuan, a young Shanghai propagandist, to write a critical essay of Wu's play. The article, entitled "Comment On the Newly Composed Historical Play," was published in the Shanghai-based *Wen Hui Pao*, on November 10, 1965, marking the beginning of the Cultural Revolution. The article pointed out that the hidden purpose of the play was to defend the dismissed Defense Minister P'eng Te-huai. Obviously, the Maoists wanted to turn the issue into a political affair, taking their first stab at the "power-holders." From the end of 1965 to the spring of 1966, articles against Wu Han were published almost daily. Teng To, who shared a newspaper column with Wu Han, was also attacked.

Lo Jui-ch'ing, Chief of Staff of the PLA, was the first "power-holder" to fall from power.[3] He was Liu's and Teng's principal supporter in the army. Lo's dismissal gave Lin Piao unconditional sway over the army which in turn helped strengthen Mao's position.

Although Teng disagreed with Mao in many ways, he had no intention of overthrowing Mao. Now that he realized that Mao was fighting back, he became hesitant. He seconded Mao in criticizing P'eng Chen for being too protective of Wu Han.[4] P'eng was the leading minister in charge of cultural affairs in the Secretariat who headed a Cultural Revolution Group of Five to study the Wu Han case.

On February 7, 1966, the Group of Five submitted a report which concluded that the Wu Han issue was "academic in character" and that further criticism by the press should be limited. It also referred to the critics of Wu Han as "scholar tyrants,"

---

3. Before his dismissal, Lo Jui-ch'ing also looked after the military affairs in the CCP Central Secretariat. After his removal from office, Yeh Chien-ying assumed his position in the Secretariat and Yang Ch'eng-wu succeeded him as the Chief of Staff.

4. "Chieh-k'ai Teng Hsiao-p'ing Kao 'Pei-to-fei' Chu-lu-pu Te Hei-mu," p. 28; and Lowell Dittmer, *Liu Shao-ch'i and the Chinese Cultural Revolution* (Berkeley, Cal.: University of California Press, 1974), p. 74.

and "dogmatic and forceful."[5] The report was accepted by the Standing Committee of the Politburo as a guideline for the Cultural Revolution.[6] Liu Shao-ch'i and Teng both supported its adoption. However, Teng later defended his approval of the report by saying he was deceived by P'eng. "I ratified it because I was told that the Chairman had agreed to it," Teng said. A Red Guard pamphlet later confirmed Teng's remark.[7]

It was rumored in February 1966 that P'eng Chen, Lo Jui-ch'ing, Lu Ting-i and Yang Shang-k'un were planning a coup to overthrow Mao. According to the Red Gaurds, the Peking "authorities" had called the army to the capital to await further orders.[8] Teng dismissed these accusations. He said, "We have made investigations.... P'eng Chen cannot order the army, nor can I."[9] But Lin Pao insisted that the story was true and hinted that Teng might have been involved in the conspiracy.[10] Once, the Red Guards even urged that Liu Shao-ch'i, P'eng Chen, Lo Jui-ch'ing, Lu Ting-i, Yang Shang-k'un, and Teng Hsiao-p'ing be sentenced to death.[11] But Chou En-lai threw his influence behind Teng and denied that there was any February mutiny. K'ang Sheng, who led the secret police, also dismissed the authenticity of the story. (But he said it was "useful" to let people believe that there was a mutiny!)[12] Although Mao did not say anything about the "February Mutiny" officially, he remarked, "Liu and Teng have always done their work in the open, not in secret. They are different from P'eng Chen."[13]

5. *Chung-kung Chi-mi Wen-chien Hui-pien* (Collection of the CCP Secret Documents) (Taipei: Kuo-li Cheng-chih Ta-hsueh kwo-chi Kuan-hsi Yen-chiu Chung-hsin, 1977), pp. 164-165.

6. Parris Chang, *Power and Policy*, p. 164; and "Teng Hsiao-p'ing Fan-Mao Yu-lu," p. 73.

7. Dittmer, *Liu Shao-ch'i* p. 74.

8. Esmein, *The Chinese Cultural Revolution*, p. 77.

9. "Teng Hsiao-p'ing Fan Mao Yu-lu," p. 77; "Teng Hsiao-p'ing Wen-ti" (The Problems of Teng Hsiao-p'ing), a Red Guard pamphlet.

10. *Yomiuri*, February 15, 1967.

11. Esmein, *Cultural Revolution*, pp. 77-78.

12. Rue, *Mao's Way*, p. 264.

13. Mao Tse-tung, *Wan-sui*, p. 655.

At a Secretariat meeting held from April 9th to 12th, Teng joined the Maoists in condemning P'eng Chen for making so many errors, which included opposition to Mao. The meeting suggested that the Five-Man Group be dissolved and that its reports and instructions be withdrawn. A proposal to appoint a new group to direct the Cultural Revolution was adopted at the April 16 Hangchow meeting.[14] The new group was called the CCP Central Cultural Revolutionary Group, and was subordinate to the Politburo's Standing Committee. Ch'en Po-ta and Chiang Ch'ing headed the group which included the likes of Chang Ch'un-ch'iao, a Shanghai Party cadre. After a grueling round of criticism, the Hangchow conference removed P'eng Chen from the Mayorship of Peking. Lu Ting-i, Director of the CCP Propaganda Department and Minister of Culture, also lost his job. The so-called "May 16th Circular" now replaced the "February Thesis," the original guiding principles for the Cultural Revolution, calling for an intensification of class struggle.[15]

P'eng had been Teng's longtime confidant. Mao once remarked that Teng had relied heavily on P'eng Chen in the Secretariat.[16] P'eng was, in essence, the Deputy Secretary General. He had accompanied Teng on many trips in and out of the country. The two were good friends and their families had maintained close ties for years.[17] Teng stood on Mao's side in the P'eng affair because he thought Mao would be appeased and therefore limit the dimensions of his latest radical undertaking. He, and Liu Shao-ch'i as well, underestimated the ruthlessness of Mao's tactics. In Mao's scheme defaming such cultural leaders as Wu Han, Teng To, and Liao Mo-sha was the first step. With the downfall of the "Three Family Village" (Wu, Teng

---

14. Dittmer, *Liu Shao-ch'i*, p. 76.

15. *Chung-kung Chi-mi Wen-chien Hui-pien*, pp. 167-171; and Ssu-ma Ch'ang-feng, *Wen-ko Shih-mi*, Vol. I, p. 77.

16. *Mao Tse-tung Ssu-hsiang Wan-sui*, p. 661. Mao's remark came in October 1966.

17. "Pa Teng Hsiao-p'ing Tsung Hei-wo Li Wa-ch'u-lai Shih-chung," p. 27.

To, and Liao), the Maoists directed their attacks toward the so called "Four-family Shop" of P'eng Chen, Lo Jui-ch'ing, Lu Ting-i, and Yang Shangk'un — all four members of the Central Secretariat. Now they turned their attention to the ultimate targets —Liu and Teng.

In April 1966, an Albanian delegation came to visit China. A welcome party was given by the Shanghai workers on May 6th. Teng addressed the meeting, referring specifically to the Thoughts of Mao Tse-tung as the guideline for all Party work.[18] This renewed emphasis of Mao's authority was a major turn around of party policy since the Eighth Party Congress. Liu Shao-ch'i, who received the same delegation earlier, did not mention anything about the Thoughts of Mao Tse-tung.[19] The Albanian delegation then went to Hangchow to hold talks with Mao. The hosts and the guests were photographed together. Lin Piao, Chou En-lai and Teng were seen standing beside Mao, but Liu was left out of the picture.[20] It appears that Mao wanted to favor Teng for the time being as a means of isolating Liu.

Although Teng tried to appear more like a radical, he still could not agree with Mao in letting the Cultural Revolution develop spontaneously. The students' response to the May 16th Circular was enthusiastic and soon after its publication Red Guard organizations grew. As the Party's organization man, Teng could not allow any autonomous political groups to exist outside the Party. On May 25th, Nieh Yuan-tzu, an assistant lecturer at Peking University, posted a big-character poster on the campus wall attacking the University's chancellor, Lu P'ing, and the Party's other affiliates. Nieh's poster was the first of its kind to appear since the onset of the Cultural Revolution. Mao-ists were excited and eager to publicize the event immediately. Teng managed to delay the news until June 1st, after which

18. Ting Wang, ed., *Chung-kung Wen-hua-ta-ko-ming Tzu-liao Hui-pien* (Selected Materials of the Chinese Cultural Revolution), Vol. I (Hong Kong: Ming Pao Yueh-kan She, 1972), p. 500.

19. Dittmer, *Liu Shao-ch'i*, p. 77.

20. *Peking Review*, May 13, 1966, p. 8.

Mao intervened and gave the story to the New China News Agency.[21]

When Liu and Teng realized that student radicalism was growing stronger, they employed their old tactic of sending work teams to be stationed in the colleges and schools. They hoped that these work teams would bring the student movement back in line. They prohibited the posting of big-character posters on the streets, the holding of rallies and demonstrations, and violence of any kind.[22] Of course, moderate counter action was contrary to Mao's wishes. What Mao really wanted was to give a free hand to the masses for smashing the Party apparatus.

Mao disliked the idea of the work teams. Ch'en Po-ta also urged that the work teams be dissolved to allow spontaneous participation by the masses. He wrote a letter to Teng recommending the dissolution of the work teams but Teng could not agree.[23] "Now that the Party affiliations in schools are no longer functioning," said Liu and Teng, "who should assume the Party's role? The work team must represent the Party." They said that work teams should be sent to schools and colleges as fast as "the first engine rushing to the fire." Teng said that if the "babies" (Red Guards) were allowed to have their way, everything would be turned upside down.[24] Consequently, in the capital area of Peking alone more than four hundred work teams were organized with more than 10,000 cadres. Teng said: "A genuine leftist will cooperate with the Party; he will trust the work teams in schools." Once he called a school work team to his house and instructed the students to rebuild the Party organizations in their school and absorb the Red Guard organs into the Youth League.

---

21. "Teng Hsiao-p'ing Yu-lu" ("Quotations from Teng Hsiao-p'ing"), in *Chan-wang*, No. 191, and Jacques Guillermaz, *The Chinese Communist Party in Power 1949-1976*, trans. by Anne Destenay (Boulder, Colorado: Westview Press, 1976), p. 382.

22. "Teng Hsiao-p'ing Fan Mao Yu-lu," p. 74.

23. Teng Hsiao-p'ing, "Chien-t'ao," p. 288; and "Pa Teng Hsiao-p'ing Tsung Hei-wo Li Wa-ch'u-lai Shih-chung," p. 26.

24. "Teng Hsiao-p'ing Fan Mao Yu-lu," pp. 74-75.

The work-team policy was carried out for about fifty days until July 24th when Mao returned to Peking.[25] Mao later condemned work teams as the product of "bourgeois dictatorship" and a "white terror" aimed at sabotaging the Cultural Revolution.[26]

In July a rumor spread which claimed that a conspiracy was underway to remove Mao. According to a Yugoslav reporter B. Gugunovic, Liu planned to call an emergency Central Committee meeting to vote for Mao's retirement. P'eng Chen and Yang Shang-k'un were sent earlier to the northeast and the northwest to prepare these regions for the meeting. In early July, members of the Central Committee began to arrive in Peking for the anticipated meeting on July 21st. It was cancelled, however, because of Teng's opposition.

When Lin Piao's army had secured control of the capital, Mao returned to Peking.[27] The Eleventh Plenum of the Eighth Central Committee was convened on August 1st. A number of the moderate members absented themselves because of threats on their lives. Thus, only 80 of the 173 Central Committee members appeared at the meeting, which did not meet the quorum requirements of at least half the total membership.[28] Many young rebels were invited to the conference as voting delegates.[29] During the conference period Mao wrote his own poster to attract a radical constituency. "Bombard the Headquarters," it screamed in bold face.

25. Liu Shao-ch'i, "Tsai Chung-kung Chung-yang Kung-tso Hui-i Shang Te Chien-t'ao" ("Confessions at the CCP Central Work Conference"), reproduced in Hsu Kuan-san, *Liu Shao-ch'i Yu Liu Shao-chi Lu-hsien* (Liu Shao-ch'i and the Liu Shao-ch'i Line) (Hong Kong: Chung Tao Ch'u-pan-she, 1980), p. 410.

26. Mao Tse-Tung, "Pao-ta Ssu-ling-pu" ("Bombard the Headquarters"), reproduced in *Liu Shao-ch'i* (Hong Kong: Ming-jen Tsung-kan she).

27. "I-chiu-liu-liu-nien Ch'i-yueh Ta-feng-pao" ("The July Thunderstorm of 1966"), reproduced in *Teng Hsiao-p'ing*, pp. 51-54.

28. Franz Michael, "The Struggle for Power," in *Problems of Communism* (May/June 1967), p. 19.

29. Esmein, *Cultural Revolution*, p. 80; David and Nancy Milton, *The Wind Will Not Subside* (New York: Pantheon Books, 1976), p. 140.

Sure enough, the conference was dominated by the radicals. But their victories were uneasy ones. Even Mao admitted that he had won the "consent of slightly more than half of those present."[30] The conference adopted Maoist guidelines and announced that the aim of the Cultural Revolution was to war with the "capitalist-roaders" inside the Party. It acknowledged the legitimacy of the Red Guards,[31] which meant that spontaneous movements were admissible even though they bypassed the Party machinery. It also elected Lin Piao as the sole Vice-Chairman of the Party. Lin became the acknowledged heir-designate of Mao. The Politburo was reorganized: Teng retained his position in the Secretariat; T'ao Chu, Party boss of the Kwangtung Province and a new member of the Central Secretariat, was elected to the Politburo with higher position than Teng in the Standing Committee; and Liu Shao-ch'i was demoted to the eighth position and lost his Vice Chairmanship.[32] Although many of the so-called "power-holders" remained in the Politburo, their positions were no longer secure since the Red Gaurds dominated the Party line. One by one, the moderates were to being purged.

A statement released on August 12th at the close of the Party conference extolled Mao's "First Ten Points" and his "Twenty-three Points." Teng's "Late Ten Points" were not mentioned. In addition, the statement emphasized that the proposed "General Line of the International Communist Movement" (The 25 Points) was prepared under the personal guidance of Mao, neglecting to mention any of Teng's contributions.[33]

---

30. Mao Tse-Tung, *Wan-sui*, p. 674.

31. *Jen-min Jih-pao*, October 9, 1966.

32. The Politburo then consisted of Mao Tse-Tung, Lin Piao, Chou En-lai, T'ao Chu, Ch'en Po-ta, Teng Hsiao-p'ing, K'ang Sheng, Liu Shao-ch'i, Chu Te, Li Fu-ch'un, Ch'en Yun, Tung Pi-wu, Ch'en I, Liu Po-ch'eng, Ho Lung, Li Hsien-nien, T'an Chen-lin, Li Ching-ch'uan, Hsu Hsiang-ch'ien, Nieh Jung-chen, and Yeh Chien-ying. The first ten were members of the Standing Committee.

33. "Chung-kuo Kung-ch'an-tang Ti-pa-chieh Chung-yang Weiyuan-hui Ti Shih-i-tse Ch'uan-ti Hui-i Kung-pao" ("Conference Statement of the CCP

On October 8th Mao called a work conference which included leading cadres from the provinces. The 17-day conference was virtually a continuation of the Eleventh Plenum.[34] Both Liu and Teng were subjected to criticism — most severely by Ch'en Po-ta and Lin Piao. Among other things Ch'en declared, "Teng is the pioneer of the mistaken path. In the past, everyone was afraid to criticize Teng's mistakes because he believes he knows everything. He never studies the issue and yet he makes decisions. His mistakes are obvious and serious. He never consults the masses, nor is he interested in the mass movements. It would be easier to climb to heaven than to talk with Teng about problems."[35] Lin, on the other hand, hinted that Teng had something to do with the so-called "February Mutiny."[36]

On October 23rd, Liu and Teng criticized themselves to the conference. Teng spoke humbly. He said he was a "petty bourgeois" who had not remolded himself. "I have not upheld the great banner of the Thoughts of Mao Tse-tung," Teng said. He admitted three mistakes: supporting the rightists in 1962, sabotaging the Socialist Education Campaign, and dispatching work teams to schools and colleges in early 1966. He also acknowledged having seldom reported to Mao. Teng made the appearance of being cooperative. He paid tribute to the Thoughts of Mao Tse-tung and spoke very highly of Lin Piao.[37] Political survival left him with little other recourse.

Mao commented on Teng's self-criticism October 24th and 25th. He said he was displeased that Teng did not come to him

Eleventh Plenum of the Eighth Party Congress"), *Jen-min Jih-pao*, August 14, 1966.

34. Esmein, *Cultural Revolution*, pp. 142-143.

35. Ssu-ma Ch'ang-fang, *Wen-ko Shih-mo*, Vol. I (Hong Kong: Pa Yeh Shu-she, 1976), p. 143; and Tseng Hsien-kuang, "Teng Hsiao-p'ing Fan Mao Chiu Mao Chih Mi" ("The Pro-Maoist Teng Hsiao-p'ing and the Anti-Maoist Teng Hsiao-p'ing: A Mystery") in *Ch'un-ch'iu* (Hong Kong), No. 305 (March, 1970), p. 6.

36. *Yomiuri*, February 15, 1967.

37. Teng, "Chien-t'ao," pp. 286-294.

regularly after 1959 to report on Party affairs. "Teng is hard of hearing, but at meetings he used to sit far away from me. In the six years since 1959 he has not reported to me about his work.... He tries to avoid me," Mao said.[38] But Mao refrained from vindictiveness before the conference. "We cannot lay every responsibility on Comrade Liu and Comrade Teng," Mao stated. "They have responsibilities and the Central Committee has responsibilities, too. The Central Committee has not done its work well.... Allow them to rejoin the revolution. Let them repent."[39] However, this proved to be lip-service only. Mao did not adhere to his fine speech.

Although Liu and Teng appeared in public occasionally, they were no longer politically important. The function of the Secretariat was assumed by the Central Cultural Revolutionary Group.[40] Toward the end of October, the Peking media began openly criticizing Teng.[41] On November 8th, an article written by Nieh Yuan-tzu and ten other Maoists called Teng a "capitalist-roader." It said Liu was the Number One and Teng the Number Two "capitalist-roader."[42] On November 15th, the Red Guards of Peking University broadcast the article.

Eight rallies of the Red Guards were held between August

38. Mao Tse-tung, *Wan-sui*, pp. 655, 661-662. Teng admitted years later that Mao's complaint was true. He said that he did that intentionally because he was displeased with Mao's patriarchal style of leadership. He claimed that Mao would never accept or listen to others' opinions. (Fallaci's interview with Teng.)

39. Mao Tse-tung, *Wan-sui*, pp. 656, 660.

40. Edward E. Rice, *Mao's Way* (Berkeley, Cal.: University of California Press, 1974), p. 266. Chou En-lai told the army and the masses at a 1967 conference that the CCP Cultural Revolutionary Group functioned as the Secretariat. *See Kung-fei Wen-hua Ta-ko-ming Chung-yao Wen-chien Hui-pien* (Selected Documents of the Chinese Cultural Revolution) (Taipei: Kuo-fang-pu Ch'ing-pao-chu, 1968), p. 251. After the Cultural Revolution, the Secretariat was abolished and its function was taken over by the Central Administrative Office headed by Wang Tung-hsing.

41. Dittmer, *Liu Shao-chi*, p. 136.

42. "Teng Hsiao-p'ing Shih Tso Tzu-pan Chu-i Te Tang-ch'uan-pai" ("Teng Hsiao-p'ing is the Capitalist Roader in Power"), a Red Guard pamphlet reproduced in C. B. Kok, ed., *Teng Hsiao-p'ing*, p. 45.

18th and November 26th. On every occasion Liu and Teng accompanied Mao to receive the Red Guards. Apparently neither Liu nor Teng felt comfortable on these occasions, appearing downcast or indifferent in the photos taken.[43]

Teng's last public appearance was made on December 14th at a funeral of the late Wu Yu-chang, head of the People's University and one of the founders of the Work-and-Study Program of the twenties.[44] On December 25, a Ch'ing Hua University student, K'uai Ta-fu, carried out the orders of Chang Ch'un-ch'iao, by leading his fellow Red Guards to put up posters denouncing Liu and Teng on street walls.[45] On December 27th, 100,000 people gathered at the Peking Worker's Stadium to criticize Liu and Teng.[46] That same day Teng's October self-criticism was reproduced in the big-character posters.[47] From then on, Red Guard posters and pamphlets poured out attacks on Teng. Teng was even forced to read these posters.

Beginning early in 1967, the Red Guards dragged Teng out of privacy for public trials. Although Teng admitted that he had opposed Mao's policy, he denied he had opposed Mao personally.[48]

Mao wanted to give the purge the trappings of legitimacy. But he was not sure whether the Central Committee would vote in favor of removing Liu and Teng. Therefore instead of calling a Central Committee meeting, he summoned a meeting of the Politburo Standing Committee at the end of March 1967. The Standing Committee had been enlarged from 7 people to 11 people; the four newly added members were Ch'en Po-ta, K'ang Sheng, Li Fu-ch'un, and T'ao Chu. A ballot was taken. Lin Piao, Chou En-lai, Ch'en Po-ta, K'ang Sheng, and Li Fu-ch'un

43. Harold Hinton, *An Introduction to Chinese Politics* (New York: Praeger Publishers, 1973), p. 63.

44. Tseng Hsien-kuang, "Teng Hsiao-p'ing," p. 5.

45. *Chuan-chi*, pp. 227-228.

46. *Asahi*, December 27, 1966; and *Chung-kung Chi-mi Wen-chien Hui-pien*, p. 185.

47. *Chung-kung Chi-min Wen-chien Hui-pien*, p. 185.

48. Dittmer, *Liu Shao-ch'i*, p. 102.

voted for Mao, while Chu Te, Ch'en Yun, T'ao Chu voted for Liu and Teng. Mao won by only one vote![49]

One of the accusations made against Teng was that he propagated the idea of the cessation of class struggle. The Red Guards condemned him for making the following remarks:

In recent times, the situation has fundamentally changed — workers and office employees represent a division of labour within the same class. Poor peasants and rich peasants have all become members of cooperatives. Very soon, the differences between them will have historical meaning only. The vast majority of our intellectuals have also come over politically to the side of the working class.... What is the point, then, of classifying these occupational groups into two different categories? And even if we were to try and devise a classification, how could we make it neat and clear-cut? [Report given at the Eighth Party Congress]

Our previous job was to fight for the revolution. Now that job is accomplished. Our next job is construction. For the most part, the contradictions between classes have been solved. [1956.]

With the extinction of class struggle, any remaining contradictions would be internal contradictions among individuals. We would not use class struggle methods to solve internal contradictions or we would be making a mistake. [1956.]

Stalin kept on agitating for class struggle when there was no longer a class struggle.... When there exists no class, it would only exaggerate problems if class struggle were stressed. The same case can be applied to China, too. [1957.][50]

Teng was also censured because of his opposition to the Maoist cult. The Red Guards accused Teng of having been responsible for the deletion of the Thoughts of Mao Tse-tung from the new Constitution adopted by the Eighth Party Congress. His speech responding to Soviet de-Stalinization was also criticized. He was charged with having edited out the sentence

---

49. Karnow, *Mao and China*, p. 323.

50. "Teng Hsiao-p'ing Fan Mao Tse-tung Ssu-hsiang Yen-lun I-pai Li," pp. 131, 132; and "Ch'e-ti Ch'ing-suan Teng Hsiaop'ing Fan Tang Fan She-hui Chu-i Fan Mao Tse-tung Ssu-hsiang Te T'ao-t'ien Tsui-hsing," p. 105, and 131-132.

"Comrade Mao Tse-tung has supreme prestige among the Chinese people, and he has supreme prestige among the revolutionary people in the world, too" from the July 1, 1966 editorial of the *Jen-min Jih-pao*.[51] The radicals also attacked Teng for making the following remarks about Mao:

> Chairman Mao has never said that he will not make mistakes. [At a 1957 conference.]

> Is it possible to hold different ideas from the Chairman? Certainly, it is possible. [Chengtu Conference, 1958.]

> Everyone is subjective to some extent; Chairman Mao included.

> All [the Communist Youth League report] talks about is the thought of Mao Tse-tung. Where is Marxism-Leninism? It is not necessary to issue this report.

> "The Four Old Essays" should be read, but if we read only them they won't be too helpful.[52]

Teng's personal life was also the subject of criticism. He was said to be so addicted to playing bridge that he had allegedly ordered the construction of a club in Peking. Teng's bridge partners included Wan Li (member of the Peking Municipal Party Committee), Wu Han, Hu Yao-pang (General Secretary of the Communist Youth League), and Hu Ko-shih. Even when Teng was out of Peking on business, he would still play bridge. It was said that once when he was on an investigative trip in northeast China, he suddenly wanted to start a bridge game. He supposedly called his friends in Peking and had them flown to Harbin on a special plane just for that purpose.[53] Teng was also attacked for leading a life of luxury. He was reported to

---

51. "Teng Hsiao-p'ing Fan-tui Ko-jen Tsung-pai Yu-lu" (Quotations of Teng Hsiao-p'ing on Opposition to Personality Cult), a Red Guard pamphlet reproduced in *Teng Hsiao-p'ing*, pp. 80, 82 and 85-86.

52. "Teng Hsiao-p'ing Fan-tui Ko-jen Tsung-pai Yu-lu," pp. 85-86. (The "Four Old Essays" are: "The Foolish Old Man Who Moved the Mountains," "To Serve the People," "In Memory of Dr. Bethune," and "Against Liberalism.")

53. "Chieh-k'ai Teng Hsiao-p'ing Kao 'Pei-to-fei' Chu-lo-pu Te Hei-mu," pp. 24-25.

have once said that nobody could understand civilization if one did not dine out.[54]

Teng's last public trial, according to sources, was held on August 5, 1967, the anniversary publication date of Mao's poster. Cho Lin was also present. Elsewhere on the same day, Liu Shao-ch'i was held and ridiculed by the rabble. The aging Liu could not stand the mob torture and his leg was broken within twenty minutes. Teng withstood the so-called "flying plane" torture better than Liu because he was shorter. At the trial he removed his hearing aid so that he could not hear what people said about him.[55] Liu appeared very dignified and held his ground throughout the ordeal. Teng, on the other hand, seemed rather playful. He said he was a "counter-revolutionary" who had eluded Mao's control for years.[56]

During the Twelfth Plenary Session held on October 13, 1968, Liu was removed from all posts and expelled from the Party. The verdict was made in accordance with a report made by a special investigation committee. Liu was called a renegade, traitor, and labor thief.[57] Teng, however, was not investigated and was allowed to remain in the Party.[58] Evidently, Mao reserved a chance for his old comrade at arms.

Mao's treatment of Liu and Teng was extremely unequal. Liu was tortured repeatedly until he finally died in 1969. The Lin Piao and the Chiang Ch'ing group tried to have Teng

54. "Teng Hsiao-p'ing Tsui-hsing Tiao-cha Pao-kao," pp. 41-43; and "Pa Teng Hsiao-p'ing Tsung Hei-wo Li Wa-ch'u-lai Shih-chung," p. 30.

55. Liu Ying, "Chung-nan-hai Te Feng-yen" ("Battles in the Chung-nan-hai"), *Cheng Ming*, December 1979, p. 33; Chi Hsi-chen, "Erh-yueh Ni-liu Shih-mo Chi" ("The February Reverse Tide, Its Beginning and End"), *Cheng Ming*, July, 1980, p. 70.

56. Stanley Karnow, *Mao and China*, pp. 390-392.

57. "Kuan-yu P'an-t'u Nei-chien Kung-tsei Liu Shao-ch'i Tsui-hsing Te Shen-ch'a Pao-kao" (A Report on the Crimes of Liu Shao-ch'i: Renegade, Traitor, and Labor Thief), *Chung-kung Chi-mi Wen-chien Hui-pien*, pp. 24-28.

58. Ch'en Li-sheng, "Teng Hsiao-p'ing Tsai Chih-se wu-t'a Shang Te Paio-yen" ("Teng's Performance in the Red Theater"), in *Ching-nien Chan-shih Pao*, April 14, 1977; and Dittmer, pp. 108-109.

killed as well, but Mao ordered that Teng be protected.[59] The most probable explanation for Liu's ruin and Teng's survival is that Liu alone was Mao's principal enemy. Liu was a more prestigeous figure than Teng and, since the sixties, was considered Mao's equal on many occasions.[60] He was better informed about Marxist theories than Teng and was thus a more dangerous ideological competitor to Mao as demigod. Liu's wife, Wang Kuang-mei, was also a rival figure to Madame Mao. She had the charm, cultivation and popularity that Chiang Ch'ing seemed to lack. But this fails adequately to explain why Teng was protected while many other important figures such as Wu Han and P'eng Te-huai were tortured to death. Mao's and Teng's love-and-hate relationship was complex indeed.

In 1967 and 1968, Teng and Cho Lin lived in disgrace in a small, isolated house in Chung-nan-hai. Everyday they did their own menial chores — sweeping, laundry and cooking.[61] A border conflict between China and the Soviet Union broke out in March 1969 over the sovereignty of the Chenpo Island on the Ussuri River. An emergency order dispatched discredited senior cadres to different locations for the sake of "preparation for war." Teng was sent to Kiangsi. Teng and Cho Lin lived in the suburbs of Nanchang, where they cultivated vegetables in the backyard and raised chickens. Everyday Teng went to a nearby factory to do manual labor. His job was smoothing newly made screws.[62] Mao was concerned about the safety of Teng and continued to post guards to protect him.

Before Teng left Peking Mao reportedly asked him what he wanted to do. Teng replied that it did not matter to him. Mao told Teng that he was an articulate and brilliant person, but that he failed to understand the importance of class struggle.

---

59. Fallaci's interview with Teng.

60. Liu was Chairman of the State and Mao was Chairman of the Party.

61. Yu wen, "Teng Hsiao-p'ing Te Chien-k'ang Ch'ing-k'uang" ("The Health Conditions of Teng Hsiao-p'ing"), *Cheng-ming*, No. 35 (September 1980), p. 37.

62. Yu Wen, p. 37.

Mao wanted Teng to live among the masses so that he could learn from them. Teng said mockingly that he should learn instead from the example of Lin Piao, who dismissed everything and destroyed everything.[63]

The Cultural Revolution was not only a great blow to Teng's career, but to the prosperity of his family as well. Cho Lin was purged from political office along with her husband. Their children were attacked viciously as the offspring of the "black gang." Although Teng had told them to renounce their father without mercy to protect themselves, they could not escape being tortured.[64] Teng's eldest son, Teng P'u-fang, was to graduate from Peking University. One day, while he was being held for subversive activity, he fell from the stairs and injured his spinal cord. The radicals accused him of trying to commit suicide. Teng P'u-fang, however, said that someone had pushed him from behind. He has been paralyzed ever since.[65] Teng's younger brother, Su-p'ing, killed himself in March 1967 in the Kweichow Province because he could not bear the harassment.[66] The rest of Teng's children were sent away to different places in the countryside. The Cultural Revolution was a personal nightmare for Teng.

The Cultural Revolution confirmed some of Teng's beliefs that he had developed since the fifties. These included his distrust of spontaneous mass movements, his support for collective leadership, and his fear of excessive personal glorification. He also learned that the army was the most important weapon to hold on to.

Teng was a disciplinarian. He was disgusted by the uncon-

---

63. "Teng Hsiao-p'ing Tsai Chung-kung Shih-chieh San Chung Ch'uan hui Lin-shih Tso-t'an-Hui Te Chiang-hua" ("Teng Hsiao-p'ing's Speech at a Forum of the Third Plenary Session of the Tenth Congress"), in *Fei-ch'ing Yueh-pao* (The Communist Affairs, Taipei), December 1977, p. 82.

64. "Pa Teng Hsiao-p'ing Tsung Hei-wo Li Wa-ch'u-lai Shih-chung," p. 31.

65. Ying Lan, "Erh-nu-men," p. 30.

66. "Teng Hsiao-p'ing Tsui-hsing Tiao-ch'a Pao-kao," p. 29.

trollable destruction brought about by the Red Guards. While mob hysteria reigned, the Party apparatus lay demolished. Many people were killed without reason. The Cultural Revolution proved to Teng that mass movements needed to be Party directed or they would lead to catastrophe.

The Cultural Revolution was launched by Mao personally and in opposition to the wishes of the Party center. Mao's actions denied the principle of collective leadership laid down at the Eighth Party Congress. In order to prevent another disastrous dictatorship, Teng was determined, after his second rehabilitation in 1977, to strengthen collective leadership in the Party.

Personal deification was always unacceptable to Teng because it encouraged the glorified person to lose his touch with reality. Lin Pao succeeded in building up Mao as a god-like being to the army which enabled Mao to mobilize the masses to oppose the Party even though he and the radical group represented a minority. When Teng gained prominence in the Party after his second reinstatement in 1977, he insisted that personal worship be discouraged.

"Power proceeds out of the barrel of a gun," Mao once said. How far Teng would agree with Mao in this respect, we do not know. But he certainly realized how important it was to take control of the military in Communist politics. Teng knew that if he did not have army support, he could not have full sway. Therefore, although he has resigned from many posts in recent years, Teng has not let go of his hold on military power. In 1975 he was appointed Chief-of-Staff and currently he is Chairman of both the Party's Military Commission and the State Military Commission. In the seventies, the radicals and the moderates fought hard to control power. The radicals failed because they did not secure the army.

Chapter 10

The Second Rehabilitation (1973-1976)

On April 12, 1973, Teng made a dramatic return to political favor. He surprised the world by appearing at a banquet given by Chou En-lai for Prince Norodom Sihanouk, the Cambodian leader in exile. When Teng first arrived at the entrance, he hesitated. Wang Hai-jung, the Deputy Foreign Minister, approached him encouragingly and accompanied him to the hall. An applause of welcome thundered across the Great Hall of the People when the Chinese officials saw Teng come in. The unexpected presence of Teng surprised foreign visitors. Chou introduced him to the guests and called him the Vice Premier.[1] Teng had, since 1954, held that position.

It was Chou's idea to reinstate Teng. He proposed to Mao that Teng be restored to work in the State Council.[2] The

---

1. Edward Rice, "The Second Rise and Fall of Teng Hsiao-p'ing," in *China Quarterly*, No. 67 (Sept. 1976), p. 494; Ssu-ma Ch'ang-feng, *Wen-ko Ho Te Chung-kung* (China After the Cultural Revolution) (Taipei: Shih-pao Wen-hua Ch'u-pan Kung-ssu, 1977), p. 273; and Mei Jo-ch'iu, "Teng Hsiao-p'ing Fu-ch'u Te Ch'ien-yin Hou-kuo" ("Events Leading to Teng Hsiao-p'ing's Rehabilitation"), in *Chan-wang*, No. 270 (May 1, 1973), p. 4.

2. According to Hu Yao-pang, Teng's protegé. See Hu Yao-pang, "I-chiu-ch'i-pa-nien Shih-i-yueh Tsai Chung-kung Chung-yang Tang-hsiao Yen-chiang"

radicals opposed it, bu Mao gave his approval to the idea. Mao said that Teng was capable, that he could be both tough and easy-going, and that he knew both economic and military affairs.[3] Teng later recalled, "Chairman Mao took me back and returned me to government as Vice Premier. He said that my mistakes were only 30 percent, my merits 70 percent, and he resurrected me on the basis of that score."[4] Teng's remark about Mao's consent is undoubtedly credible given the fact that he was escorted by Mao's darling niece on the occasion of his first public appearance since his purge.

It was the circumstances of the time that made Teng's return possible. In September 1971, Mao's heir designate, Lin Piao, was killed in an aircraft accident as he allegedly fled to the Soviet Union following an abortive coup. Lin had been the leader of the Fourth Field Army. During the Cultural Revolution, Lin and his followers all gained prominence in the Party, but now that this group had fallen from favor, Mao turned to the Second and the Third Armies for support. (The First Army had long been discredited since the downfall of P'eng Te-huai). Because the Second Army was Teng's army and because Teng had cultivated a good relationship with the Third Army, he was the logical person to win the backing of the military men. Mao needed him.

In addition to that, Mao was anxious to halt the growing influence of the military commanders. After many years of immobilization, the armies had entrenched themselves politically in their designated territories. The power of the commanders was further strengthened during the Cultural Revolution when many of them assumed posts formerly reserved for civilians. This development contradicted Mao's principle that the guns

---

("Speech at the CCP Central Party Cadre School, November 9, 1978"), in *Chung-kuo-jen* (China Monthly, Hong Kong), May 1980, p. 22.

3. According to Informant No. 3, these remarks were contained in a CCP Central Committee Document.

4. Fallaci's interview with Teng, August 1980.

should always be placed under the Party's command. Mao was determined to turn things around. Because of Teng's popularity with the army, his working in the Party Center would make the reorientation easier to carry out.

There was a third factor. Chou En-lai was in bad health. As early as 1972 it was found that Chou had cancer.[5] The State Council needed an experienced administrator to help Chou direct daily affairs. The Cultural Revolution had destroyed many government and Party organs and had thrown the nation's economy into disarray. Thus the most urgent task was to restore the efficiency of the government apparatus and to build the economy. Externally, China's relationship with the Soviet Union was going from bad to worse. After the Soviet invasion of Czechoslovakia in 1968 and the Chen-pao Island incident, the Russians stationed a huge army along the Sino-Soviet border which constituted a major threat to China. By contrast, Sino-American relations were on the upswing. President Nixon's visit to China in 1972 opened the way for diplomatic relations where each country was represented by a liaison office in the other's capital. But further advances which necessarily involved a solution to the Taiwan issue required patient and skillful maneuvering. Chou needed someone capable enough to assume the challenging job. Teng was the ideal candidate because of his many years of experience in handling foreign affairs. Teng had, after all, been Acting Premier during the absence of Chou in 1963 and 1965. When asked the secret that kept him undefeated, Teng replied, "No secret. At a certain moment they thought that I could be useful again and they took me out of the grave. That's all."[6]

Chou En-lai was pleased to see Teng reinstated. With the fall of Lin Piao, Chou became the second man in the Party. But he was also the subject of attacks by the radical group. With the

5. According to Teng's speech given at the funeral of Chou En-lai, 1976. See "Teng Hsiao-p'ing Fu-chu-hsi Chih Tao-tzu" ("Memorial Speech by Vice-Chairman Teng Hsiao-p'ing"), *Jen-min Jih-pao,* January 16, 1976.
6. Fallaci's interview with Teng.

return of Teng, Chou hoped that the strength of the veteran group would be increased. He also hoped that Teng would implement his pragmatic policies. The two were on fairly good terms. During the Cultural Revolution, Chou tried to stop the Red Guards from calling a public trial for Teng.[7] After Teng's reinstatement, Chou made every effort to make him his successor.

Mao's attitude, however, was markedly different. In Mao's mind to let Teng live during the Cultural Revolution was one thing, but to return him to power was quite another. Before Teng's actual reinstatement Mao had Teng promise that he would never overturn the status quo.[8] Mao had no intention of letting Teng assume too much power.

Before the Cultural Revolution the State Council consisted of ten Vice Premiers. After the Cultural Revolution only four Vice Premiers remained and, of these, only Li Hsien-nien was active.[9] Teng was now added as the fifth Vice-Premier, but soon emerged as the most active member of the State Council. By the end of 1973, he had appeared in public on 125 occasions. He was excluded, however, from the Party power core and held only ordinary membership.

After the Lin Piao Incident, Mao sought the support of the moderates and the army to clear away the remnants of Lin's adherents. The radicalism of the Cultural Revolution was suppressed for the time being. Material incentives were restored to promote production in the villages and factories. In schools, a normal schedule was resumed and ideology was deemphasized. Purged veterans were reinstated in great numbers. In the middle of 1973, however, Mao decided to halt the rightist swing.

Mao started two campaigns simultaneously the "Anti-Con-

---

7. Chou had, on the second day after Liu and Teng had made their self-criticism (October 24, 1967), said that they should be given a chance "to carry on the revolution." See Ssu-ma Ch'ang-feng, *Wen-ko Hou Te Chung-kung*, p. 271.

8. "Wei-ta Te Sheng-li" ("The Great Victory"), *Jen-min Jih-pao*, editorial, April 10, 1976.

9. The other surviving Vice Premiers were Ch'en Yun, Li Fu-ch'un, and Nieh Jung-chen.

fucius Campaign" and the "Against the Tide Campaign." Confucius was described as a revisionist who aimed at restoring the feudal system and the outcast feudal lords. Clearly the Maoists used Confucius as a metaphor to condemn the pragmatists who brought back many of the pre-Cultural Revolution practices and who restored many of the purged cadres. The "Against the Tide" campaign called on the masses to oppose the pragmatist policies.[10] The renewed upheaval was timed just before the opening of the Tenth Party Congress in August, 1973. The radicals hoped that the two campaigns would strengthen their position regarding the appointment of officials in the coming congress.

Although some sixty moderate veterans were elected to the Central Committee, the Politburo and its Standing Committee, the core of the Party, was dominated by the radicals.[11] Chiang Ch'ing, Chang Ch'un-ch'iao, Wang Hung-wen, and Yao Wen-yuan, later known as the "Gang of Four," were elected to the Politburo. Chang and Wang also took places in the Standing Committee.[12] The most surprising change in personnel was the election of the 36-year-old Shanghai factory worker, Wang Hung-wen, to the Politburo. Wang, who was unknown to the outside world before the Tenth Congress, was also elected second Vice Chairman after Chou En-lai. Although Chou was the acknowledged second man in the Party, Mao did not confer special recognition on him as he had done earlier on Lin Piao. Instead, the Party now had five Vice Chairmen. Teng remained an outsider, excluded from the Politburo. The political shuffling at the Tenth Party Congress obviously indicated that Mao was

---

10. The radicals also pointed out that the moderate veterans were hostile to many of the "innovations" which appeared since the Cultural Revolution. These included the "triple union of the old, the middle-aged and the youth," "the selection of college students from workers and peasants," "young intellectuals work with peasants," "the May Seventh Cadre School," "research by the mass," and "bare-foot doctor."

11. Among the 21 Politburo Members, 13 were Maoists and five were elected to the nine-person Standing Committee.

12. Chiang, Chang, and Yao had been Politburo members since 1969.

working to prepare for his succession by the Chiang Ch'ing group.

The "Anti-Confucius Campaign" and the "Against the Tide Campaign," continued to cause trouble for the pragmatists after the Tenth Party Congress. Faced with an unstable situation, the pragmatists adopted a new strategy for extracting the teeth from the tiger. First, they linked the anti-rightist Anti-Confucius Campaign with the Anti-Lin Piao Campaign, a movement set in motion after the Lin Piao Incident. Due to Lin Piao's radical bent, the campaign's character became more of an anti-leftist movement. On February 2, 1974, the pragmatists succeeded in formalizing the name of the campaign, calling it the "Anti-Confucius and Anti-Lin Piao Campaign,"[13] thus linking the two different movements together. Secondly, they turned the tide on the "Against the Tide Campaign" by emphasizing Party discipline. They interpreted the "Tide" to mean some leftist policies.

In January 1974, eight of the ten regional military commanders were transferred from their posts. Mao hoped that the shift would prevent the commanders from becoming warlords and threatening regional autonomy. In their new posts, the military commanders no longer simultaneously held government and Party titles. The change of policy was carried out fairly smoothly by Teng. In fact, six of the eight transferred commanders had been Teng's subordinates during the years of the Civil War.[14] Before the actual implementation of the new policy, Teng was admitted to the Politburo in December 1973 and appointed Vice Chairman of the Party's Military Commission.[15] His appointment to the military bureaucracy was necessary because it gave him the capacity to effect military personnel shifts. Similarly, Teng was admitted to the Politburo because

13. *Jen-min Jih-pao*, February 2, 1974.
14. They were Li Te-sheng, Ch'en Hsi-lien, Yang Te-chih, Tseng Ssu-yu, Han Hsien-ch'u, and Hsu Shih-yu.
15. Parris Chang, "Mao's Last Stand?" *Problems of Communism,* Vol. XXV, No. 4 (1976), p. 5.

the Vice Chairman of the Military Commission was tradition-
ally a member of the Politburo. His admittance, however, bypassed formal procedures. On February 11, in the memorial service conducted for the late Deputy Defense Minister Wang
Shu-sheng, Teng was included in the list of names of people
who sent wreaths. Teng's name occupied the ninth position,
after the eight Politburo Standing Committee members. This
was an indication that he occupied a high position in the
Politburo.[16]

Behing Teng's high standing is an unconfirmed, but probable story. Wang Hung-wen and Teng were both sent on an
investigative tour across the country toward the end of 1973.
Upon their return to Peking, Mao asked what would happen to
China if he were to die. Wang replied obsequiously, "The
whole country will certainly follow Chairman Mao's revolutionary line and unite firmly to carry the revolution to the end."
Teng, however, said that "civil war will break out and there
will be confusion throughout the country." Mao agreed with
Teng and decided once again to implement new policies
immediately.[17]

Chou was admitted into the hospital in May 1974. During
the Premier's absence, Teng assumed most of his duties which
included presiding over the State Council and administering
China's foreign policy. Chou remained in the hospital until his
death 19 months later.[18]

On May 11, when Mao received Pakistan's Premier Butto,
Teng sat beside Mao, a seat usually reserved for Chou. After
that, Teng consistently occupied the Premier's seat when Mao
received foreign visitors.[19] A month earlier, in April, Teng led a

---

16. See Ssu-ma Ch'ang-feng, *Wen-ko Hou Te Chung-kung*, p. 279.

17. Chi Hsin, *The Case of the Gang of Four* (Hong Kong: Cosmos Book
Ltd., 1977), pp. 147-148.

18. During this period, Chou left the hospital three times to appear in
public — the August 1st Army Day, the National Day, and the Fourth People's
Congress (which was held in January 1975). He received visitors in the hospital,
but by the end of 1975 he was too sick to do anything.

19. Rice, "The Second Rise and Fall of Teng Hsiao-p'ing," p. 495.

Chinese delegation to attend the Sixth Special Session of the United Nations General Assembly, where his speech won great acclaim.

In his United Nations address Teng stated that there no longer existed a unified Communist camp nor a unified capitalist camp. He pointed out that the world was now divided into three worlds.[20] The two super powers, the United States and the Soviet Union, constituted the First World both seeking world hegemony. Teng called the two countries "the biggest international exploiters and oppressors of today." Teng stressed particularly that "the superpower which flaunts the label of socialism is especially vicious."

The Second World, Teng said, consisted of industrially developed countries as in Europe and Japan. These countries, he observed, were more or less threatened or bullied by either the U.S.A. or the Soviet Union. "In varying degrees, all these countries have the desire to shake off superpower control and safeguard their national independence and the integrity of their sovereignty."

The Third World, he declared, consisted of the developing and underdeveloped countries in Asia, Africa, and Latin America. "These countries constitute a revolutionary force propelling the wheel of world history and are the main force combatting the imperialism of the superpowers.... China is a socialist country, and a developing country as well. China belongs to the Third World.... China is not a superpower, nor will she ever seek to be one."

This was the first time that a Chinese leader explicitly spelled out the premise of China's foreign policy to an international forum. The speech distinguished China from the Soviet

---

20. *Teng Hsiao-p'ing T'uan-chang Tsai Lien-ho-kuo Ta-hui Ti-liu-chieh Te-pieh Hui-i Shang Te Fa-yen* (Speech by Teng Hsiao-p'ing, Chairman of the Delegation of the People's Republic of China, at the Sixth Special Session of the U.N. General Assembly) (Peking: Jen-min Ch'u Pan-she, 1974), p. 2.

164

Union and identified China with the majority of the underdeveloped countries. It impressed the assembly that China might become the leader of the Third World someday. Teng also appealed to the Second World, hoping to win its support to strengthen China's position in the international arena. Teng's speech at the United Nations greatly enhanced his prestige. On his return to Peking, all the important politicians (except Mao) came to welcome him, including the radicals. This scene was reminiscent of a decade earlier, when Teng had also been given a similar grand welcome home from Moscow.

At home, however, the radicals kept attacking the pragmatists. They described the pragmatists as Confucian-like reactionaries. And they identified themselves with the legalists, who were portrayed as being progressive. They boosted the historical role of Empress Lu, wife of Liu Pang, the founder of the Han Dynasty, and Empress Wu, who ruled China between 683 and 705 A.D., labelling them legalist politicians. Their aim, obviously, was to create the image that Chiang Ch'ing was the ideal successor to Mao. The Chiang Ch'ing group worked hard to establish their prominence before the leadership was reshuffled again. Prior to the opening of the Fourth People's Congress, they published an article urging that the "Legalists" be appointed to work in the Party's highest councils and that "legalist leadership" be established.[21]

The group also attacked Teng over the issue of the *Feng-ch'ing* boat. The *Feng-ch'ing* was a Chinese-built ocean-going vessel which was launched in May 1974. Teng was said to have remarked that Chinese ships were substandard when compared with foreign ships. The radicals labelled Teng a "traitor" for this opinion.[22] At a Politburo meeting on October 17, Chiang

21. Ting Wang, *Yao Wen-yuan Mao Yuan-hsin P'ing-chuan* (Critical Biographies of Yao Wan-yuan and Mao Yuan-hsin) (Hong Kong: Ming Pao Yueh-kan She, 1979), p. 94.
22. According to Informant No. 3; and Chi Hsin, *The Case of the Gang of Four*, p. 199.

and Teng were involved in a heated quarrel over the matter.[23] That same evening Chiang decided that Wang Hung-wen should report to Changsha in Hunan where Mao had been residing since July.

Wang's trip to Changsha was intended to accomplish more than angering Mao about the quarrel in the Politburo. With the approach of the Second Plenary Session of the Tenth Party Congress, Wang tried his best to sway Mao's decisions about political appointees. The radicals especially wanted to block Teng from being appointed First Vice Premier.[24] Wang told Mao that Chou and Teng were working on a conspiracy behind the scenes. He said that although Chou was sick and stayed in the hospital, he received visitors as usual and held talks with them until late in the evening. He said that Teng, Yeh Chien-ying, and Li Hsien-nien were Chou's most frequent visitors. Such frequency, he added, "must have something to do with the arrangement of personnel in the coming Fourth Congress.... The atmosphere in Peking today reminds me of what happened on the eve of the Lushan conference."[25] The aim of the Chiang Ch'ing group was to replace Chou as well as Teng. Under their rule Chang Ch'un-ch'iao would be the Premier and Wang Hung-wen would be the Chairman of the People's Congress. Chiang Ch'ing, of course, would succeed Mao as Chair-person of the CCP, and Yao Wen-yuan would become the Party's Secretary General.

Mao wrote to Chiang Ch'ing on November 12, saying that she was not yet popular enough to initiate any major personnel

---

23. *Shen-p'an Lin Piao, Chiang ch'ing Fan-ko-ming Chi-t'uan an Tzu-liao Ch'uan-chi* (Selected Documents of the Trial of the Lin Piao, Chiang Ch'ing Anti-Revolutionary Group) (Peking: Chung-kuo Jen-min Ta-hsueh Shu-pao Tzu-liao She, 1980), p. 60 (hereafter referred as *Chuan-chi*); and Chi Hsin, *The Case of the Gang of Four*, p. 149.

24. *Chuan Chi*, pp. 38, 61.

25. Ibid. The Lushan conference refers to the Second Plenum of the Ninth Party Congress held in the autumn of 1970. According to some sources, Lin Piao and his associates had planned to capture the important positions in the Party.

changes in the Party or the government. "You have too many enemies and you have yet to unite the majority," Mao wrote. "One should know one's limitations and try not to do anything beyond them." Although Mao leaned towards the Chiang ch'ing group both ideologically and sentimentally, he realized that they were not strong enough to win a showdown with the veteran majority. He had openly repudiated them in the July 1974 meeting, telling them not to form a small faction of four. He repeated this warning in May 1975, "I told you not to organize any form of a 'gang of four.' Why are you still doing this?"[26] Mao did not approve of the group completely because he knew that their time was not yet ripe.

The Second Plenum of the Tenth Party Congress and the Fourth National People's Congress were convened one after the other in January 1975. Seven of the 12 Vice Premiers were Maoists.[27] Chang Ch'un-ch'iao was appointed Second Vice Premier and Director of the PLA Political Department. The Fourth Congress also adopted a constitution which abolished the Chairmanship of the Republic, a post hated by Mao. The Constitution also empowered Mao with the supreme role of leading the military.[28] However, Chiang Ch'ing, Wang Hung-wen and Yao Wen-yuan were excluded from the State Council and the Standing Committee of the National People's Congress. The Maoists gained only five of the 27 ministerial posts in the State Council.[29] The most telling example of the moderates' success was Teng's ascendency. Teng replaced Li Te-sheng to become the fifth Vice Chairman of the Party under Chou En-lai, Wang

---

26. Ibid. p. 62.

27. The 12 Vice premiers were (in order): Teng Hsiao-p'ing, Chang Ch'un-chiao, Li Hsien-nien, Ch'en Hsi-lien, Chi Teng-k'uei, Hua Kuo-feng, Ch'en Yung-kuei, Wu Kuei-hsien, Wang Chen, Yu Ch'iu-li, Ku Mu and Sun Chien. Chang, Ch'en, Chi, Hua, Ch'en, Wu, and Sun were acknowledged Maoists.

28. See Article 15 of the Constitution, *Hung Ch'i*, No. 2, 1975.

29. They were Ch'iao Kuan-hua (Foreign Minister), Hua Kuo-feng (Minister of Public Security), Yu Hui-yung (Minister of Culture), Liu Hsiang-p'ing (Minister of Health), and Chuang Tse-tung (Minister of Physical Health).

Hung-wen, K'ang Sheng and Yeh Chien-ying. He was also elected to the Standing Committee of the Politburo.[30] Furthermore, Teng was appointed First Vice Premier—in practice the acting premier—Chief of Staff of the PLA, and Vice Chairman of the Military Commission. For the first time in his life Teng held a leading position simultaneously in the government, the Party, and the army. He was now acknowledged to be a possible heir to Mao.

In addition, the State Constitution also adopted some practical programs, which in the eyes of the radicals were nothing but "bourgeois rights." For example, it formally endorsed the right of peasants to farm private plots and engage in sideline production, reaffirmed the principle of income distribution according to labor output, and guaranteed the citizens the right of private ownership.[31]

Chou also delivered a report at the Congress which was said to have been prepared by Teng.[32] The report set forth an outline of the Four Modernizations. It called for modernization in agriculture, industry, national defense and science before the end of the century.[33] In summary, the moderates, and Teng Hsiao-p'ing in particular, were the winners at the Congress.

When, in 1980, the "Gang of Four" was on trial, a court statement asserted that Teng's appointment to the Vice Premiership had been personally proposed by Mao on October 4, 1974.[34] However, Mao had no desire to see Teng rise to dominance. He was more than likely forced to conceded because of strong pressure from the moderates. The moderates realized the urgency of putting Teng into Chou's position before the Premier died. In actuality, Mao was highly displeased with the results of the Congress. He reminded the people that China was still practic-

---

30. Li Te-sheng was demoted but still remained in the Politburo.
31. See Articles 7 and 9 of the State Constitution.
32. *Chung-kuo Shih-pao* (China Times, Taipei), March 17, 1978.
33. Chou En-lai, "Cheng-fu Kung-tso Pao-kao" ("Report on the Work of the Government"), *Jen-min Jih-pao*, January 21, 1975.
34. *Chuan-chi*, p. 38.

ing a wage system that observed "distribution to each according to his work, and exchange by means of money." This system, Mao said, was modelled after the capitalist system and was dangerous to socialism without a solid proletarian dictatorship. "Otherwise," Mao warned, "once there emerges a Lin Piao type of traitor to leadership, there is every possibility of reverting back to capitalism."[35] The so-called "Lin Piao type," admitted Hua Kuo-feng in later years, referred to Teng Hsiao-p'ing.[36] It should be noted that after his death Lin was condemned by Maoists as an ultra-rightist in order to disassociate themselves from him.

Mao refused to attend the Congress as a gesture of protest. This never happened before. Although Chou En-lai told the delegates that Mao could not attend because of health reasons,[37] Mao was not so ill as to prevent him from receiving foreign visitors while the Congress was in progress. On one occasion he received Prime Minister Dominic Mintoff of Malta; on another he met Franz-Josef Strauss, head of West Germany's Christian Social Union Party.[38] Mao's two receptions were publicized.

Immediately after the Congresses, Mao launched a campaign "to study the theory of the dictatorship of the proletariat."[39] Yao Wen-yuan and Chang Ch'un-ch'iao each published an article to promote the event.[40] The moderates responded.

35. Mao's speech was not publicized until February 9, 1975, as quoted by the *Jen-min Jih-pao* editorial.

36. "Hua Kuo-feng Tung-chih I-chiu-chi-liu-nien Erh-yueh Erh-shih-wu-jih Kuan-yu Fan-chi Yu-ch'ing Fan-an Feng Han P'i-p'an Teng Hsiao-p'ing Wen-ti Te Chiang-hua" ("Comrade Hua Kuo-feng's Speech on the Anti-Rightist and Anti-Teng Campaign, February 26, 1976"), in *Teng Hsiao-p'ing*, p. 304.

37. Ch'en Chung-p'ing. "Tsung Liang-feng T'a-pien-shu Kan Chung-kung Te 'Chieh-p'i' Yun-tung," *Shih-pao Tsa-chih*, October 8, 1979, p. 14.

38. *Peking Review*, Vol. 18, Nos. 3 and 4 (January 17 and 24, 1975).

39. The call for the campaign came in a *Jen-min Jih-pao* editorial of February 9, 1975, entitled "Study Well the Theory of Dictatorship of the Proletariat."

40. Yao's article, "Lun Lin Piao Fan-tang Chi-tuan Te She-hui Chi-ch'u" ("On the Social Basis of the Lin Piao Anti-Party Group") was published in *Hung Ch'i*, No. 3, 1975. The article was reprinted in *Jen-min Jih-pao* on March

Teng said that he found no fault with the principle of more reward for more work. "Why must everything be called 'bourgeois rights'?" Teng demanded.[41] "There is no material basis for a bourgeoisie in China."[42] Mao's campaign persisted for another six months.

The year 1975 was the most active for Teng after his reinstatement. To Teng the most urgent task was to push forward his modernization programs. In order to accomplish his goals, the radicalist obstacles had to be removed. While the Maoists were busily engaged in the Study Campaign, Teng occupied himself in the task of economic reconstruction. Teng said that China after the Cultural Revolution was a mess. "There were no regulations and no discipline." He refused to shake the hands of attendants at a conference on industry because he said industry was not doing well enough. In order to promote his programs of modernization, he called for a series of conferences between May and October 1975 to study problems in defense, agriculture, education and science and technology. That summer, Teng produced three important documents: the General Outline of the Party Tasks and the National Tasks; a Report Outline on Work of the Academy of Sciences; and Certain Problems in Speeding Up Industrial Development.[43]

The General Outline was prepared by a theoretical group

1. Chang's article, "Lun Tui Tse-ch'an-che-chi Te Ch'uan-mien Chuan-cheng" ("On Exercising All-round Dictatorship over the Bourgeoisie"), was published in *Hung Ch'i*, No. 4, 1975.

41. Wen Kung-hsiao, "Teng Hsiao-p'ing Yu Erh-shih-t'iao" ("Teng Hsiaop'ing and the Twenty Articles"), *Hsueh-hsi Yu P'i-p'an* (Studies and Criticisms, Shanghai), No. 6 (June 1976).

42. Jaap Van Ginneken, *The Rise and Fall of Lin Piao*, trans. Danielle Adkinson (New York: Avon Books, 1977), p. 307.

43. The three documents were not officially published until 1976 as appendices to the pamphlet "Criticism of the Three Poisonous Weeds." According to *Jen-min Jih-pao* (July 7, 1977), these appendices "gave the full draft of 'On the General Program,' the third section of the first draft of the 'Outline Report,' and one of the several drafts of 'Some Problems in Accelerating Industrial Development.'" They were translated as appendices in Chi Hsin's *The Case of the Gang of Four*.

led by Hu Ch'iao-mu, Teng's ideologue.[44] Finalized in October, the Outline was a blueprint for the coming 25 years to the end of the century, emphasizing economic development and the Four Modernizations. It called for the setting up of regulations, and a comprehensive revision of existing policies in nine fields, including the Party and the military.[45] The Report Outline, drafted by Hu Yao-pang, Teng's right-hand man and now General Secretary of the CCP,[46] also contained ten items advocating professionalism in scientific research and development.[47] The "Report Outline" recognized the old Liu-Teng advocacy of

---

44. Formerly Deputy Secretary of the CCP Secretariat and Deputy Minister of Propaganda Department, Hu was purged during the Cultural Revolution. In 1974, he was restored to his former position and was the acknowledged leading theoretician of Teng's group.

45. Chi Hsin, *The Gang of Four*, pp. 203-283. See also Cheng Yueh, "Lun Ch'uan-tang Ch'uan-kuo Ko-hsiang Kung-tso Te Tsung-kang P'o-hsi" ("A Diagnosis of the 'General Outline' "), in *Hung Ch'i*, No. 4 (April 1976); and Hung Hsuan, "P'ing Teng Hsiao-p'ing Te Fan-ko-ming Yu-lun Kung-shih" ("On Teng Hsiao-p'ing's Anti-Revolutionary Propaganda Campaign"), in *Hsueh-hsi Yu P'i-p'an*, No. 6 (1976).

46. During the war against Japan, Hu served under Teng in the Central Military Committee as head of the Organization Department in the Political Department. On the eve of Liberation he was Director of the Political Department of the Eighteenth Army Corps of the North China Field Army. The Corps fought hand in hand with the second Field Army which invaded Szechuan in 1949. Hu then worked under Teng in the Southwest region in the next two years. His ups and downs followed Teng's closely. In 1952 he was transferred to Peking and led the Communist Youth League. He was elected to the Central Committee at the Eighth Party Congress in 1956. He fell in disgrace during the Cultural Revolution. In 1972, he was reinstated. In July 1975, he was appointed Party Secretary and Vice Chancellor of the Institute of Sciences. The Maoists called him the "capitalist-roader" in the Institute of Science and the "never repenting capitalist-roader in science field." The "twin-Hu's" (Hu Yao-pang and Hu Ch'iao-mu) were acknowledged as Teng's most reliable aides. See "Chung-kung Hsin Chu-hsi Hu Yao-pang Hsiao-chuan" ("A Brief Biography of Hu Yao-pang, CCP's New Chairman"), *Hua-ch'iao Jih-pao*, July 1, 1981.

47. Chi Hsin, *The Case of the Gang of Four*, pp. 277-286. See also K'ang Li and Yen Feng, "Hui-pao-t'i-kang Ch'u-lung Te Ch'ien-ch'ien-ho-ho" ("Before and after the production of the 'Report Outlines' "), in *Hsueh-hsi Yu P'i p'an*, No. 4 (April 1976), and "P'ing Ko-hsueh-yuan Kung-tso Hui-pao T'i-kang" ("On the Report Outline on Works of the Institute of Sciences"), *Hung Ch'i*, No. 8 (August 1976).

"Expertise over Redness," while the Industrial Development document stressed production, material incentives, and importation of foreign technology and theories. In many ways "Industrial Development" duplicated Teng's "Seventy Articles" of the sixties.[48]

The General Outline attacked the Maoists unreservedly:

> The anti-Marxist class enemies, Lin Piao's successors... mix up black and white, turn truths upside down... wave the banner of combatting revisionism to carry out revisionism, and wave the banner of opposing restoration to carry out restoration. They toppled good Party cadres... usurped the leadership in some places.... They have a mania for "creating mountain strongholds," and engaging in factional fights. They are inextricably entangled in the struggle between this faction and that faction, between the so-called rebellious faction and conservative faction, between the so-called new and old cadres....

> Some of our comrades.... talk only about politics and revolution and never about economics and production. As soon as they hear someone talking about properly grasping production and developing our economic sector, they put a [bourgeois] hat on him and say that he is practicing revisionism....

> The view that once revolution is grasped, production will increase naturally and without effort is believed by those who indulge in fairy tales.[49]

Teng remarked that the principal task at hand was to examine the performance of people in office.[50] His reorganization programs made the radicals nervous. In the eyes of the Maoists, Teng was preparing for a coup. Teng had no admiration for those who emerged quickly during the Cultural Revolution. He said disapprovingly that the rise of these people was as fast as riding a helicopter. Conversely, he expressed his eagerness to see

---

48. Wen Kung-hsiao, p. 141.
49. Chi Hsin, *The Case of the Gang of Four*, pp. 207-209, 223, and 227.
50. Wen Kung-hsiao, p. 134.

the old cadres restored to power.[51] By the end of 1975, most of the disgraced old guard was back at work. Some of them were given higher positions than they had previously held.[52]

Teng grew bold in criticizing the byproducts of the Cultural Revolution. He dismissed any excuses for the poor standards in educational and scientific research. These deficiencies, he complained, would only hamper the prospects of the Four Modernizations. Teng said that illiteracy and cultural ignorance were the greatest dangers and greatest crises of the day.[53] He regarded the intellectuals as workers too. "Scientific research is production," he argued. He added that scientists, the so-called "white experts," should be protected and respected. "If the 'white experts' are working for the good of the country, they are undoubtedly better than those who eat from the bowl but do nothing."[54] As for economic development, Teng said that he cared only about the results, not about how it was done. Chiang Ch'ing's modern drama, he complained, permitted only her pet themes to flourish,[55] which made the plays hard to sell.

Teng said that the accomplishments of the Cultural Revolution should be weighed against all the trouble it caused. "The press reports successful stories only and never mentions anything about failures.... What is revolution? Is it merely arousing impatience, hysteria, outrage, and cries of revolution? Who can believe that? It is self-deception."[56] Teng noted that "we cannot

51. Liang Hsiao and Jen Ming, "P'ing 'San-hsiang-chih-shih' Wei Kang" ("Criticism of 'Taking the Three Directives as the Key Link"), *Jen-min Jih-pao*, February 29, 1976.

52. Among those reinstated, 31 were appointed to the ministerial posts, 58 were appointed departmental heads, and 44 were appointed provincial posts. See *1976 Fei-ch'ing Nien-pao* (The Yearbook of Chinese Communism,1976) (Taipei: Kuo-fang-pu Ch'ing-pao-chu, 1976), pp. (V) 19-20. In the single year of 1975, seven reinstated cadres were appointed First Secretary of the Provincial Party Committee.

53. Liang and Jen.

54. K'ang and Yen, pp. 160-161.

55. "Ti, Fu, Fan, Huai, Yu Te Tsung-Tai-P'aio Teng Hsiao-p'ing" ('Teng Hsiao-p'ing, the Stereotype of Landlord-Rich, Anti-party Bad Element, and Rightist"), reproduced in C. B. Kok, ed., p. 142.

56. *1976 Fei-ch'ing Nien-pao*, p. (V) 17.

talk of class struggle everyday."[57]

After seven and eight years of struggle, Teng admitted it was difficult to forget the feelings of enmity he had cultivated for the radicals.[58] He described himself as a Sinkiang native girl who "had many pigtails" which enabled others to catch him easily.[59] But he urged the reinstated cadres to forget the past. "I have a bad memory: I forget everything," he said.[60] "The veteran cadres should be unwavering and should not be afraid of being purged a second time."[61] He added, "When others accuse you of being restorationists, it means you are doing a good job...."[62]

Teng's actions and speeches set the example and angered Mao. The old demigod refused to retire. In August 1975 Mao launched yet another campaign, this time against the classical novel *Shui Hu*. *Shui Hu* or *The Water Margin* had been one of Mao's favorite classics. It describes the struggles of a band of Robin Hood-like outlaws who fight corrupt officials and rob from the rich to give to the poor. The story concludes when the rebels follow their leader, Sung Chiang, out of the mountains to surrender to the government and became government functionaries themselves. Mao, and many of the official literary commentators too, used to speak highly of the novel. But Mao changed his view now. He said Sung's surrender was an old form of revisionism. "The good point of the novel is that it describes surrender. We can use the book as a 'negative' teaching aid. It enables us to know who are our traitors."[63] The Sung

57. Chi Yen, "Teng Hsiao-p'ing Wei-she-mo San-po Che-chi-tou-cheng Hsi-mieh-lun" ("Why Teng Hsiao-p'ing Propagated the Idea of Cessation of Class Struggle"), *Jen-min Jih-pao*, April 19, 1979.

58. Hung Hsuan, p. 170.

59. K'ang and Yen, p. 161.

60. "Fan-an Fu-p'i Te Tzu-kung-chuang" ("A Confession on Reversing the Verdict and Restoration"), *Jen-min Jih-pao*, April 3, 1976.

61. *1976 Fei-ch'ing Nien-Pao*, p. (V) 83.

62. Chi Yen.

63. "K'ai-chan Tui 'Shui Hu' Te P'ing-lun" ("Unfold Criticism of Shui Hu"), *Jen-min Jih-pao*, editorial, September 4, 1975. According to Lu Ti, Mao's aide who used to read him books in his last years, Mao spoke of these on August

Chiang-like traitors implicitly meant Chou and Teng.

An article written by a Maoist commented, "Sung Chiang.... works very hard to win government favor. He even calls the landlords and government officials to Liangshan to settle the dispute. Lu Chun-i is a typical example of a landlord.... And Lu is made the rebels' second leader. Sung Chiang now has an able man to help him sell out the revolution."[64] Sung here implies Chou while Lu implies Teng. In another article Teng is identified as the modern Sung Chiang. The article discloses that Teng regarded himself as Sung Chiang during the fifties when he worked in the southwest.[65] Chiang Ch'ing also made her feelings known about the novel. She said that the story describes how the original rebel leader, Ts'ao Kai, was overshadowed by Sung Chiang. "In the Party Central, Chairman Mao is now being overshadowed," she said. Hua Kuo-feng admitted later that Chiang's comment was directed against Chou and Teng.[66]

Mao's remarks about "revisionism" and "surrenderism" were aimed of course at the pragmatic line advocated by Chou and Teng. Surrenderism was supposedly a denial of class struggle and a capitulation with the bourgeoisie. Maoists also accused the pragmatists of selling out the "national interest" by promoting exports abroad. When such a policy was pursued, they argued, it made China subordinate to the imperialists.[67]

In response to this war of words, Teng used the old tactics. He deemphasized the political character of the *Shui Hu* campaign and tried to limit the controversy over the novel to a

13, 1975. See also Yang Chieh-yeh, "Tsai Mao Chu-hsi Shen-pien Tu-shu" ("Reading beside Chairman Mao"), *Kuang-ming Jih-pao,* December 19, 1978.

64. *Hung Ch'i,* No. 9, 1975.

65. Hung Hsuan, p. 147; "Shih Jen-min Tou Chih-tao Tou-hsing-p'ai" ("Let People Know Who the Surrenderists Are"), *Jen-min Jih-pao,* June 2, 1976.

66. Speech delivered by Hua Kuo-feng at the Eleventh Congress.

67. "Tou-hsiang-chu-i Te chan-ko" ("The Hymn of Surrenderism"), *Jen-min Jih-pao,* September 5, 1975; "Teng Hsiao-p'ing Te So-wei Hsien-tai-hua Chi Tzu-pan-chu-i Hua" ("Teng Hsiao-p'ing's So-Called 'Modernization' is 'Bourgeoisation' "), *Jen-min Jih-pao,* August 6, 1976; and Wen Kung-hsiao, p. 136.

purely academic issue.[68] Publically Teng said the primary purpose of the campaign was to reevaluate past interpretations of the novel. Privately, he told his men that the new critiques did not relate at all to reality. "Some people nowadays are too sensitive," he said. When they hear the wind blowing, they fear the rain is going to fall. They would make any irrelevant issue a big deal. The criticism of Sung Chiang's surrenderism is thought by many people to be the beginning of another political purge. "What are you afraid of? You are not Sung Chiang and you are not a surrenderist."[69] Teng denied the existence of any surrenderist in the Party.

In August and September, Liu Ping, the Deputy Party Secretary of the Tsinghua University, wrote Mao two letters complaining about the low academic standards caused by the Maoist educational reform program. "Unless the system is changed," Liu Ping wrote, "young people will leave the university without the ability to read a book."[70] The letters expressed discontent with Ch'ih Ch'un, a Party official at the university and a follower of Chiang Ch'ing.

Liu's letters were seen by Mao as a challenge to the Cultural Revolution. The Chairman also interpreted aspersions against Ch'ih to be an attack on him. Thus he used the letters as an excuse to launch another anti-rightist campaign, specifically the Anti-Rightist Deviationism Campaign. The pragmatists were accused of having held many "subversive talks" during the summer months which attacked the "new things" in the fields of education, science and culture. "[The pragmatists] want to reappraise and reverse the innovations of the Cultural Revolution," the radicals claimed. With regard to education, the radicals accused the pragmatists of emphasizing basic knowledge

---

68. T'ien Chih-sung, "P'ing Teng Hsiao-p'ing Kuan-yu Shui-hu Te I-tse T'an-hua" ("A Commentation on one of Teng Hsiao-p'ing's Speeches on Shui-Hu"), in *Hung Ch'i*, No. 7, 1976.

69. Hung Hsuan, p. 172.

70. Terrill, p. 401; and John Gittings, "Research Note: New Material on Teng Hsiao-p'ing," *The China Quarterly*, No. 67 (September 1976), pp. 489-493.

and theories instead of manual labor. The radicals also objected to the pragmatists' attempt to separate scientific research from politics. As for art and literature, the radicals were insulted that the pragmatists thought their work to be poor and boring. "How can eight hundred million people be content with having only eight model dramas?" demanded the pragmatists.[71]

With Chou En-lai still alive, the Maoists were cautious not to push anything too far. Chou was the most important moderate because he had the stature and popularity to compete with Mao. If Chou died after Mao, he would probably make every effort to appoint Teng his successor. But his health was deteriorating rapidly. In late December, Julie Nixon and David Eisenhower visited Peking. At a banquet, both guests and hosts discussed a recent publication of Mao's poetry. Teng sat there silently, adjusting his watch.[72] Evidently, Teng was preoccupied by thoughts about his uncertain future.

Chou died on January 8, 1976. According to a popular, though unconfirmed account, Chou called eight military region commanders to his bedside on January 6. He urged them to support and protect Teng. Chou allegedly said:

> Comrade Teng Hsiao-p'ing's accomplishments are visible everywhere. The Liu-Teng Army fought bravely under fire to help build the country. I have worked with Comrade Hsiao-p'ing for several decades and I understand him very well. He has contributed much to the country. After his reinstatement, he worked hard for the good of the nation. He sleeps only two or three hours a day for the sake of the country's future. His intentions are good. However, some people still cannot accept him. Is there a cam-

71. "P'i-p'an Tang-nei Na-ko Pu-ken Kai-hui Te Tzo-Tzu-p'ai" ("Criticize That 'Never Repenting Capitalist-Roader' Inside the Party"), *Jen-min Jih-pao*, March 3, 1976; Cheng Hsueh-chia, *Tsung Wen-ko Tao Shih-i-ta* (From the Cultural Revolution to the Eleventh Party Congress) (Taipei: Li-ming Wen-hua Shih-yeh Kung-ssu, 1978), p. 100; and Yen Kung-hsiu, "So-wei Hui-chi Ko-chi-chieh Te Yu-ch'ing-fan-an-feng" ("The So-Called Counterattack on the Rightist Deviationist Wind in Sciences Field"), *Ta-lu Kuan-ch'a* (Mainland Review, Taipei) March 1, 1976, p. 8.

72. See Ssu-ma Ch'ang-feng, *Wen-ko Hou Te Chung-kung*, p. 469.

paign in progress not directed at him? You should support Comrade Hsiao-p'ing, and take good care of him. You have the responsibility to protect your old comrades. In the past our enemies could not kill us by knife or gun, but now some people want to kill us by political means, by pens.... You should use the revolutionary gun to suppress the anti-revolutionary pen.... My death will probably lead to the destruction of Hsiao-p'ing and other comrades....[73]

Another account says that Chou made out a will on December 29, expressing his wish of having Teng preside over the funeral after his death.[74] The Maoists, however, said that the so-called "Premier's will" was forged by Teng.[75] Scholars cannot take the so-called "Premier's will" or Chou's bedside harangue too seriously. According to Chou's physicians, the Premier had lapsed into a coma in late December.[76] However unlikely the stories are, they serve to illustrate an affinity between Chou and Teng.

Chou died in the morning. When the news spread members of the Politburo rushed to the hospital. Teng stayed silently beside Chou. Seven days later Teng delivered a memorial speech at the funeral.[77] Mao did not show up. After the funeral, Teng disappeared from the public eye. He was supposedly seen at three o'clock the next morning, standing solemnly before the Heroes' Monument in Tien-an-men Square, mourning Chou.[78]

The most urgent task following Chou's death was to fill the power vacuum and appoint a new Premier. It was said that at a Politburo meeting someone nominated Teng to be the Premier. The Chiang Ch'ing group reportedly opposed the motion, saying they would refuse to serve under him if he were appointed. They

---

73. Ssu-ma Ch'ang-feng, *Wen-ko Hou Te Chung-kung*, pp. 499, 501-502.

74. Yang K'uang-man and Kuo Pao-ch'en, "Ming Yun" ("The Fate"), *Cheng-ming*, January, 1980, p. 72.

75. Hung Hsuan, p. 178.

76. Yang and Kuo, p. 72.

77. *Jen-min Jih-pao*, January 16, 1976.

78. Yang and Kuo, p. 70.

suggested instead that Chang Ch'un-ch'iao take the post. But supporters of Teng blocked the motion.[79] Mao did not want Teng to become the Premier. Seeing that both sides were unwilling to yield, Mao proposed that Sixth Vice Premier Hua Kuo-feng be appointed the Acting Premier. This was acceptable to both parties for the time being. Although Hua was a Moist, he kept his distance from the ultra-radical Chiang Ch'ing group. The appointment was made official on February 3. Hua was also commissioned to take charge of the work of the Party Central.[80]

Hua Kuo-feng had worked in Hunan, Mao's native province, and had won Mao's favor during the Cultural Revolution. In 1969 he was elected to the Central Committee of the Ninth Congress. In 1971 he was transferred to work in Peking where, at the Fourth National People's Congress, he was appointed Vice Premier and Minister of Public Security. Earlier in 1968 the Chiang Ch'ing group attempted to exclude him from the Hunan Revolutionary Committee.[81] They were not, of course, content for long seeing Hua appointed Premier. In their plan, Chang Ch'un-ch'iao was to succeed Chou.[82] On February 3 Chang Ch'un-ch'iao wrote a sour essay:

> "Here's another Number One document. Last year we had a Number One document too.... It came fast, it came violently, and it fell fast."[83]

The Number One Document referred to by Chang was the mandate appointing Teng as Vice Chairman of the Military Com-

---

79. Terrill, *Mao,* pp. 406-407.

80. The CCPCC Central Issued No. 24 Document, p. 64.

81. Ting Wang, *Hua Kuo-feng Chi Teng-kui Han Hsin Ch'i-te I-tai (Hua Kuo-feng, Chi Teng-kui and the Rising Generation)* (Hong Kong: Ming Pao Yueh-k'an She, 1970, pp. 43-44.

82. "Chieh ch'uan 'Ssu-jen-pang' P'ing Shui-hu Te Cheng-chih P'ien-chu" ("Exposing the Political Lies of the Gang of Four's Critique of Shui-hu"), reproduced in *Ssu-jen-pang Yu Teng Hsiao-p'ing* (The Gang of Four and Teng Hsiao-p'ing) (Taipei: Kuo-li Cheng-chih Ta hsueh tung-ya Yen-chiu-so, 1979), p. 196.

83. *Chuan-chi,* p. 38. The article has never been published in China.

mission and Chief of Staff of the PLA. The pragmatists did not give up pushing Teng for premiership either. Mao later commented that they had "surreptitiously plotted to write letters to the Party Central Committee to demand Teng's appointment as premier."[84]

After Chou's death, Mao stepped up the Anti-Rightist Deviationism Campaign. The Maoists concentrated on attacking Teng. On February 6 the *People's Daily* published an article announcing that the anti-rightist campaign was initiated by Mao personally as a continuation of the Cultural Revolution. The campaign, it said, was to bring the struggle between the classes and the political polarities to the surface. The article said that the rightist deviationists were "capitalist roaders" who had been restored to their political offices but who refused to repent. "[The rightists] madly threaten the proletariat from all sides — politically, ideologically, and organizationally," the radicals charged.[85] On February 25, Ch'ih Ch'un, Party official of Ch'inghua University, told visiting U.S. President Nixon that "the never-to-repent capitalist-roader" was none other than Teng. On the same day a forum was held in Peking. Hua Kuo-feng made the following remarks:

> Our struggle with the "unrepenting capitalist-roader" is not just a struggle for the apparent differences over the reappraisals or for what he calls "same end but different means." No. This is a struggle for the leadership between the proletariat and the bourgeoisie. This is a campaign determining China's future.[86]

---

84. "T'ien-an-men Kuang-ch'ang Shih-chien So-ming Lo She-mo?" ("What Did the T'ien-an-men Square Incident Tell Us?"), *Jen-min Jih-pao*, editorial, April 18, 1976.

85. "Wu-chan-che-chi Wen-hua-ta-ko-ming Te Chi-hsu Han Shen-ju" ("The Continuation and Deepening of the Cultural Revolution"), *Jen-min Jih-pao*, February 6, 1976.

86. "Hua Kuo-feng Tung-chih Kuan-yu Fan-chi Yu-ch'ing-fan-an-feng Han P'i-p'an Teng Hsiao-p'ing Wen-ti Te Chiang-hua" ("Comrade Hua Kuo-feng's Speech on the Anti-Rightist Deviationism Wind and Anti-Teng Hsiao-p'ing Campaign"), in *Teng Hsiao-p'ing*, p. 304.

On March 2, Chiang Ch'ing spoke at a conference of provincial leaders and described Teng as a "fascist" and the "boss of the 'rumor company.' " She also accused Teng of selling fuel to foreign countries and of acting as an agent for the international bourgeoisie. "Teng," she said, "is a traitor."[87] On March 10 the *People's Daily* printed an editorial which said, "the man who blows the Rightist Deviationist Wind follows Liu Shaoch'i's line of revisionism. He was criticized during the Cultural Revolution for repeatedly opposing the socialist revolutions and yet he refuses to repent. Although he paid us lip service by saying he would never reverse the previous innovations, he is up to his old tricks again now that he is back in power. He keeps upholding the capitalist line." Mao was quoted by the paper as saying that: "This person does not grasp class struggle and never refers to this key link. His theme is still 'white cat, black cat....' "[88] Although everyone knew that Teng was the target of the campaign, his name was not mentioned in the press until the Tien-an-men Square Incident on April 5.

Needless to say, the three documents written in the autumn of 1975 under Teng's guidance were now targets of criticism. The Maoists said that these documents were written to oppose the dictatorship of the proletariat, and to propagate "productionism," "pro-foreignism" and "the non-existence of class struggle." The documents became three "poisonous weeds." Teng was condemned for attempting to restore capitalism under the name of rectification.[89]

Teng was criticized most severely for having distorted Mao's three directives. In the autumn of 1974 and spring of 1975, Mao had issued in succession three directives, namely, "To Study the

87. *Chuan-ch'i*, pp. 39 and 63.

88. *Jen-min Jih-pao*, March 28, 1976.

89. "P'ing 'Ko-hsueh-yuan Kung-tso Hui-pao T'i-kang' " ("A Comment on the Report Outline of the Institute of Sciences"), reproduced in *Teng Hsiaop'ing*, pp. 118-119; "P'ing 'Tang-nai Na-ko Pu-ken Kai-hui Te Tso-tzu-p'ai' P'ao-chih Te I-p'ien Wen-chang" ("A Comment on an Article Initiated by that 'Never Repenting Capitalist-roader Inside the Party' "), *Jen-min Jih-pao*, April 3, 1976.

Theory of Proletarian Dictatorship," "To Promote Stability and Unity," and to "Develop the Economy." Teng gave the three directives equal importance in his General Outline. He said they should be observed as the guiding principles of national construction over the next twenty-five years. The Maoists, on the other hand, maintained that the first directive — "To Study The Theory of Proletarian Dictatorship" — was the supreme task guiding the other two. Said Mao, "To study the theory of proletarian dictatorship is of utmost importance. The other two are of secondary importance. The three should not be given equal status." Mao was displeased with Teng's interpretation. He sneered, " What a saying — Observing the three directives as the key link! Stability and unity do not mean writing off class struggle; class struggle is the key link, and everything else hinges on it."[90] People who are familiar with Mao's thinking would know that he was consistent in stressing the importance of class struggle. Placing the three directives on an equal basis was indeed a distortion of Mao's ideas. Teng was, however, employing the old technique of "upholding the red banner to oppose the red banner" for what he considered best for the country.

During this period Teng was forced to read the latest onslaught of posters attacking him. Once he was forced to attend a student meeting and was asked to make a critical evaluation of himself. He replied, "I am an old man, and my hearing is not very good — I don't hear a word of what you say." He retired from the meeting early.[91]

The April Fifth Incident (T'ien-an-men Square Incident) was the first real spontaneous mass movement China had experienced since 1949. People were disgusted with Mao's radicalism

---

90. When Mao said this is uncertain. It was first quoted by the *Jen-min Jih-pao* in an editorial on January 1, 1976. The entire speech was quoted in an article by Liang Hsiao and Jen Ming ("Ping San-hsiang Chih-shih Wei-kang") ("A Comment on the Three Directives as the Key Link"), published in *Jen-min Jih-pao*, February 29, 1976.

91. Ginneken, *Lin Piao*, p. 315.

and despised the Chiang Ch-ing group. The economy was stagnating and the standard of living showed no signs of improving. People wanted changes. They found that Chou and Teng's pragmatism was more beneficial to the people and preferred the pagmatists to the radicals. Because many looked upon Chou as their idol, they were angry to see a disrespectful attitude during the few months following Chou's death: Mao did not attend the funeral, the Chiang Ch'ing group obstructed any public mourning in memory for Chou,[92] and articles were published which implicitly denounced Chou.[93] The antirightist campaign ran counter to the people's wishes because it was aimed at Teng, who some saw as their only hope for the future. Toward the end of March, the people expressed their anger by posting anti-Maoist posters on the walls.[94]

The immediate cause leading to the outburst on April Fifth was removal of wreaths placed at the Hero's Monument in memory of Chou. A week before the April 5 Ch'ing Ming Festival, a day in Chinese custom for commemorating one's deceased ancestors, wreaths were placed before the monument by streams of people coming to pay their last respects to the late Premier. The number of mourners grew daily as the Ch'ing Ming Festival drew near. The day before the festival, over a million people gathered at the monument. Several thousand wreaths were placed around the memorial bearing words and phrases which praised Chou, repudiated the radicals, and expressed sympathy for Teng. The Maoists could not tolerate the opposition. Late at night they ordered the wreaths removed. When people discovered a barren monument the next morning, they rioted. They battled both police and Public Security Guards. By noon, the people seemed to disperse, but the Maoists came again that

92. *Jen-min Jih-pao,* November 28, 1976.

93. For example, there was published in *Jen-min Jih-pao* on February 13, 1976, a hateful article against Chou. The article was entitled "Yao Chi-hsu P'i-k'ung" ("The Need to Carry on the Anti-Confucian Campaign").

94. *Teng Hsiao-p'ing Fu-ch'u Nei-mu* (The Inside Story of Teng's Rehabilitation) (Taipei: Shih-pao Wen-hua Ch'u-pan Kung-ssu, 1977), p. 78.

afternoon to remove more wreaths and portraits of Chou. A violent mob swarmed after them. The violence went unchecked until the militia and armed forces were brought in. Over 100,000 people wer reported to have participated in the riot.[95]

One of the most striking banners held by the people read, "The time of Emperor Ch'in Shih Huang has gone forever," a reference to Mao's hero, looked upon by orthodox historians as a tyrant. Other banners blasted Chiang Ch'ing — "Down with the Empress Dowager" and "Down with Indira Gandhi." Still other banners supported Teng — "The current Anti-Rightist Deviationism Campaign is the campaign of a small handful of ambitionists to reverse the verdict," "Long live the Four Modernizations," "Teng Hsiao-p'ing should direct the work of the Party," and "We want true Marxism-Leninism, not false Marxism-Leninism."[96] People urged the return of Teng. They demanded that Teng be appointed Premier.[97]

No evidence exists that Teng instigated the riot. In fact, the violence could have been avoided altogether had the leftists kept their hands off the wreaths. The Maoists, however, used the incident as an excuse to blame Teng. Two days after the incident, the Politburo called a meeting "to discuss the anti-revolutionary outburst before the Tien-an-men Square and the involvement of Teng Hsiao-p'ing." According to the New China News Agency, Party members belived that Teng's attitude had changed from a craftiness to open hostility. The Politburo adopted a resolution, on Mao's recommendation, to strip Teng of his offices "while allowing him to keep his Party membership so as to see how he will behave in the future."[98] A second

95. "T'ien-an-men Kuang-ch'ang Te Fan-ko-ming Shih-Chien" ("The Anti-Revolutionary Incident in the T'ien-an-men Square"), *Jen-min Jih-pao*, April 8, 1976; and *Teng Hsiao-p'ing Fu-ch'u Nei-mu*, pp. 78-84.

96. Jurgen Domes, "The Gang of Four and Hua Kuo-feng," *The China Quarterly*, No. 71 (September 1977), p. 490.

97. Liang Hsiao, "Tang Nei Ch'ueh-shih Yu Tzu-chan-che-chi" ("There Exist Absolutely in the Party Bourgeois Elements"), *Jen-min Jih-pao*, May 18, 1976.

98. *Jen-min Jih-pao*, April 6, 1976.

resolution appointed Hua Kuo-feng as the First Vice Chairman of the Party (a new position), and Premier of the State Council. These appointments officially recognized Hua as Mao's successor. Chu Te reportedly was the only one who spoke on Teng's behalf during the meeting.[99] Teng did not lose his Party membership because everyone knew he had nothing to do with the April 5 Incident. However, Teng was effectively ousted for the third time. When the resolutions were made public, protests broke out across the country.[100]

After the April 5 Incident, the Anti-rightist Deviationist Campaign became the "Criticize Teng and Anti-Rightist Campaign." Teng was accused of having inspired the Incident[101] and for being "the villain working behind the scenes."[102] The Incident was described as an anti-revolutionary uprising bearing the same stamp as the 1956 Hungarian revolt. Teng was referred to once again as a revisionist. Chang Ch'un-ch'iao even called him "Nagy," the former revisionist leader of Hungary, face to face.[103] The April 10 editorial of the *People's Daily* quoted Mao as saying, "[Teng] knows nothing of Mar xism-Leninism. He represents the bourgeoisie. He swore that he would never reverse our innovations — but that is simply not true."[104] On April 25, Hua Kuo-feng and Chiang Ch'ing, among others, received representatives of the forces that had crushed the riot. Chiang Ch'ing told her guests that Teng was the boss of the anti-revolutionaries.[105] The radicals were not content to have Teng merely discredited and still retain his Party membership. They wanted to

---

99. *Teng Hsiao-p'ing Fu-ch'u Nei-mu*, p. 210.

100. *1976 Fei-ch'ing Nien-pao*, p. (V) 10.

101. Hung Kuang-ssu, "Teng Hsiao-p'ing shih T'ien-an-men Kuang-ch'ang Shih-chien Te Tsui-k'ui-ho-sho" ("Teng Is the Principal Villain of the T'ien-an-men Sqaure Incident"), *Hung Ch'i*, No. 5, May 1976.

102. Liang Hsiao.

103. *Hua-ch'iao Jih-pao*, December 1, 1980.

104. "Wei-ta Te Sheng-li" ("The Great Victory").

105. Cheng Hsueh-chia, p. 126. Other hosts included Chang Ch'un-ch'iao, Yao Wen-yuan, Wang Hung-wen, Ch'en Hsi-lien, Chi Teng-k'uei, Wang Tung-hsing, Wu Te, Ch'en Yung-kuei and Ni Chih-fu.

use his "conspiracy" as an excuse to remove all other "capitalist-roaders" from the Party. One Maoist wrote an article in the *People's Daily*, saying that the "downfall of one representative figure will not cause the other capitalist-roaders to disappear." "They remain able to use their title as 'Communist Party members' and their identity as 'leading cadres' to usurp power and push through the revisionist line in 'legitimate form.' "[106] Teng's close associates — Hu Yao-pang, Hu Ch'iao-mu, Wan Li, Chou Jung-chin, Hsu Li-ch'un, and Ch'ien Hsin-chung were all subjected to ridicule and dismissed from their positions.[107] Chou Jung-chin was tortured to death. The radicals did not halt their campaign against the rightists even during the violent earthquake in T'ang-shan that killed over 1 million inhabitants.

After his downfall, Teng was kept under house arrest.[108] Teng later said that he remained in Peking until his reinstatement in July 1977;[109] however, a more exciting version of the interim gives us this story: Teng escaped to Kwangtung province, riding in a car sent by Hsu Shih-yu, commander of the Canton Military Region. Ch'en Hsi-lien, who was then in command of Peking security, tried vainly to stop Teng. While Teng was in Kwangtung, many Party, government, and military leaders came to see him. Chao Tze-yang, then first secretary of the Szechuan province (now Premier of the State Coun-

---

106. Kuei Chih, "Tzo-tzu-pai Hai-tsai Tzo" ("The Capitalist Roaders Are Still on their Way"), *Jen-min Jih-pao*, April 21.

107. Chou Jung-chin was Minister of Education. Hsu Li-ch'un, formerly Deputy Minister of Propaganda, fell in disgrace during the Cultural Revolution and was reinstated in 1974. He was another theoretician of the Teng group. Ch'ien Hsin-chung was a veteran of the Second Field Army, formerly Minister of Health. He fell during the Cultural Revolution and became Deputy Minister of Health after his reinstatement.

108. Ying Lan, p. 31.

109. As told by Teng to Franz-Josef Strauss, head of West Germany's Christian Social Union Party, during his visit to China in 1982. See Li Ssu, "Teng Hsiao-p'ing Tsai Tan Wang-shih" ("Teng Recalled the Old Days"), *Hua-chiao Jih-pao*, April 12, 1982. Yu Wen's article "Teng Hsiao-p'ing Te Chien-k'ang Ch'ing-k'uang" (Teng Hsiao-p'ing's Health Condition) also said the same thing.

cil), for example, had a long talk with Teng. On one occasion, Teng gave a public speech:

> Either we admit we are impotent and wait to be slaughtered, allowing four people to move our country back a century, or we fight with them while we still have a mouthful of breath. If we win, every problem will be solved. If we lose, those who survive can go into the mountains and carry on the fighting or go overseas to wait for another chance. We have for the time being bases in Canton, Foochow, and Nanking where we can still fight them. But we will lose everything if we do not act now.[110]

If the story is true, Teng's every move in Canton was kept secret. Once he went to see Yeh Chin-ying, reportedly riding in a paddy wagon. The Chiang Ch'ing group sent Chu Chia-yao, Deputy Public Security Minister, to Kwangtung to search for Teng's whereabouts but he returned emptyhanded. Teng's enemies believed he had gone to Szechuan. They later discovered he was in Kwangtung, but Hsu Shih-yu refused to hand Teng over to them.[111]

Despite another major disgrace in 1976, the Teng Hsiao-p'ing Era truly began with the Fourth People's Congress in 1975. Although Teng was recognized as one of the top leaders of the country before this time, he remained more or less a shadow of his patrons: first with Mao, then Liu, and finally Chou. Since the Fourth People's Congress, however, Teng emerged a national leader in his own right and serious competition to Mao. It was in 1975 that Teng unveiled his blueprint for tomorrow's China. The slogan, the Four Modernizations, was suggested by Chou En-lai, but Teng contributed the greater part of its formulation. Although the Tien-an-men Square Incident brought about Teng's third downfall, the important role he played in 1975 anticipated his future role as the leader of China.

---

110. See CCP Propaganda Minister Chang P'ing-hua's speech made at the July 23, 1978 conference. The speech was reprinted in *Tung Hsi Fang* (The East and the West Monthly, Hong Kong), February 1979, pp. 18-19.

111. Ibid. See also Wan Sou, "Pai-chan Ying-hsiung Hsu Shih-yu" ("The Battlefield Hero, Hsu Shih-yu"), *Chung-kuo-jen*, July 1980, p. 17.

Chapter 11

The Beginning of a Teng Era (1976-1982)

Nineteen seventy-six, the year of the dragon, was a troubled year for the Chinese. It was a year of deaths, of natural disasters, and of political upheaval. Chou En-lai died in January, Chu Te died in July, and finally Mao died in September. A violent earthquake killed millions of people in T'ang-shan. A massive demonstration brokeout spontaneously at the Tien-an-men Square. Teng was disgraced for the third time. And a bitter struggle ensued over the succession to chairmanship.

After Mao's death, it appeared that the Chiang Ch'ing group had Mao's blessings to succeed him. They distributed the so-called "Last Testimonial" of Mao. According to the testimonial, Mao had gathered Hua Kuo-feng, Yeh Chien-ying, Wang Hung-wen, Chang Ch'un-ch'iao, Yao Wen-yuan, Li Hsien-nien and Ch'en Yung-kuei before his death bed and urged them to help Chiang Ch'ing "uphold the Red Banner."[1] In other words, Chiang Ch'ing was to succeed Mao as the Chairman of the CCP. The "Gang of Four" also claimed that

---

1. Chen Hsueh-chia, "Tsung Wen-ko Tao Shih I ta," pp. 150-151.

Mao had instructed them to carry on everything according to the "established direction." On the other hand, Hua Kuo-feng, First Vice Chairman of the CCP, also claimed that he had Mao's approval to take the chairmanship. He showed the people a personal note from Mao which said, "with you [Hua] in charge, I am at ease." After the October coup, the Chiang Ch'ing group was charged with forging the last will of Mao. However, Mao's April 30 note to Hua could not be viewed as a will either because it was made by Mao when Hua reported to him on the progress of the Anti-Teng Campaign.[2] It probably referred to Hua's performance in that campaign only.

At a Politburo Standing Committee meeting held in late September, Chiang Ch'ing formally proposed that she be elected to head the Central Committee. She said that Hua was too "incompetent" to lead the Party. Hua retorted that he was "competent" enough and added that at least he knew "how to solve problems.[3] On October 4, The Chiang Ch'ing group published an article entitled "To Follow the Established Direction in our Work." The article stated, "The revisionist who wants to distort Chairman Mao's established directives is sure to be condemned."[4] Contending that a "revisionist" was now "standing before the people," the radicals heaped their poisoned propaganda on Hua. The radicals, however, were prepared for more than a mere volley of words. They planned to call the armies of Shenyang and Shensi into Peking on October 2nd. Plans were postponed because of the intervention of Yeh Chien-ying, but mobilization occurred at the radical homebase in Shanghai.[5]

---

2. Andres D. Onate "Hua Kuo-feng and the Arrest of the 'Gang of Four,' " *China Quarterly*, No. 75 (September 1978), p. 548; and Ssu-ma Ch'ang-feng, *Teng Hsiao-p'ing Fu-chih Shih-mo* (The Rehabilitation of Teng Hsiao-p'ing) (Hong Kong: Bo Wen Shu-chu, 1980), p. 117.

3. *South China Morning Post*, October 17, 1976.

4. Liang Hsiao, "Yung-yuan An Chi Ting Fung-chen Pan" ("To Work Forever According to the Established Rule"), *Jen-min Jih-pao*, October 4, 1976.

5. Chia Yu-ch'un, "Ssu-jen-pan Pei Pu Ch'ien Ho" ("Before and After the Arrest of the Gang of Four"), *Chung Pao Yueh-kan*, No. 8 (September, 1980), p. 18.

The militia received modern weapons to prepare it for possible confrontation with factional troops.[6] The 38th Army garrison at Paoting was to initiate the coup on October 9th.[7]

In a quick reflex for survival, Hua Kuo-feng allied himself with Yeh Chien-ying, Li Hsien-nien, Wang Tung-hsing and Ch'en Hsi-lien to arrest the "Gang of Four."[8] Other important activists in the Chiang Ch'ing clique followed their "ringleaders" to jail: Yu Hui-hung, Ch'ih Ch'un, Hsieh Ching-i, Liu Hsiang-p'ing, and Mao Yuan-hsin. In the south, Hsu Shih-yu, Commander of the Canton Military Region, put all the radical elements in Shanghai and Nanking under intensive surveillance.[9] Two days after the arrest, the Politburo adopted a resolution that Hua Kuo-feng be appointed the Chairman of the Party and Chairman of the CCP Central Military Commission.

Although the "Gang of Four" was toppled, Teng did not find favor immediately. On October 10th, he wrote Hua a letter expressing his delight and pledging his support.[10] But Hua's response was cold. He wrote back, "You made mistakes and remain to be criticized."[11] The Teng Hsiao-p'ing Criticism Campaign continued.

Party leaders held different opinions as to returning Teng to power. Wang Tung-hsing, Ch'en Hsi-lien, Wu Te, and Chi Teng-k'uei stood on the side of Hua Kuo-feng in opposing reinstatement. Although these officials played a significant role in deposing the "Gang of Four," they were Maoists too. They had gained their prominence during the Cultural Revolution and

---

6. Cheng Hsueh-chia, "Tsung Wen-ko Tao Shih I Ta," p. 160.

7. Chia Yu-ch'un, p. 19; and Li Yen-wu, "Lin Chiang Liang Pang Fu-mo Chi" ("The Downfall of the Lin Piao Clique and the Chiang Ch'ing Clique"), *Cheng Ming*, No. 37 (November 1980), p. 43.

8. Chia Yu-chun, p. 19.

9. Wan Shou, "Pai Chan Ying-hsiung Shu Shih-yu" ("The Hundred-battle Hero Hsu Shih-yu"), *Chung Kuo Jen*, Vol. II, No. 6, (July 1980), p. 15.

10. Letter of Teng Hsiao-p'ing on October 10th. It was reprinted in Ssu-ma Ch'ang-feng, *Fu-chih Shih-mo*, pp. 185-186.

11. *I-chiu-chi-liu Nien Fei Ch'ing Nien-pao*, p. (II) 5.

had taken considerable part in the Teng Hsiao-p'ing Criticism Campaign. If Teng were allowed to come back, their credibility would be jeopardized. Worse still, to dishonor Mao's wishes, even posthumously, would threaten their claim to the succession. To Hua personally, there was another consideration. His appointment to the premiership was made at the same time as Teng's dismissal from office. Hua was worried that should the resolution against Teng be withdrawn, his appointment as Premier would be withdrawn too. Thus to these Maoists, the purge of the "Gang of Four" had little to do with reinstating Teng Hsiao-p'ing.

On the other hand, Yeh Chien-ying and Li Hsien-nien believed that Teng should be reinstated, but not before they had entrenched their own power. Yeh supported Hua in carrying on the campaign of criticism against Teng[12] and Li remarked on several occasions that Teng had made mistakes.[13] Yeh and Li's caution was due primarily to the benefit they had received from the Cultural Revolution. Despite some heckling in the beginning of the turmoil, they emerged with stronger positions in the Party than before. They feared that if Teng were reinstated immediately, he might call for reappointments. They were pleased to have Hua chairing the Party because Hua was politically immature and needed the counsel of old veterans such as themselves. If Teng again became the senior statesman, their positions would be less prestigious. Li remembered well that his importance in the State Council declined when Teng recovered from his second purge in April, 1973.

The most eager advocates of Teng's reinstatement were Hsu Shih-yu and Wei Kuo-ch'ing, both of whom had been Teng's subordinates. Hsu had served under Teng in the 129th Division during the Sino-Japanese War and Wei was with Teng in Kwangsi province in the late twenties. Hsu reportedly accom-

---

12. Chen Chung-p'ing, p. 14.
13. Ssu-ma Ch'ang-feng, *Fu-chih Shih-mo*, p. 80.

panied Teng on his flight back to Peking after the downfall of the Gang of Four.[14]

In general, military leaders in the southeast and southwest wanted to see Teng reinstated. In the north, military leaders like Ch'en Hsi-lien and Li Te-sheng supported Hua Kuo-feng. A tense situation emerged over the issue of Teng's reinstatement which ultimately divided north and south into contending camps.[15]

Criticisms against Teng began to disappear after November, but the Hua Kuo-feng group remained firm in their opposition. On December 30th, Hua told the delegates of the "Second National Agricultural Conference of Learning From Tachai" that criticism of Teng should continue. He said:

> We have mentioned little about the Teng Hsiao-p'ing Criticism Campaign at this conference and some people doubted if we would continue the campaign initiated personally by Chairman Mao.... Teng Hsiao-p'ing had sharp contradictions with the "Gang of Four," but they are all revisionists. Each of them keeps a book of his deeds in opposing the Party, socialism, the Thoughts of Mao Tse-tung, and Chairman Mao. The overthrow of the "Gang of Four" does not mean that Teng will be spared. But the major contradictions at the present time are not Teng's.... [16]

Hua's remarks indicated that the first priority was to deal with the Chiang Ch'ing group before returning to the Teng issue. Clearly Teng would not be allowed to resume his office.

In January 1977, the first anniversary year of Chou En-lai's death, posters went up and rallies were held by the masses in memory of the late Premier. From January 6 to 15, over one million people gathered before the Tien-an-men Square to pay

---

14. *Teng Hsiao-p'ing Fu-ch'u Nei-mu* (The Inside Story of the Rehabilitation of Teng Hsiao-p'ing), (Taipei, Shih-Pao Wan-hua ch'u-pan Shih-yeh Yu-hsien Kung-ssu, 1977), p. 242. (Hereafter referred to as *Fu-ch'u Nei-mu*.)

15. Wan Sho, p. 17.

16. *Fu-ch'u Nei-mu*, pp. 239-240.

tribute to Chou En-lai. They demanded that Teng be reinstated and that the April 5th Incident be reassessed.

Under public pressure the Party met to discuss Teng's future and debated the issue furiously. Finally, the Maoists conceded that Teng be rehabilitated providing earlier resolutions on the Tien-an-men Square Incident be left untouched.[17] Hua's supporters knew that if any re-examination of the April 5th incident was made, the Party might come to the conclusion that the April 7th resolutions were unjustified, including the resolution that appointed Hua Premier.

Another condition to the Maoist concession was that Teng admit his mistakes. On February 7th, Yao Lien-wei, a member of the Hua Kuo-feng group, hinted that Teng was still a Party member and was therefore entitled to a Party job. First, however, he needed to make a self-cirticism. On the same day, Teng Ken, Teng's brother and former Vice Mayor of Wuhan, reappeared from house arrest to preside over a mass meeting in Wuhan. Then in March, Hua Kuo-feng commented on the issue of Teng's reinstatement at the Central Work Conference. He summed up his views in four points. First, Teng had nothing to do with the April Fifth Incident personally. Second, Teng had done a decent job during his tenure in the State Council with only 30 percent error. Third, the Party Central needed to help correct Teng's error and give him a chance to work, but that reinstatement had to be accomplished gradually. Fourth, dialog for and against Teng's reinstatement would continue at the upcoming Eleventh Party Congress.[18]

Teng responded by writing a letter to Hua on April 10th, thanking him for clearing up any connection between him and

---

17. Ch'i Mao-chi, "Tsung Wang Tung-hsing Te 'Tzu-wo Chien-t'ao' K'an chung-kung Te Ch'uan-li Tou-cheng" ("A View on Power Struggle Inside the CCP from the Study of Wang Tung-hsing's Self Criticism"), *Chung-kuo Shih-pao*, January 16, 1980; and Tu Feng, "Wang Tung-hsing Wei She Mo Hui Hsia-tai?" ("Why Wang Tung-hsing Fell?"), *Cheng Ming*, No. 30 (April, 1980), p. 37.

18. *Fu-ch'u Nei-mu*, pp. 233-234; pp. 199-200.

the Tien-an-men Square Incident. He admitted having made mistakes during his involvement in the State Council in 1975 and expressed his readiness to accept criticism. Finally he said he would accept the decision of the Party with regard to a return position.[19] Once again, Teng impressed people by his pragmatism.

On May 3, the Party Central distributed Teng's October and April conciliatory letters for discussion.[20] The first sign that Teng's return was imminent was the withdrawal of accusations against him. In April, the fifth volume of Mao's selected works was published, containing compliments to Teng. Many of Teng's purged adherents were returned to work — men like Hu Yao-pang, Wan Li, and Hu Ch'iao-mu.

The reinstatement of Teng was a slow process due to the resistance of the Maoists. They knew that if Teng regained his former stature he would be harsh with them and reverse the gains they had made in the Cultural Revolution. Thus they needed time to build up their prestige and strength. Hua had many local leaders transferred in order to build up his following. He made frequent tours around the country and attended the Agricultural Conference and the Industry Conference. Hua hoped to build an image that showed his concern for economic reconstruction. He tried to build a cult following to make himself look like another Mao Tse-tung. To prevent Teng's effort to reverse his gains, Hua declared that "We wholeheartedly support whatever decisions were made by Chairman Mao and we absolutely observe his instructions."[21] Hua's views were officially published in the *People's Daily* on February 7.[22]

---

19. Letter of Teng Hsiao-p'ing on April 10. It was reprinted in Ssu-ma Ch'ang-feng, *Fu-chih Shih-mo*, pp. 187-188.

20. See CCP Central Committee Document No. 15. The document was quoted in Ssu-ma Ch'ang-feng, *Fu-chih Shih-mo*, p. 183.

21. *Hua-ch'iao Jih-pao*, July 22, 1980; and Pi Ming, "Lueh Lun Hua Kuo-feng Te Tso-wu" ("A Brief Study of Hua Kuo-feng's Mistakes"), *Tung-hsiang*, No. 28 (January, 1981), p. 9.

22. See *Jen-min Jih-pao*, editorial, February 7, 1977.

Teng made his official comeback at the Third Plenary Session of the Tenth Party Congress held in July 1977. He was restored to all the posts he formerly held: Vice Chairman of the Party, member of the Politburo Standing Committee, Vice Premier, and Vice Chairman of the Military Commission. The session also elected Hua as Chairman of the Party and Chairman of the Military Commission. The membership of the "Gang of Four" was removed.[23]

The Eleventh Party Congress, called in August, featured major reports by Hua Kuo-feng and Yeh Chien-ying. Both reports sang lengthy praises to Mao and urged the continuation of Mao's will by following the revolutionary lein. Hua even quoted Mao as saying that "solidarity does not imply absence of class struggle." Yeh patronized Hua here and there and even proclaimed him as Mao's chosen successor. Yeh warned:

> If there returns any capitalist-roader who wants to usurp Party and state power, we will, under the leadership of Chairman Hua and the Party Central, get rid of him by using the same methods we used during the Cultural Revolution — mass mobilization and grand democracy.

Clearly these words were meant to intimidate Teng.

Teng presided over the last meeting of the Conference and delivered a closing speech. His speech was brief in comparison to Hua's four hour major opus and did not suggest the prominent role of the new Chairman. Although Teng paid Hua lip service by saying that Mao's line should be carried on, he added that "we should *restore* and develop the *practical* tradition that Chairman Mao founded for our party." In other words, Teng hinted that the present doings of the Party were not practical enough and he legitimized this assertion by claiming that Mao's line was practical too.

Teng was elected second Vice Chairman after Yeh Chien-ying and re-elected a member of the Politburo Standing Com-

---

23. Ssu-ma Chang-feng, *Fu-chih Shih-mo*, pp. 158-159.

mittee. While many Maoists retained their seats, many discredited veterans were restored to office, Teng's men Hu Yao-pang, Wan Li, and Chao Tse-yang were elected to the Central Committee. Later that year, Hu Yao-pang was appointed to head the CCP Organization Department.

Teng was also appointed the PLA's Chief of Staff. Many of his friends simultaneously received positions in the army. For example, Wei Kuo-ch'ing was appointed Secretary General of the Military Commission and Yang Yung was appointed Deputy Chief of Staff of the PLA. Although on the surface the Party was ruled by the triumvirate of Hua Kuo-feng, Yeh Chien-ying, and Teng, Teng's power increased daily. Hua and Yeh soon found themselves on the defense. Teng frequently accepted foreign visitors, discussing with them China's foreign policies and internal affairs. He appeared to foreigners as the de facto prime minister of the country.

The Fifth National People's Congress was called on February 26, 1978. Yeh Chien-ying was elected Chairman of the Standing Committee of the People's Congress, a position equivalent to the head of the state.   Since Mao Tse-tung had never been a Premier, people assumed that Hua would retain the Party Chairmanship and give up the post of Premier in the State Council. But the People's Congress appointed Hua once again to the head of State affairs and Teng was still the first Vice Premier. Teng delivered the closing speech on the last day of the congress. The speech emphasized the importance of the Four Modernizations.

The differences between Hua and Teng became more distinct at consecutive meetings. In March, both Teng and Hua made speeches at the National Science Conference. Teng raised a number of controversial issues in his report. He said that the difference between manual and mental labor was a matter of labor division only and not a matter of class. Teng added that whoever loved his country and whoever was willing to serve his country was "red" enough. In other words the professionals were "reds" if they did their job well. There was no distinction between "expertise" and "redness." Teng contradicted the traditional Party concept that "redness" implied political consciousness. He even asked the scientists to read fewer political books, to attend fewer less irrelevant meetings, and to concentrate their time and energy on their own business. Teng did not believe that the Party should lead and direct research in the science field. He stated that scientific affairs should be managed by the scientists themselves and that the Party should back them up as an auxiliary service only. Teng volunteered to administer such a service. In addition, he dismissed seclusionism and irrational anti-foreignism. He said that China needed more contact with foreign countries to exchange views with them on scientific and technological knowledge. Teng believed it an urgent task to train a group of first-rate scientists, technicians, and engineers. His concern was professionalism and an atmosphere conducive to experimentation.[24]

A few days later, Hua Kuo-feng gave his speech at the same conference. He stressed the primacy of politics and urged the scientists to learn the thoughts of Mao Tse-tung. The Party, he said, should lead scientific teams. Hua upheld the Maoist concept of "mass voluntarism" instead of elitism to further science.

In the Army Political Work Conference held in May and June, Teng and Hua presented differing viewpoints on military affairs. Hua upheld Mao's emphasis of human factors and politics. He said that revolution was the principal expression of all warfare. Teng, on the other hand, believed that the army should rival the best international armed forces. In a technological age, he said, weapons were as important as men. He added that the use of modern equipment meant conforming to a modern training system. Hua repeated over and over the Maoist theme of class struggle while Teng ignored the issue. Hua reaffirmed the Cultural Revolution and called for "solidarity" among cadres. Obviously he hoped that Teng would not carry the purge of the

---

24. *Ta Kung Pao*, March 22, 1978.

Maoists to the extreme. But Teng stressed "rectification," calling for all the remnants of the "Gang of Four" to be removed.

Teng realized that in order to win a total victory for his Four Modernizations, the die-hard Maoists needed to be cleared away. On May 11th, the Teng group published an article in the *Kuang-ming Jih-pao* which the *Jen-min Jih-pao* reprinted the following day. The article repudiated anyone who took Mao's every word as sacred and proposed instead that all problems be approached realistically. Following the publication of this article, a heated debate broke out between the pragmatists and the Maoists. Wang Tung-hsing, the spokesman for the Maoists, said that the article was theoretically faulty, intellectually reactionary, and politically hostile to the thoughts of Mao Tse-tung. He insisted that Mao's teachings were the only criteria to verify truth. Teng returned the volley at the Army Political Work Conference. He accused the Maoists of being concerned exclusively with theories. He said:

> Some comrades talk about thoughts of Mao Tse-tung everyday but they often forget, or even oppose, Chairman Mao's pragmatism. They ignore a basic tenet of Marxism that theories and practices should be combined. Worse than that, they believe that whoever upholds pragmatism, or insists on the synthesis of theory and practice, is committing serious crimes. In essence, they only want to spout off the words or sayings of Marx, Lenin and the Chairman Mao, and that's all.[25]

Teng urged his fellow communists to liberate their thoughts.

The debate brought the two camps into direct confrontation. This time the Maoists were in the unfavorable position because Party secretaries and military commanders of most provinces and regions supported Teng. Many of those who kept

---

25. Teng Hsiao-p'ing, *Teng Fu-chu-hsi Tsai Ch'uan-chun Chang-chih Kung-tso Hui-i Shang Te Chiang-hua* (Speech of Vice Chairman Teng Hsiao-p'ing at the Military Political Work Conference), p. 28.

singing Mao's praises soon found themselves out of a job.[26] The debate reached its climax when in September the first issue of the revived *Chinese Youth*, was released. It featured an article by Hu Yao-pang (under a pseudonym) on verifying truth with means other than Mao's sayings. Other articles praised the April 5th Incident. Wang Tung-hsing ordered the magazine to be withheld from circulation, but Teng reversed the censorship when he returned from an official trip to Pyongyang. The magazine was released on September 20th, roughly the day Teng began his purge against the nuclei of the Maoists.[27]

The first victim was Wu Te, the Mayor of Peking. Chi Teng-k'uei was also removed from his post as First Political Commissar of the Peking Military Region. Ch'en Hsi-lien retained his office but most of his power was stripped away. Seeing some of his best men tumble, Hua was forced to condone the release of *Chinese Youth* for distribution. Another development which symbolized the victory of the Teng group was a declaration calling the Tien-an-men Square Incident a "revolutionary act."[28]

On November 11th a Central Work Conference was held. The issue of economic construction was slated for discussion, but the discontented Maoists again brought up the subject of verifying truth.[29] Upon hearing the news, Teng hurried back from a state visit to southeast Asia to deal with the Maoists. He dismissed them scornfully:

---

26. Such as Wang Huai-hsiang of Kirin, Liu Kuang-t'ao of Heilungkiang, Tseng Shao-shan of Liaoling, Liu Chien-hsun of Honan, Hsieh Hsueh-kung of Tientsin, Chao Hsin-ch'u of Hupeh, and Sai Fu-ting of Sinkiang.

27. Chi Hsin,"Chung-kung Te Hsin Ch'uan-li Tou-cheng" ("New Power Struggle in the CCP"), *Chi Shih Nien-tai*, No. 106 (November, 1978), p. 9.

28. Ch'i Mao-chi,"Hua Kuo-feng Cheng-chih Sheng-ming Te Po-sui" ("The Collapse of Hua Kuo-feng's Political Life"), *Shih-pao Chou-kan*, No. 188 (July 4, 1981), p. 55.

29. Hu Chung-hua, "Chung-kung Shan-chung-ch'uan-hui Nei-mu" (The Inside Story of the CCP's Third Plenary Session), *Chung-kuo-jen*, Vol. I, No. 4, p. 111.

Some people only know how to threaten others. Every chance they get they accuse others of chopping up the revolutionary banner. To hell with them![30]

Teng won the conference over. Wang Tung-hsing, Wu Te, Chi Teng-k'uei, and Ch'en Hsi-lien were all forced to criticize themselves before the audience.[31] Although they still held their positions in the Politburo, the surrendered their government and military posts to Teng's followers. Also in favor of the pragmatists, the conference reappraised "ten major historical events," including the 1957 Anti-Rightist Movement, the Tien-an-men Square Incident, the Resolution against Teng Hsiao-p'ing, the P'eng Te-huai case, the Liu Shao-ch'i case, the P'eng-Lo-Lu-Yang case and the Wu Han case. The meeting lasted more than a month.

The Third Plenary Session opened on December 18th and marked a milestone in the history of Chinese Communism. The leftist line that had dominated Party doctrine and practice for years was replaced by a more practical line. The conference stressed economic construction and modernization, not, as the Eleventh Party Congress emphasized, class struggle and political indoctrination. It also emphasized discipline and routinization. Hua Kuo-feng's plans for a "New Leap Forward," which emphasized mass mobilization and heavy industries, was abandoned. Mao's supremacy was not officially denounced, but the conference agreed that it was not Marxist to expect a leader never to make mistakes, a view that contradicted "Comrade Mao's judgement of himself." P'eng Te-huai (deceased), Po I-po, Yang Shang-k'un, and T'ao Chu (deceased) were restored to Party membership. The conference acknowledged the April Fifth Incident as a revolutionary movement and withdrew all proclamations related to the "Anti-Rightist Deviationism Campaign."

---

30. Tu Feng, p. 38.
31. Hu Chung-hua, p. 114; *Ming-pao*, February 8, 1979; and Ch'i Mao-chi, p. 56.

It endorsed Teng's pragmatism and voted for the principle of "practice as the only criterion for verifying truth."[32]

Accompanying the change in policy came a new arrangement of personnel. Ch'en Yun, Teng Ying-ch'ao (Madam Chou En-lai), Hu Yao-pang and Wang Chen were admitted to the Politburo. Ch'en was elected the fourth Vice Chairman of the Party, a position higher now than that of Wang Tung-hsing. This promotion rewarded Ch'en Yun for his importance as an economic planner during the sixties when Liu and Teng led the "first line" of the Party. His reinstatement indicated that he would be given a supervisory role in reconstructing the state's economy. All other departments were filled by Teng's supporters. Hu Yao-pang assumed the post of Secretary-General of the CCP and Minister of Propaganda. Hu Ch'iao-mu and Yao I-lin became Deputy Secretary-Generals of the Party. Sung Jen-ch'ing[33] succeeded Hu as head of the Organization Department. Wang Tung-hsing managed to retain his position as the fifth Vice Chairman of the Party, but his other posts were given to Teng's people. Yao I-lin replaced Wang as Director of the Party's Central Administrative Office, Hu Yao-pan replaced him as Vice Chancellor of the Party School, Hu Ch'iao-mu ousted him as Chairman of the Committee for Publication of Selected Works of Mao Tse-tung, and Yang Yung took over his leadership of the "8341" brigade.[34] The 8341 brigade and Ch'en Hsi-lien's Peking Garrison were depended on by the Maoists as their front line defense forces but now Teng successfully took control. The Maoists were more vulnerable than ever.

As soon as the populace of Peking heard that the Tien-an-

---

32. *Chung-kung Shan-chung-ch'uan-hui Kung-pao* (Communique of the CCP's Third Plenum), *Pei-mei Jih-pao*, December 27, 1978.

33. *Hua-ch'iao Jih-pao*, January 23, 1979. Sung had been working for a long time under Teng. He was formerly Deputy Director of the Political Department of the 129th Division and the Second Field Army. He served as Deputy Secretary-General while Teng was the Secretary-General in 1954. In 1961 he took full charge of the Party apparatus in Northeast China. He was purged in the Cultural Revolution.

34. Ch'i Mao-chi, p. 56.

men Square Incident was officially a revolutionary act, big character posters flooded the city.[35] Posters everywhere in Peking attacked Hua Kuo-feng, Wu Te, Wang Tung-hsing, Ch'en Hsi-lien and other Maoists, accusing them of spilling blood at Tien-an-men Square. The posters demanded that the two resolutions stemming from the incident — the dismissal of Teng Hsiao-p'ing and the appointment of Hua kuo-feng to the Premiership — be nullified. They urged that Teng take the supreme chair in the Party. They also stated that "With Teng Hsiao-p'ing in charge, the people of the entire nation are ease," ridiculing what Mao had written to Hua: "With you in charge, I am at ease." Some of the posters went so far as to describe Mao as the fascist who patronized the "Gang of Four." Some demanded the implementation of western-style liberalism and democracy.[36] Teng responded to the protesting posters with a tolerant attitude so long as they did not go beyond the limits of the constitution. "We should have an active and easy political life," he said.[37] Teng's tolerance encouraged more posters to go up and the people staged rallies and demonstrations.

The Maoists used these developments as an excuse to denigrate Teng's leadership. Under pressure to crack down, Teng changed his tone. He proclaimed in March 1979 the four "insistences": insistence of socialism, insistence of a proletarian dictatorship, insistence of the CCP leadership, and insistence of Marxist-Leninist-Mao Tse-tung Thought. Liberal activities and big-character posters were forbidden while dissidents were arrested. In reality, Teng had always disapproved of the big-character posters. As an organization man, he opposed uncontrolled, democratic movements. He had tolerated the mass protests only because they were directed against the radicals, which helped him consolidate his strength in the Party. The

---

35. *Pei-mei Jih-pao*, November 16, 1978.

36. *Hsing-tai Jih-pao*, November 21, 23 and 28, December 4, 1978; *Chung-yang Jih-pao*, November 23, 1978; and *Far Eastern Economic Review*, December 1, 1978.

37. *Hua-ch'iao Jih-pao*, November 28 and 29, 1978.

short-lived democratic movement reminded people of the "Hundred Flowers" period when democrats and liberals were encouraged to speak out and then attacked.

The insignificant war gains in Vietnam and the liberal protests at home gave the Maoists ammunition to fight back. At a Central Work Conference held in April 1979, Wang Tung-hsing remarked that the Third Plenary Session was a "right-turn" conference. "Are we following the path of socialism or capitalism?" Wang challenged.[38] In Hunan, the home base of Hua Kuo-feng, the provincial media called for the continuation of "class struggle" in China. They propagated the Tachai model zealously, stressing the importance of revolutionary enthusiasm in emulating production.[39] Nevertheless, the Maoist counter offensive did not bring much in the way of eroding Teng's influence. At the Second Plenary Session of the Fifth People's Congress, Teng's supporters — Ch'en Yun, Po I-po and Yao I-lin — were elected Vice Premiers. P'eng Chen became the Vice Chairman of the Committee of the People's Congress.

In September, the Fourth Plenary Session of the Eleventh Central Committee reaffirmed the spirit of the last Plenum. The Maoists were subjected to criticism once again.[40] A preliminary study of the Cultural Revolution pronounced it "a disaster." P'eng Chen and Chao Tzu-yang, both supporters of Teng, were admitted to the Politburo. Until his transferral to Peking in January 1980 Chao Tzu-yang had ruled Teng's home province of Szechuan since 1975 as its First Party Secretary. He adopted Teng's economic line and made Szechuan a model province of the country.[41]

Teng triumphed again at the Fifth Plenary Session of the Eleventh Central Committee held late in February. At this ses-

---

38. Tu Feng, p. 39.

39. *Shih-cheh Jih-pao*, May 30, 1979.

40. Tu Feng, p. 40.

41. Chao had worked in the Chin-Chi-Lu-Yu Border Region under Teng during the war against Japan. After 1949 he became the First Party Secretary of the Kwantung Province. He was purged during the Cultural Revolution, but was rehabilitated in 1971. In 1974 he resumed his post in Kwangtung. In 1975 he

sion he finally succeeded in expelling the "petty Gang of Four" —Ch'en Hsi-lien, Wu Te, Chi Teng-k'uei, and Wang Tung-hsing, from the Politburo, thereby removing the last vestige of opposition influence from the power center. Hu Yao-pang and Chao Tzu-yang were admitted to the Standing Committee of the Politburo, which enabled Teng to control the core of the Party.[42] The Fifth Plenary Session also rebuilt the apparatus of the Secretariat. Hu Yao-pang was placed in charge of the Secretariat as the General Secreatary, rising from the post of the Secretary-General of the Party as Teng had ascended in the fifties. The Secretariat included ten other secretaries who were all veteran Party members. Most of them had followed Teng since the war against Japan.[43] Hua had virtually lost his control of the Party organization. The triumvirate began to fall apart.

---

was transferred to First Party Secretary of the Szechuan Province. According to Chang P'ing-hua, former Propaganda Minister, Chao had visited Teng while Teng supposedly hid himself in Kwangtung in 1976. After the arrest of the "Gang of Four," Szechuan under Chao was the first province in the country to take action against the followers of the Chiang Ch'ing group. He stood on the side of Teng in the 1978-79 struggle against the Maoists. However, Chao was less intimate with Teng than Hu Yao-pang, Hu Ch'iao-mu, Wan Li, and Sung Jen-ch'iung.

42. The Standing Committee of the Politburo consisted of seven members: Hua Kuo-feng, Yeh Chien-ying, Teng Hsiao-p'ing, Li Hsien-nien, Ch'en Yun, Hu Yao-pang, Chao Tzu-yang. Ch'en, Hu, and Chao were enthusiastic supporters of Teng. Thus Teng gained majority support in the Politburo.

43. Teng's war-year followers included Wan Li, Hu Ch'iao-mu, Sung Jen-ch'iung, and Wan Jen-Chung.

Wan Li studied in France during his youth. He had worked under Teng since 1939 starting in the Chin-Chi-Lu-Yu Border Region. Later he worked in the Second Field Army and then in the Southwest. After transferring to Peking, he became the Deputy Mayor. He fell during the Cultural Revolution. After rehabilitation he became Minister of Railroads only to fall again in 1976. He became the First Party Secretary of Anhwei province in 1977. Under his leadership the agricultural output of Anhwei increased significantly. He was also one of the fans of Teng's "bridge club."

Sung had also worked in the Chin-Chi-Lu-Yu Border Region. He became First Secretary of Hupeh after 1949. He fell during the Cultural Revolution, but became First Party Secretary of Shansi in 1978. After the Third Plenum of the Tenth Party Congress, he was appointed leader of agricultural planning and development.

One of the important ideological decisions made at the Fifth Plenary Session was to return the deceased Liu Shao-ch'i to full Party standing. The conference adopted a resolution praising Liu as "a great Marxist" and called his purge the most mistaken case ever made in the history of Chinese Communism. It also denied that the Party under Liu contained "an anti-revolutionary revisionist line," any "bourgeois headquarters," or any "capitalist roaders."[44] The resolution defended the Liu-Teng line before the Cultural Revolution, saying that their methodology was correct. The restoration of Liu's historical stature consummated Teng's legitimacy and paid a debt to an esteemed comrade. A memorial service for Liu Shao-ch'i was held on May 17th in Peking. Teng praised Liu as a great contributor to Chinese Communism, rescinding the condemnation he had been forced to make at the Third Plenary Session of the Tenth Party Congress in 1977.[45] The rehabilitation of Liu Shao-ch'i, Mao's chief villain, was a snub to the memory of the late Chairman. Yeh Chien-ying and Li Hsien-nien did not attend the service as a gesture of protest.[46]

Although the Cultural Revolution was termed a disaster and Liu Shao-ch'i was commemorated, the CCP was cautious in making any final judgment on Mao Tse-tung. The Chinese leaders each used a different scale for evaluating Mao. Teng believed that Mao had damaged the Party and the country in his last years. He attributed at least four major mistakes to Mao —intensification of the Anti-Rightist Movement of 1957, enforcement of the Three Red Banners Movement, overemphasis of class struggle, and instigation of the Cultural Revolution. Teng

---

44. "Wu-chung-ch'uan-hui Kung-pao"(Communique of the Fifth Plenary Session), *Pei-mei Jih-Pao*, March 7, 1980.

45. Speech of Teng Hsiao-p'ing at one of the forums of the Third Plenum of the Tenth Party Congress. The speech was reprinted by *Ming Pao*, October 20 and 21, 1977.

46. *New York Times*, May 18, 1980. While the memorial service was held, Yeh was in Kwangtung and Li Hsien-nien was visiting New Zealand. However, according to CCP customs, people in their position should have attented the memorials.

also blamed Mao for doing nothing to stop the ultra-radicalism of the Chiang Ch'ing group. He concluded, however, that Mao had done more good deeds than harm and that the Party should not denounce Mao the same way as Khrushchev had done to Stalin.[47] Hua Kuo-feng on the other hand, defended Mao with every breath. He said it was the "Party" that committed serious mistakes during the decade from 1966 to 1976 and that Mao, as Party Chairman, bore the responsibility. Hua blamed the excesses of the Cultural Revolution on the "Gang of Four" and stated that they deceived Mao. The late Chairman, he said, was so sick in his last years that he could do very little to stop the Chiang Ch'ing group from wreaking havoc.[48]

Teng remarked several times that the Party needed to be separate from the government. He also mentioned that he would resign from some of the positions he held to become an advisor at the age of 80. In February 1980, before the meeting of the Fifth Plenary Session, Teng resigned as Chief of Staff of the Armed Forces. Yang Te-chih, a loyal supporter, succeeded him to the post.[49] At the Fifth Plenary Session, it was also disclosed that Teng planned to resign from the position of Vice Premier at the coming meeting of the National People's Congress.[50] After the Fifth Plenum Teng virtually withdrew from government administration and let Chao Tzu-yang (who became the executive Vice Premier in April) look after the daily work.[51]

One of the reasons that Teng gave up some of his power

---

47. Fallaci's interview with Teng; and Wang Ching-tao, "Chung-kung Tang Nei Fei Mao Hua Yun-tung Te Fa-chan yu Wei-lai" ("The Trend and Prediction of De-Maoization in CCP"), *Chung-kuo-jen*, No. 22, November, 1980, p. 15.

48. *Chung-yang Jih-pao*, October 13, 1980; and *Pei-mei Jih-pao*, August 12 and 16, 1980.

49. Yang had served under Teng during the Sino-Japanese War as Commander of the Chi-Lu-Yu Military Region. K'ang Ming-shu, "Yang Te-chih Jen Kung-chun Tsung-ch'an-mo-chang Te Ch'u-pu Kuan-cha" ("A Preliminary Observation of Yang Te-chih's Assumption to Chief of Staff"), *Chung-kuo Shih-pao*, February 27, 1980.

50. *New York Times*, March 17, 1980.

51. *New York Times*, April 18, 1980.

was that he wanted his opponents to surrender some of their power too. In particular, Teng aimed at taking Hua Kuo-feng and Yeh Chien-ying down a notch. He hoped to be an example which would motivate Hua to resign from the Premiership and Yeh to resign as Chairman of the People's Congress. His assurances that he would retire at 80 were aimed at Yeh Chien-ying, who was five years older than Teng. In fact, the principle of separation between the Party and the government was never meant to be followed closely. It was fundamentally a tactic used by the Teng group to decrease the opposition's strength.

Teng's ruse gained results. At the Third Plenary Session of the Fifth People's Congress held in late August, Teng resigned from Vice Premiership.[52] Although Yeh Chien-ying remained Chairman of the People's Congress, Chao Tsu-yang replaced Hua as the Premier. Wan Li, Teng's old friend, became the First Vice Premier.[53] The State Council had at last fallen into the hands of Teng's colleagues.

The pressure was now on Hua to resign the chairmanship. The Teng group stepped up criticism of him in the media, an onslaught which intensified after Hua's resignation from the Premiership. One article in *People's Daily* hinted that Mao had no right to appoint anyone his successor since such a practice was feudalistic. The "Gang of Four" was put on trial in November. The trial embarrassed Hua Kuo-feng because he had stood on the same ground as the "Gang of Four" during the Tien-an-men Square Incident and Teng Hsiao-p'ing Criticism Campaign. Ultimately Hua was forced to submit his resignation in late November. Hu Yao-pang replaced him as Chairman of the Party, and Teng succeeded him as Chairman of the Party's Military Commission. At first it was suggested that Teng assume both posts, but Teng recommended that Hu Yao-pang be the

---

52. Also resigning at the same time were Ch'en Yun, Li Hsien-nien, Hsu Hsiang-ch'ien, Wang Chen, and Wang Jen-chung. Ch'en Yung-k'uei, a Maoist, was dismissed.

53. *Shih-cheh Jih-pao*, September 11, 1980.

Chairman of the Party.[54] Teng knew that the Chairman of the Military Commission was at least as powerful as the Party Chairman because he controlled the army. Teng's long-standing relationship with the army made him uniquely qualified to take that position. On the one hand he could ensure the army's loyalty to the pragmatists and on the other hand he could carry out the necessary reforms in the army. The change of personnel did not please Yeh Chien-ying, however. Yeh went to Canton and stayed there for some six months until June 1981 when an envoy of Teng's persuaded him to return north.[55]

At the Sixth Plenary Session held in June 1981, Teng refused for the second time to become the Party Chairman.[56] In an interview he told Cha Liang-yung, publisher of the *Ming Pao Daily*, that "I have already had fame, so what's the use of getting more? I need to look farther and not be shortsighted. I am in good health now but I am an old man and can work only 8 hours a day or I will get tired." Hua Kuo-feng became the sixth (and the lowest ranking) Vice Chairman in the Party.

In September 1982, the CCP called its Twelfth Party Congress. In his opening speech Teng announced that the CCP had three major tasks in the 1980's: to speed up modernization and economic construction; to reunite Taiwan; and to oppose hegemony. Before the end of the century Teng said the CCP had to finish reforming the economy, educating the cadres, building a healthy socialist culture, and reforming the Party structure. He insisted that China would continue its present open door policy with the exclusion of "corruptive" thinking and fashion.[57]

---

54. Lo Ping, "Chung-kung Ho-hsin Kai-chu Chi" ("The Reorganization of the CCP Power Core"), *Cheng Ming*, January 1981, p. 8.

55. *Yuan-tung Shih-pao* (Far East Times, San Francisco), June 4, 1981.

56. *Hua-ch'iao Jih-pao*, February 20, 1982; *Jen-min Jih-pao*, April 2, 1982; and *Shih-chieh Jih-pao* February 8, 1982. See "Teng Hsiao-p'ing Yu Cha Liang-yung Teng-hua Chi-lu" ("Talks between Teng Hsiao-p'ing and Cha Liang-yung").

57. *Chung Pao*, September 2, 1982.

The conference introduced new changes to the Party structure. The positions of Chairman and Vice Chairman were abolished and replaced by a General Secretary as head of the Party. The General Secretary is responsible not only for administering the Secretariat, but for calling meetings of the Politburo Standing Committee. In actuality, the Secretariat was the leading organ of the party before 1945. It was only at the Seventh Party Congress that Mao created a supreme office for himself to distinguish his improtance from previous general secretaries. In terrms of power, the CCP Secretariat differs from the Soviet Secretariat. In the Soviet Union the party's General Secretary controls the Politburo while in China the General Secretary is not the "leader", but the "convener" of Politburo meetings. A Central Advisory Committee was also created as a way to tap the wisdom of political veterans. These changes were obviously intended to take collective leadership one step forward and to prevent concentration of power in one person.[58] The conference adopted a new Party Constitution containing articles which would help prevent personal dictatorships. "All members, regardless of position, cannot make decisions alone on major issues," it said. "No leader is allowed to cultivate personal rule, or to place himself above the Party."[59]

Hu Yao-pang assumed the post of General Secretary. Teng took the chairmanship of both the Central Advisory Committee and the CCP Military Commission. The Standing Committee of the new Politburo included Hu Yao-pang, Yeh Chien-ying, Teng, Chao Tse-yang, Li Hsien-nien and Ch'en Yun. Hua Kuo-feng was excluded from both the Standing Committee and the Politburo. The new recruits to the Politburo were Wan Li, Hsi Chung-hsun, Yang Shang-k'un, Yang Te-chih, Sung Jen-ch'iung, Hu Ch'aio-mu, Yao I-lin, Liao Ch'eng-chih, and Ch'in Chi-wei — all close to Teng.[60] If the Seventh Party Con-

---

58. See *Chung-kuo Shih-pao*, September 15, 1982.
59. *Shih-chieh Jih-pao*, September 8, 1982.
60. See *Hua-ch'iao Jih-pao*, September 14, 1982.

gress was "Mao's Congress," the Twelfth Party Congress was certainly "Teng's Congress." The Congress concluded the power struggle between the pragmatists and the Maoists and symbolized the end of the transitional period after Mao's death. It began the era of Teng Hsiao-p'ing.

Since his reinstatement in 1977, Teng's policies were implemented one after the other. The economic sector now emphasized material incentives while in agriculture the government offered better prices for produce. More land was reserved for private cultivation and a free market was encouraged. In factories, wages were paid according to the volume of production, and a reward system was observed. The country was more open than before, importing foreign capital and technology. The status of intellectuals and experts was recognized and a great number of students were sent abroad to study. Universities restored the academic degree system. In the military, a million soldiers were disbanded and eight military commanders were transferred once again to prevent the growth of regionalism.

Beginning in 1982, Teng concentrated on improving the performance of the bureaucracy by simplifying the cumbersome apparatus. Almost one-third of the 600,000 government cadres were designated for gradual removal. Again cadres were requested to retire early or take an advisory role. Corrupt or radical leftist cadres were marked for dismissal. The plan emphasized "rejuvenation, intellectualization, and professionalism." In addition, the post of the Republic Chairman, The Chief of State, abolished under the 1975 Constitution, was restored. A State Central Military Commission was set up to lead the army. The village political system was to be restored to take the administrative burden off communes and give them a stronger economic function. All this undeniably bore Teng's imprint.

Chapter 12

Teng Hsiao-p'ing and the Future of China

Teng Hsiao-p'ing has been extremely fortunate. He has survived the searches of the Kuomintang, the crossfire of the Japanese, and the purges of his own Party. One who survives so many misfortunes, according to a Chinese proverb, will surely be rewarded. The ups and downs of Teng Hsiao-p'ing constitute not only a dramatic testament to the person himself, but a unique story in Communist politics. There are many more examples of individuals who were unable to make a comeback after being purged. But Teng did — three times. Even more surprising, each time Teng was reinstated he was given more power. Teng Hsiao-p'ing is the de facto ruler of China today.

What kind of person is the man who guides China's future? Physically, he is short in stature, about four feet and 11 inches tall, and his round face is set with piercing eyes. He speaks in a strong Szechuanese accent. While Teng is upstanding, tough, brave, and intelligent, he can also be rude, arrogant, vengeful, and ruthless. He possesses exceptional organizational talent and administrative ability. Moreover, he is witty and talks lucidly, often coining his own aphorisms. Because of his stocky build, he has been described by some western journalists as a "peppery Napoleon."[1]

He is "uncivilized" by some western standards because he has a taste for dog meat and will spit noisily into a handy spittoon. He was once called by Henry Kissinger a "nasty little man."[2] Yet he is also highly cultivated. In 1981, for example, he was named bridge personality of the year by the International Press Association. Teng once said that only when he played bridge could he take his mind from worries and relax.[3] Swimming, strolling, hiking, billiards and soccer have all rated at one time or other as Teng's favorite leisure-time activities. In the twenties, while Teng was in France, he often went to sports events and once pawned his overcoat to buy a ticket for a soccer match. Teng is no ascetic: he loves good food and, in leisure hours, will retreat to a villa in the quiet and well-guarded "Jade Spring Mountain" in the western suburb of Peking.[4] Perhaps he enjoys talking most of all for he never tires of showing off his cloquence.

Mao, on the other hand, wrote poems, practiced calligraphy, and was addicted to the ancient Chinese classics. Many Chinese leaders of less talent and originality attempted to follow Mao's example so they, too, could impress people by appearing cultivated. Hua Kuo-feng is a sorry example. During his difficult term as the Party Chairman, Hua copied every style of the late Chairman. But Hua appeared to people as an unconvincing and even embarrassing imitation of Mao. He was known pejoratively as "Mao Tse-tung the Second." Teng Hsaio-p'ing, however, eschewed pastimes that did not interest him. Teng was no poet, no calligrapher, and he never had a library filled with thousands of books. He humbly referred to himself as "one of

---

1. Boorman, "Teng Hsiao-p'ing," p. 125.

2. Kissinger said that Teng was too arrogant. He said he would rather deal with Chou En-lai. See *Pei-mei Jih-pao*, January 29, 1979.

3. Yu Wen, p. 36. Teng learned bridge in Szechuan during the fifties and soon became a great fan of the game.

4. *Shih-chieh Jih-pao*, November 11, 1980.

the common folk."[5]

In many ways Teng is not typical for a Chinese leader. He does not seem to have an "emperor complex" nor does he represent the traditional ministerial servant. Mao's temperament was obviously inclined to despotism — he was mysterious, distant, lordly, quiet, and suspicious. Mao was so well versed in Chinese history that he knew to an art how to play "in-court" politics, how to initiate a coup, and how to dispose of his enemies by a sudden stratagem. Mao seldom attacked an enemy directly. More often he would pick a scapegoat and divert the enemy's attention so the latter would be taken unawares. The Cultural Revolution and the ousting of Lin Piao resembles, in many ways, the classical court intrigue of Chinese history. Chou En-lai, on the other hand, remained until his last breath a loyal servant of Mao. Chou was like a Prime Minister of the old Chinese Empire clothed in revolutionary ideology. He never thought of overthrowing Mao and refused to oppose the Chairman even if he disagreed with him. By contrast, Teng never dreamt of becoming an emperor nor did he act like a courtier of old China. Although Teng holds supreme power in China today, he does not appear to people to be infatuated with this status like Mao, Lin Piao, and Hua Kuo-feng. It seems that Teng would accept any position so long as it helped him accomplish his plans. At the same time Teng found it difficult to be falsely agreeable, even to protect himself. He spoke out against Mao for what he thought was right. In Teng, China found one of its most significant modern leaders.

If we call Mao a revolutionary, Chou a politician, Liu Shao-ch'i a bureaucrat, Lin Piao a soldier, and Hua Kuo-feng a policeman, we must call Teng a practitioner. Mao built a people's army to liberate China and inspired revolutions in the Third World. Chou proved himself an outstanding diplomat in the public eye at home and abroad. Liu was the able administra-

---

5. *Pei-mei Jih-pao,* January 29, 1979.

tor, Lin the fierce warrior, and Hua the man for established law and order. Teng has played different roles during his political career. He too was a revolutionary (before 1949), a bureaucrat (after 1949), and a soldier (during the Sino-Japanese War and the Civil War). And yet above all Teng is a practitioner. His job was to put theories and programs into practice. Of necessity he was cautious because a mistake on a grand scale could bring disastrous results. It was because of his caution that Teng was so often looked upon as an anti-revolutionary. His less orthodox and more adaptable approach to predicaments gave Teng his reputation for being a rightist. A revolutionary brings forth change, a politician promotes legitimacy, a bureaucrat structures the system, and a soldier defends it. A practitioner, however, simply works to make everything else work. A practitioner is utilitarian. According to Teng, a good cat is a cat that catches mice, regardless of its color. As long as the goal is achieved, the means are inconsequential.

Teng is no theoretician. He generally avoids hypothetical issues and his understanding of Marxism seems limited. The comparison of Mao to the young Marx and Teng to the mature Marx is based more on their methodology than on their actual understanding of Marxism. Strictly speaking, none of the living Chinese Communist leaders can be called an ideologue. Even the late Mao's knowledge of Marxism was second-hand, fragmented, and utilitarian. Although Teng's ideological contribution to Marxism is certainly more limited, his practical approach to problems attempts to affirm an orthodox Marxist proposition, that is, unless the production force is liberated from want by a surplus of wealth, socialism can never be actualized.

Because of their limited understanding of the theoretical foundations, most Chinese Communists interpret Communism as simply the nationalization of properties. China today is practicing a state-controlled, or more accurately a bureaucrat-controlled economy. Although in Marxist theory a socialist economy is ideally geared toward decentralization, it is the state apparatus in China and not the Chinese people that dictates production goals. From every indication, it appears tha Chinese totalitarian state will determine the livelihood of ι citizenry for decades to come.

In 1983, the *Selected Works of Teng Hsiao-p'ing* was published. We know that Teng has never been a prolific writer and that forty-seven pieces featured in his *Selected Works* are all speeches or interviews dated after 1975. A survey of the *Selected Works* reveals a continued heavy reliance on Mao as an ideologue. Mao's name is mentioned 517 times. In terms of theory, Teng extrapolates nothing original from Mao, but limits his thoughts to technical issues. The rehabilitated Liu Shao-chi is mentioned only 17 times. Despite the fact that many of Liu's practical policies have been restored, Liu was unable to provide Teng the needed intellectual fodder. The Teng Hsiao-p'ing Line is therefore more a managerial than a philosophical phenomenon. Its formation is the result of what the man has done, not of what he has conceptualized.

One of the most dramatic aspects of Teng's personality is his ability to recover from defeat and regain control. He was repeatedly purged because he dared contradict his superiors and carry out policies unpopular with the power core. In the 1930's he was purged because he stood on the side of Mao who was then a pragmatist. In the 1960's, he fell from favor because he introduced a series of practical policies which were "revisionist" in eyes of the leftists. In the 1970's he was disgraced again because he was anxious to reconstruct the disastrous economy caused by the Cultural Revolution. Several reasons explain Teng's resiliency. For one, he rarely committed errors of judgement. After each purge it was Teng's ideas that were proven right. Teng was also a highly experienced official in almost every aspect of the government, the Party, and the army. Few other cadres in the Party could compete with Teng's experience. Teng, furthermore, enjoyed wide support. Both cadres and the masses alike looked upon him as a better and more trusted leader than many other Communists in the power core. The army, in particular, played a significant role in Teng's second and third rehabilitation in 1973 and 1977.[6]

Teng's utmost concern is the Four Modernizations through which it is hoped that China will become fully industrialized by the early 21st century. To Teng's mind, industrialization is a prerequisite for improving the livelihood of the Chinese. But the process of industrialization is hindered by the underexploitation of resources, a dense population, and the lack of professionals and experts. Politically, the ultraleftist remnants do not genuinely cooperate with Teng. Moreover, people have lost confidence in the government after repeated disastrous campaigns. The fundamental problem, however, is that Teng's modernization program is not compatible to Communism. Teng's modernization is westernization. He wants a technology as sophisticated, and a living standard as high, as the West's. While he looks upon the United States and Japan as models of modernization, he refuses to adopt western institutions — the political and economic systems. He refuses to adopt the capitalist free market, but he hopes to build China, under a state-controlled economy, into a consumer economy. The dilemma of Teng's program of modernization is that on the one hand it aspires to the example of advanced capitalist countries, while on the other hand it will not abandon the Communist system.

It is tempting for historians to compare the Four Modernizations with the Yang-wu Movement which the Manchus undertook a century ago. In the mid-nineteenth century, enthusiastic reformers such as Tseng Kuo-fan and Li Hung-chang believed that unless China assimilated Western technology, it would be vulnerable to exploitation. But these reformers believed so strongly in the sacredness and superiority of Chinese culture that they failed to recognize the spirit of Western culture which

---

6. Seven of the 11 Military Region commanders appointed in November 1982 were old partners of Teng. They were Ch'in Chi-wei (Peking), Li Te-sheng (Shenyang), Hsiang Shou-chih (Nanking), Yu T'ai-chung (Canton), Chang T'saich'ien (Wuhan), Tu I-te (Lanchow), and Wang Cheng-han (Chengtu). Besides, Yang Te-chih (Chief of Staff), Yu Ch'iu-li (Director of the General Political Department), and Yang Yung (Deputy Chief of Staff).

made advanced technology possible. The Yang-wu movement proved a total failure when Japan defeated China in 1895. At that time the Manchus possessed better battleships than Japan, but China was still defeated. The Chinese Communists seem to be repeating the same mistakes as their traditionalist predecessors by upholding their idealogy religiously. Although the scope of the Four Modernizations is larger than the Yang-wu Movement, the spirit is fundamentally the same — to learn the technology of the West. Teng places no fault on the Communist system for slow development. Rather, Teng and his associates maintain that the system's mistakes are the result of human error and are therefore correctable. They blame the ultra-radicals for corrupting the system in the last decade and see China before the Great Leap Forward as moving on a steady course toward socialism. Without the violent interruption of the Cultural Revolution, they believe that China would now be fundamentally prosperous. So, the leaders of China today appear to be looking backward instead of forward. If Teng fails to seek a new framework for development, China in the next decade will, at best, gain only stability. In fact, what is happening in China today bears an uncanny resemblance to the Chinese historical concept of *Chung-hsing* ("Restoration"). In the Chinese dynastic cycle, there used to be a period of relative peace and stabilization after a preceding period of violence. The ruling class relaxed its control for the time being and concentrated on economic reconstruction.[7]

Teng's "liberal" economic policies have helped to better the livelihood of the masses but politically Teng remains a conservative. He and his associates have little faith in the people and do not trust spontaneity. They allow criticism as long as it is "constructive" but do not encourage open criticism outside the

---

7. The Tung-chih Restoration of 1860-74 is the most recent example of *Chung-hsing*. It is worthwhile to pursue further study on the resemblance of the post-Cultural Revolution China with previous restorations. For an elaboration of the content of *Chung-hsing*, see Mary Wright, *The Last Stand of Chinese Conservatism, 1860-74* (Stanford, Calif.: Stanford University Press, 1967).

Party. Teng even forbade the posting of big-character posters, a good means of expressing different opinions in China where people have little access to media. The message is clear —if the Party makes mistakes, it need no reminders. The Party men, not the people, are the watchdogs. The authority of the Party should not be questioned because the Party is the guardian of the revolution and embodies political virtue. The Leninist principle of a supreme and virtuous Party constitutes one of the main obstacles to a possible "Fifth Modernization:" political democratization.

How far Teng can accomplish his economic reform and push China a step toward democratization will affect China's policy of reunification with Taiwan. It is impractical now to unite the country by force because conditions both at home and abroad preclude a military venture on the island. Teng and other Chinese leaders have repeatedly appealed to the Nationalist Government of Taiwan for unification, promising the island republic a good deal of autonomy including its own army and political structure. The Taipei Government agrees that there is only one China, but does not trust the Chinese Communists. To them the recent overtures of reconciliation are but new tricks to lower their guard. People in Taiwan bear no love of Communism. In the last thirty years the island accomplished much in terms of economic development. The average income of the Taiwanese is more than nine times that of the people in mainland China. Politically and socially, the Taiwanese enjoy relatively more political freedom. If Teng fails to build a wealthier and freer China, the dream of unifying the country by peaceful means may be very difficult to realize.

Teng's biggest problem is his inability thus far to provide a vision for the future of China. After 30 years of turmoil, the people regard the CCP with suspicion. Maoism has lost its appeal and people seem to have lost a sense of direction. The pursuit of material well-being seems to be the only goal of the common people on mainland China today. The aged nation seems indifferent and insensitive to its future. In today's China, people under 30 constitute the greatest segment of the population. This group was born after 1949 and has been taught Communist doctrine and the thoughts of Mao Tse-tung since childhood. Once they believed that Communism was the best system, but three decades of Communist rule have disillusioned them. When the Cultural Revolution first began, the young people became excited because they believed they were making history. But they discovered that they were merely puppets of ambitious power-seekers who were using them for personal gain. They have learned to trust no one and accept no ideal. A hero today might turn out to be tomorrow's villain. Then too, promises frequently turn into lies. If Teng Hsiao-p'ing cannot inspire a new creative force, the problem of China in the next decade will be less economic in nature than psychological.

People may argue that the Four Modernizations are the way out of the current identity crisis. However, this reform is more short sighted in terms of contemplating the nation's destiny. The Four Modernizations belong to the category of the "culture of technology." While technology often brings people convenience, productivity, and abundance, technology as an end will not be enought to satisfy humanity's thirst for a spiritual greatness — greatness for their culture and society. A vision enables a nation to move forward with pride and confidence.

After more than a decade of confusion and disturbance, Teng's pragmatism has healed many of China's wounds. The problem with Teng is that although he is determined to better the lives of the Chinese people, he is unable to free himself from his old frame of reference. The Four Modernizations are not a daring new program. Despite the optimism shared by many Chinese leaders, the program's accomplishments have yet to be proven by time. Politically, the denunciation of Mao is carried on, albeit unofficially. However, there seems to be no sign of a genuine move toward liberalization. If he fails to create a breakthrough, Teng may be remembered simply as a transitional figure who helped the nation recover from the revolutionary era, and not as the leader who boldly inspired the vision of modern

China. Teng needs to do more in order to qualify as a great leader. But he has two enemies: his age, and the rigidity of the Communist system he now leads.[8]

Postscript (March, 1985)

The politics of China today seems no longer as exciting as it was when this book was completed. One cannot forget that, during the Cultural Revolution, the Chinese almost every day were frightened by unexpected and disturbing events. All were depressed by that power struggle, the sacrifice of thousands of innocent human lives and the delays in the growth and progress of the country's economy, education and technology. Although the fear of another cultural revolution cannot be totally eliminated from the mind of the Chinese populous—since there is yet no established means for the peaceful transition of power in China—the Chinese are more confident than ten years ago. The Deng Xiaoping era has been founded and the Deng reforms have been carried out quite smoothly in recent years.

The most important events in China in the last couple of years, apart from warm relations with the United States, are the passage of a new constitution in December, 1982 and the signing of an agreement between China and the United Kingdom on the return of the sovereignty of Hong Kong to China. Both events reflect important policies of Deng Xiaoping-ism: a gradual move toward collective leadership and territorial unification.

The implicit spirit of the 1982 constitution is to divide power in order to prevent the concentration of power in a single authority. Before 1982, power rested mainly with the Central Committee

---

8. Despite old age, Teng is very energetic and in good health. He says that his only problem is a certain deafness in his right ear. See *Yuan Tung Shih Pao* (Far Eastern Times, San Francisco), March 25, 1981. Also, it is known that Teng has high blood pressure and is taking medicine to prevent ulcers. See *Shih-chieh Jih-pao*, November 12, 1981.

of the party. The 1982 Constitution modified the power structure: a Central Advisory Committee and a Liaison Committee were created to decentralize the function of the Central Committee. The Central Advisory Committee acts as a planning body which formulates policy. This committee is currently headed by Deng. The Liaison Committee, on the other hand, is a judicial body to maintain the discipline of the party. The Central Committee now has become more an executive body to implement policy.

The 1982 constitution also abolished the position of party chairman. The chairmanship was replaced by the restoration of a General Secretary, who, in fact, will have less authority than that of party leader. With the creation of two balanced bodies and the evolution of the party chairmanship, Communist China is on its way to collective leadership.

The return of the British Colony of Hong Kong has been a life-long dream of the Peking leaders (most of them belong to the first generation of Communism). Although how far the idea of "two systems within in a country" can be realized remains to be seen, observers in general are not optimistic. There is no previous example of Communist-led capitalism where free competition, market economy and individualism have existed parallel with central planning and collectivism. China now generates about 40% of its external income from Hong Kong. It seems very likely that this tiny island—the Pearl of the Orient—can fulfill its present function as China's income earner even if foreign investment pulls out. Here lies a very large contradiction of Deng Xiaoping-ism: ideology versus reality. Deng has refused to be remembered in history as another Li Hung-Chang, but, on the other hand, he cannot let the golden goose be killed. The Deng mode of development in China today suffers the same dilemma: Communist ideology and economism (with western capitalism) are to be upheld at the same time.

Nevertheless, stress on economism and the growth of the economy may produce changes that, by political means alone, cannot be stopped. Examples of some of the Eastern European states (Hungary and Czechoslovakia in the sixties) have indicated that because of economic development, they have forced the deopment of liberalization. In other words, quality economic changes may lead to quality in government. A recent commentary by the *Peoples' Daily* admitted that by Marxism-Leninism alone not all problems can be solved. Thus some people including economists believe that while Deng is still alive, he should push economic modernization by all means. They believe that although there is a strange, mixed economy in China today with many problems and difficulties, the increased tempo of economic changes may create a new form of economy which will change Deng himself and the Communist limitations, thus resulting in a new social and political orientation.

Events of the past have shown that the Chinese Communists are pendulous in the formulation and execution of policies. But Deng is more cautious than Mao and will not fall into Mao's eccentric romanticism. What Mao did was "one step forward and two steps backwards." Thus he created many disasters. Whereas Deng, on the other hand, makes "two steps forward and one step backward," more in the style of a western leader. In the long run, China will surely accomplish more under Deng than in prior regimes, but much depends on the intelligence and courage of Deng Xiaoping, Deng's colleagues, his successors and the endeavor of the entire nation.

Selected Bibliography

Sources in Chinese

I. Books

Chang, Fang. *Teng Hsiao-p'ing Tse Ko Jen* (Teng Hsiao-p'ing). Taipei: Chung-Kuo Ta-lu Wen-t'i Yen-chiu-so.

Chang, Kuo-t'ao. *Wo Te Hui-i* (My Memoir). Vol. II. Hong Kong: Mingpao Monthly Press, 1973.

——————. *Tsung Wen-ko Tao Shih-i-ta* (From the Cultural Revolution to the Eleventh Party Congress). Taipei: Li-ming Wen-hua Shih-yeh Kung-ssu, 1978.

Cheng, Hsueh-chia. *Chung-kung Hsing-wang Shih* (The Rise and Fall of The Chinese Communist Party). Vol. III. Taipei: Chung-hua Tsa-chih She, 1979.

——————. *Tsung Wen-ko Tao Shih-i-ta* (From the Cultural Revolution to the Eleventh Party Congress). Taipei: Li-ming Weh-hua Shih-yeh Kung-ssu, 1978.

Chou Hsun, et al. *Teng Hsiao-p'ing.* Hong Kong: Kuang Chiao Ching Ch'u-pan-she, 1979.

Chou, Yu-jui. *Hung-ch'ao Jen-wu-chih* (The Reds). New York: Shih-chieh Jih-pao She, 1977.

Chang, Yun-hou, et al., eds. *Liu Fa Ch'in-kung Chien-hseuh Yun-tung* (The Study and Work Movement in France). Vol. I. Shanghai: Jen-min Ch'u-pan-she, 1980.

Chung-kung Chi-mi Wen-chien Hui-pien (Collected Chinese Communist Secret Documents). Taipei: Kuo-li Cheng-chih Ta-hsueh Kuo-chi Kuan-hsi Yen-chiu Chung-hsin, 1978.

Chung-kung Jen-ming-lu (Who is Who in Communist China). Taipei: Kuo-chi Kuan-hsi Yen-chiu-so, 1978.

Chung-kuo Hsien-tai-shih Tzu-liao Hui-pien (Collected Materials on Modern Chinese History). Hong Kong: Wen-hwa Tse-liao Kung-ying-she, 1976.

Chung-kung Sou-yao Shih-lueh Hui-pien (Collected Materials on the Chinese Communist Leaders), 2 vols. Taipei: Chung-kung Yen-chiu Tsa-chih she, 1969.

Chung Su Lun-chan Wen-hsien (Documents from the Sino-Soviet Debate). Hong Kong: Wen-hwa Tse-liao Kung-ying-she, 1977.

Fu Fa Ch'in-kung-chien-hsueh Yun-tung Shih-liao (Historical Materials of the Study-and-Work Movement). 3 vols. Peking: Peking Ch'u-pan-she, 1981

Ho, Kan-chih. *Chung-kuo Hsien-tai Ko-ming Shih* (A History of Modern China's Revolution). Peking: Kao-ten Chiao-yu Ch'u-pan-she, 1954.

Huai, En. *Chou-tsung-li Te ch'ing-shao-nien Shih-tai* (The Adolescent Days of Premier Chou En-lai). Szechuan: Ssu-chuan Jen-min Ch'u-pan-she, 1979.

Hui-i Ts'ai Ho-sen (In Memory of Ts'ai Ho-sen). Peking: Jen-min Ch'u-pan-she, 1980.

Kan, Yu-lan. *Mao Tse-tung Chi Ch'i Chi-tuan* (Mao Tse-tung and His Group). Hong Kong: Tzu-yu Ch'u-pan-she, 1954

K'ang, Ming-shu. *Ssu-jen-pang Shih-chien Ch'ien-hou* (Events Preceding and Following the Gang of Four Incident). Taipei: Shi-pao Wan-hwa Ch'u-pan Kung-ssu, 1978.

Kok, C.B., ed. *Teng Hsiao-p'ing*. Hong Kong: Chung-kuo Wen-hua Chung-hsin, 1977.

————, ed. *Tuan-t'ou-t'ai Hsia Te Chiang Ch'ing* (Chiang Ch'ing Facing the Guillotine). Hong Kong: Chung-kuo Wen-hua Chung-hsin, 1976.

Kuang-hsi Ko-ming Hui-i-lu (Recollections of the Kwangsi Revolutions). Nanning, Kwangsi: Jen-min Ch'u-pan-she, 1959.

Kuan-yu Teng Hsiao-p'ing (About Teng Hsiao-p'ing). Taipei: Shin-chieh Fan-kung Lien-meng Chung-hwa-min-kuo Fen-hui, 1978.

Kung, Ch'u. *Kung Ch'u Chiang-chun Hui-i-lu* (General Kung Chu's Memoirs). 2 vols. Hong Kong: Ming Pao Yueh-kan-she, 1978.

Kung-fei Chung-yai Tse-liao Hui-pien (Collection of Important Materials on the Communists). Taipei: Chung-yang Wen-wu Kung-ying-she, 1953.

Kuo, Hwa-lun. *Chung-kung Shih-lun* (Analytical History of the Chinese Communist Party). Taipei: Institute of International Relations, 1973.

224

Kung-fei Wen-hua Ta-ko-ming Chung-yao Wen-chien Hui-pien (Selected Documents of the Chinese Cultural Revolution). Taipei: Kuo-fang-pu Ch'ing-pao-chu, 1968.

Kuo, Hua-lun. *Chung-kung Shig-lun* (Analytical History of the Chinese Communist Party). 5 vols. Taipei: Chung-hua Min-kuo Kuo-chi Kuan-hsi Yen-chiu-so, 1973.

Li, Feng-ming, ed. *Chung-kung Shou-yao Shih-lu Hui-pien* (A Chronology of Chinese Communist Leaders). Taipei: Chung-kung Yen-chiu Tsa-chih she, 1969.

Li, Huang. *Hsueh-tun-shih Hui-i-lu* (Memoirs from the Ignorant Student's Studio). Taipei: Chuan-chi Wen-hsueh Ch'upan-she, 1973.

Li, T'ien-min. *Chou En-lai P'ing-chuan* (Biography of Chou En-lai). Taipei: Li-ming Wen-hua Shih-yeh Kung-ssu, 1976.

Lin Piao P'ing-chuan (Biography of Lin Piao). Hong Kong: Ming Pao Yueh-k'an-she, 1978.

Li, Yun-han, *Tsung Jung-kung Tao Ch'ing tang* (From Collaboration to Annihilation, A History of the First United Front). Taipei: Chung-kuo Hsueh-shu Chu-tso Chiang-chu Wei-yuan-hui, 1966.

Mao, Tse-tung. *Mao Tse-tung Hsuan-chi* (Selected Works of Mao Tse-tung). Peking: Jen-min Chu-pan-she, 1964.

——————, *Mao Tse-tung Ssu-hsiang Wan-sui* (Long Live the Mao Tse-tung Thought). Hong Kong: 1969.

P'eng, Te-huai. *P'eng Te-huai Tzu-shu (Memoirs of P'eng Te-huai)*. Peking: Jen-min ch'u-pan She, 1981.

Ssu-ma, Ch'ang-feng, *Mao Tse-tung Yu Chou En-lai* (Mao Tse-tung and Chou En-lai). Hong Kong: Nan-ching I-wen She, 1976.

——————. *Wen-ko Shih-mo* (The Beginning and the End of the Cultural Revolution). Hong Kong: Pai Yeh Shu-wu, 1976.

Ssu-ma, Lu, ed. *Chung-kung Tang-shih chi Wen-hsien Hsuan-ts'ui* (The History of the Chinese Communist Party and Selected Documents). Vol. V. Hong Kong: Tzu-lien ch'u-pan-she, 1977.

Teng Hsiao-p'ing. Taipei: Kuo-li Cheng-chih Ta-hsueh Tung-ya Yen-chiu-so, 1978.

Teng Hsiao-p'ing Fu-ch'u Nei-mu (The True Story of Teng Hsiao-p'ing's Reemergence). Taipei: Shi-pao Ch'u-pan Kung-ssu, 1977.

Teng Hsiao-p'ing Tzu-liao Hsuan-chi (Selected Materials of Teng Hsiao-p'ing). Hong Kong: Hsin Chung-kuo Tu-shu Kung-ssu, 1977.

Ting, Ling, *Yi-erh-chiu-shih Yu Chin-chi-lu-yu Pien Ch'u* (The 129th

Division and the Shansi, Hopei, Shang-tung and Honan Border Area). Peking: Hsin-hwa Shu-chu, 1950.

Ting, Wang, *Yao Wen-yuan Mao Yuan-hsin P'ing-chuan* (Critical Biographies of Yao Wan-yuan and Mao Yuan-hsin). Hong Kong: Ming Pao Yueh-kan She, 1979.

——————, ed. *Chung-kung Wen-hua-ta-ko-ming Tzu-liao Hui-p'ien* (Selected Materials of the Chinese Cultural Revolution). 5 vols. Hongkong: Ming Pao Yueh-kan She, 1972.

——————. *Hua Kuo-feng Chi Teng-kui Han Hsin Ch'i-te I-Tai* (Hua Kuo-feng, Chi Teng-kui and the Rising Generation). Hong Kong: Ming Pao Yueh-kan She, 1977.

——————. *Wang Hung-wen, Chang Ch'un-ch'iao P'ing-chuan* (Biographies of Wang Hung-wen and Chang Ch'un-ch'iao). Hong Kong: Ming Pao Yueh-k'an She, 1977.

Ts'ai, Hsiao-ch'ien. *Chiang-shi Su-ch'u Hung-chun Hsi-ts'uan Hui-i-lu* (The Kiangsi Soviet and the Long March, a Memoir). Hong Kong: Ta chung-hua Ch'u-pan-she, 1970.

Ts'ao, Po-i. *Chiang-hsi Su-wei-ai Te Chien-li Chi Ch'i Peng-kui* (The Rise and Fall of the Kiangsi Soviet). Taipei: Kuo-li Cheng-chih Ta-hsueh Tung-ya Yen-Chiu-so, 1969.

Wang, Chang-ling. *Chung-kuo Kung-chan Chu-i Ch'ing-nien-t'uan Shih-lun* (A Critical History of the Chinese Communist League). Taipei: Kuo-li Cheng-chih Ta-hsueh Tung-ya Yen-chiu-so, 1973.

Wang, Chien-min. *Chung-kuo Kung-chan-tang Shih-kao* (A Draft History of the Chinese Communist Party). 3 vols. Taipei: Self-published, 1965.

Wang, Hsuan. *Kuan-yu Teng Hsiao-p'ing* (About Teng Hsiao-p'ing). Taipei: Shih-chieh Fan-kung Lien-meng Chung-hua Min-kuo Fen-hui, 1978.

Wu, Min and Hsiao, Feng, eds. *Tsung Wu-ssu Tao Chung-hua Jen-min Kung-ho-kuo Te Tan-sheng* (From the May Fourth Movement to the Founding of the People's Republic). Peking: Hsin-chao Shu-tien, 1951.

Wu-ssu Shih-chi Ch'i-k'an Chieh-shao, (An Introduction of the May Fourth Publications). Vol. II, Book 1. Peking: San-lien Shu-tien, 1959.

II. Articles and Speeches

Ch'en, Yun. "Lun Chieh-chueh Tang-ch'ien Kun-ching Chih Tao" ("On Solution to the Present Dilemma"). *Ch'i-shih Nien-tai*

(*The Seventies*, Hong Kong), April, 1980.

Cheng, Yueh. "Lun Ch'uan-tang Ch'uan-kuo Ko-hsiang Kung-tso Te Tsung-kang P'o-hsi" ("A Diagnosis of the 'General Outline' "). *Hung Ch'i*, No. 4 (April, 1976).

Chi, Hsi-chen. "Erh-yueh Ni-liu-Shih-mo Chi" ("The February Reverse Tide, Its Beginning and End"). *Cheng-ming*, July, 1980.

Chou, Hsun. "Teng Hsiao-p'ing Yu Chung-kuo-shih Hsien-tai-hua" (Teng Hsiao-p'ing and the Chinese Model of Modernization). *Kuang Chiao Ching*, (*The Wide Angle*, Hongkong), No. 80 (May 16, 1979).

"Chung-kung Hsin Chu-hsi Hu Yao-pen Hsiao-chuan" ("A Brief Biography of Hu Yao-pan, CCP's New Chairman"). *Hua-ch'iao Jih-pao*, July 1, 1981.

"Chung-kuo Nung-t'sun Liang-t'iao Tao-lu Te Tou-cheng" ("Struggle between the Two Roads in China's Countryside"). *Jen-min Jih-pao*, November 23, 1967.

Hung, Hsuan. "P'ing Teng Hsiao-p'ing Te Fan-ko-ming Yu-lun Kung-shih" ("On Teng Hsiao-p'ing's Anti-Revolutionary Propaganda Campaign"). *Hsueh-hsi Yu P'i-p'an*, No. 6, (1976).

I, Ming. "Chou En-lai, Teng Hsiao-p'ing and the Red Light"). *Hua-ch'iao Jih-pao*, September 5, 1981.

K'ang, Li and Yen, Feng. "Hui-pao-t'i-kang Ch'u-lung Te Ch'ien-ch'ien-ho-ho" ("Before and After the Production of the 'Report Outlines'"). *Hsueh-hsi yu p'i-p'an*, No. 4 (April, 1976).

Kuan, Chien. "Wo Kan Teng Hsiao-p'ing," (My Views on Teng Hsiao-p'ing"). *Tung-hsiang*, No. 6 (March, 1979).

"Kung Ch'u Chiang-chun Fang-wen Chi" ("An Interview with General Kung Ch'u"). *Ming Pao Yueh-kan*, March 1976.

Li, Ta. "I Huai-hai Chan-i" ("Recollections of the Huai-hai Battle"). *Hung-ch'i P'iao-p'iao*, Vol. 18.

Liang, Hsiao and Jen, Ming. "P'ing 'San-hsiang-chih-shih' Wei Kang" ("Criticism of 'Taking the Three Directives' as the Key Link"). *Jen-min Jih-pao*, February 29, 1976.

Liu, Ying "Chung-nan-hai Te Fang-yen" ("Battles in the Chung-nan-hai"). *Cheng-ming*, December 1979.

Mo, I-te, "Jao Shu-shih Hai Ho-jo Ma?" ("Is Jao Shu-shih Still Alive?"). *Tung-hsiang*, April, 1980.

"P'i-p'an Tang-nei Na-ko Pu-ken Kai-hui Te Tzo-Tzu-p'ai" ("Criticize that 'Never Repenting Capitalist Roader Inside the Party' "). *Jen-min Jih-pao*, March 3, 1976.

"P'ing Ko-hsueh-yuan Kung-tso Hui-pao T'i-kang" ("On the Report Outline on Works of the Institute of Sciences"). *Hung Chi*,

No. 8 (August, 1976).

T'ao, Ssu-liang. "I-feng Chung-yu Fa-ch'u Te Hsin" ("A Letter Finally sent—To My Father, T'ao Chu"). *Jen-min Jih-pao*, December 10, 1978.

Tseng, Hsien-kuang. "Teng Hsiao-p'ing Fan Mao Chiu Mao Chih Mi" ("The Pro-Maoist Teng Hsiao-p'ing and the Anti-Maoist Teng Hsiao-p'ing and the Anti-Maoist Teng Hsiao-p'ing." A Mystery"). *Ch'un-ch'iu*, Hong Kong, No. 305 (March 1970).

Tso, Kwang-yu. "Hui-i Ning-tu Ch'i-i" ("Recollections of the Ningtu Uprising"). *Hung-ch'i P'iao-p'iao* (*The Red Flags Fly*). Vol. 19, pp. 271-272.

Wen, Kung-hsiao. "Teng Hsiao-p'ing Yu Erh-shih-t'iao" ("Teng Hsiao-p'ing and the Twenty Articles"). *Hsueh-hsi Yu Pi-pan* No. 6 (June 1976).

Ya, Mei-ch'ang and Huang, Chi-wei. "Chuang-chu Jen-min Te Cho-yueh Ko-ming Chan-shih" ("The Brilliant Revolutionary Warrior of the Chung People"), *Ko-ming Wen-wu*, July, 1979.

Yang, K'uang-man and Kuo, Pao-ch'en. "Ming Yun" ("The Fate"). *Cheng-ming*, January, 1980.

Yao, Sheng-hui and Ts'ui, Chiag. "Fang Ch'ing-nien Hua-chia Teng Hsiao-p'ing Nu-erh Teng Lin" ("An Interview With Teng Hsiao-p'ing's Daughter Teng Lin, the Young Artist"). *Ching Pao* (*The Mirror*, Hong Kong), September 9, 1980.

Ying, Lan. "Teng Hsiao-p'ing Te Erh-nu-men" ("Children of Teng Hsiao-p'ing"). *Cheng-ming*, February 1, 1979.

"Yu-chiang Shang-hsia Hung-ch'i Yang" ("Red Flags Fly Over the Right River"). *Ko-ming Wen-wu*, September 1978.

Sources in English

Ahn, Byung-joon. *Chinese Politics and the Cultural Revolution.* Seattle: University of Washington, Press, 1976.

Barnett, A. Doak. *Uncertain Passage: China's Transition to the Post-Mao Era.* Washington, D.C.: The Brookings Institution, 1974.

Barnett, A. Doak, ed. *Chinese Communist Politics in Action,* Seattle: University of Washington Press, 1969.

Baum, Richard and Teiwes, Frederick C. *Ssu-ch'ing: The Socialist Education Movement of 1962-1966.* Berkeley, Calif.: University of California, Center for Chinese Studies, 1968.

Baum, Richard, ed. *China in Ferment: Perspectives on the Cultural Revolution.* Englewood Cliffs, N.J.: Prentice Hall, 1971.

Belden, Jack. *China Shakes the World.* New York: Monthly Review Press, 1970.

Bloodworth, Ching Ping and Dennis. *Heirs Apparent.* New York: Farrar, Straus and Giroux, 1973.

Bowie, Robert R., and Fairbank, John K., eds. *Communist China 1955-1959: Policy Documents with Analysis.* Cambridge, Mass.: Harvard University Press, 1967.

Brandt, Conrad. *The French-Returned Elite in the Chinese Communist Party.* Berkeley, Calif.: University of California, Center for Chinese Studies, 1961.

Brezinski, Zbigniew K., *The Soviet Bloc: Unity and Conflict,* 2nd ed. Cambridge, Mass: Harvard University Press, 1967.

Brandt, Conrad, Benjamin Schwarty, and John K. Fairbank. *A Documentary History of Chinese Communism.* New York: Atheneum, 1967.

Brugger, Bill. *Contemporary China.* New York: Harper & Row Publishers, Inc., 1977.

—————, ed. *China: The Impact of the Cultural Revolution.* New York: Barnes & Noble Books, 1978.

Carlson, Evans Fordyce. *Twin Stars of China,* New York: Dodd, Mead & Co., 1940.

Chang, Parris H. *Power and Policy in China.* University Park, Pa.: The Pennsylvania State University Press, 1975.

Chang, Y.C. *Factional and Coalition Politics in China,* New York: Praeger Publishers, 1976.

Chen, Jack. *Inside the Cultural Revolution.* New York: Macmillan Publishing Co., Inc. 1975.

Chen, Jerome. *Mao and the Chinese Revolution.* London: Oxford University Press, 1965.

Ch'en, Jerome, ed., *Mao.* Englewood Cliffs, N.J.: Prentice Hall, 1969.

Chi, Hsin. *Teng Hsiao-p'ing.* Hong Kong: Cosmos Books, Ltd, 1978.

—————. *The Case of the Gang of Four.* Hong Kong: Cosmos Books, Ltd., 1978

Clubb, Edmund. *Russia and China.* New York: Columbia University Press, 1971.

Collier, John and Elsie. *China's Socialist Revolution.* New York: Monthly Review Press, 1973.

Crankshaw, Edward. *The New Cold War: Moscow vs. Peking.* New York: Penguin Books, 1963.

Croft, Michael. *Red Carpet to China*. New York: St. Martin's Press, 1959.

Daubier, Jean. *A History of the Chinese Cultural Revolution*. New York: Vintage Books, 1974.

Dittmer, Lowell. *Liu Shao-ch'i and the Cultural Revolution*. Berkeley, Calif.: University of California Press, 1974.

Domes, Jurgen. *The Internal Politics of China 1949-1972*. London: C. Hurst & Co., 1973.

Elegant, Rober S. *Mao's Great Resolution*. New York: World Publishing Co., 1971.

—————. *The Center of the World*. New York: Funk & Wagnalls, 1964.

Esmein, Jean. *The Chinese Cultural Revolution*. New York: Anchor Books, 1973.

Ginneken, Jaap Van. *The Rise and Fall of Lin Piao*. Trans. Danielle Adkinson. New York: Avon Books, 1977.

Gittings, John. *Survey of the Sino-Soviet Dispute*. New York: Oxford University Press, 1978.

—————. *The Role of The Chinese Army*. New York: Oxford University Press, 1967.

Gray, Jack and Cavendish, Patrick. *Chinese Communism in Crisis: Maoism and the Cultural Revolution*. New York: Praeger Publishers, 1968.

Griffith, William E. *The Sino-Soviet Rift*. Cambridge, Mass.: The M.I.T. Press, 1964.

Guillermax, Jacques. *A History of the Chinese Communist Party 1921-1949*. New York: Random House, 1972.

—————. *The Chinese Communist Party in Power 1949-1976*. Boulder: Westview Press, 1976.

Han, Suyin. *Wind in the Tower*. Boston: Little, Brown and Co., 1976.

Harrison, James Pinckney. *The Long March to Power: A History of the Chinese Communist Party, 1921-71*. New York: Praeger Publishers, 1972.

Hinton, Harold. *An Introduction to Chinese Politics*. New York: Praeger Publishers, 1973

—————. *China's Turbulent Quest*. New York: The Macmillan Co., 1972.

Ho, Ping-ti, and Tsou, Tang, ed. *China in Crisis*, 2 vols. Chicago: University of Chicago Press, 1968.

Houn, Franklin W. *A Short History of Chinese Communism*. Englewood Cliffs, N.J.: Prentice Hall, 1967.

Howard, Roger. *Mao Tse-tung and the Chinese People*. New York:

Monthly Review Press, 1977.

Hsiao, Tso-liang. *Power Relations Within the Chinese Communist Movement 1930-1934.* Seattle: University of Washington Press, 1961.

Hsuing, James Chieh. *Ideology and Practice: The Evoluton of Chinese Communism.* New York: Praeger Publishers, 1970.

Hsu, Kai-yu. *Chou En-lai.* New York: Doubleday and Co., Inc. 1969.

Issacs, Harold R. *The Tragedy of the Chinese Revolution.* Stanford, Calif.: Stanford University Press, 1974.

Jan, George P. ed. *Government of Communist China.* San Francisco: Chandler Publishing Co., 1966.

Jansen, Marius B. *Japan and China.* Chicago: Rand McNally College Publishing Co., 1975.

Johnson, Chalmer. *Ideology and Politics in Contemporary China.* Seattle: University of Washington Press, 1973.

Kao, Ying-mao, Paul M. Chancellor, Philip E. Ginsburg, and Pierre M. Perrolle. *The Political Work System of the Chinese Communist Military.* Providence: East Asian Language and Area Center of Brown University, 1971.

Karnow, Stanley. *Mao and China.* New York: The Viking Press, 1972.

Karol, K.S., *China: The Other Communism.* New York: Hill and Wang, 1968.

——————. *The Second Chinese Revolution.* New York: Hill and Wang, 1973.

Klein, Donald W. and Anne Clark. *Biographic Dictionary of Chinese Communism.* 2 Vols. Cambridge, Mass.: Harvard University Press, 1971.

Khrushchev, Nikita S. *Khrushchev Remembers.* New York: Little, Brown & Co., 1974.

Lee, Hong Yung. *The Politics of the Chinese Cultural Revolution.* Berkeley, Calif.: University of Calif.Press, 1978.

Lewis, John Wilson, ed. *Party Leadership and Revolutionary Power in China.* Cambridge: Cambridge University Press, 1970.

Li, Tien-min. *Liu Shao-ch'i.* Taipei: Institute of International Relations, 1975.

Lifton, Robert J. *Revolutionary Immortality: Mao Tse-tung and the Chinese Cultural Revolution.* New York: Vintage Books, 1968.

Lindbeck, John M.H. ed. *China: Management of a Revolutionary Society.* Seattle: University of Washington Press, 1971.

MacFarqhar, Roderick, ed. *China Under Mao: Politics Takes Command.* Cambridge, Mass.: The M.I.T. Press, 1966.

Menhert, Klaus. *Peking and Moscow*. New York: Mentor Books, 1964.
Meisner, Maurice. *Mao's China*. New York: The Free Press, 1977.
Michael, Franz, *Mao*. New York: Barron's 1977.
Milton, David and Nancy Dall. *The Wind Will Not Subside*. New York: Pantheon Books, 1976.
Moody, Peter R. Jr. *The Politics of the Eighth Central Committee of the Communist Party of China*. Hamden, Conn.: The Shoe String Press, Inc. 1973.
Price, James L. *Cadres, Commanders and Commissars*. Boulder, Colorado: Westview Press, 1976.
Prybyla, Jan. *The Political Economy of Communist China*, Scranton, Pa.: International Textbook Co., 1970.
Pye, Lucian W. *China*. Boston: Little, Brown & Co., 1972.
—————. *Mao Tse-tung*. New York: Basic Books, Inc. 1976.
—————. *The Spirit of Chinese Politics: A Psychocultural Study of the Authority Crisis in Political Development*. Cambridge, Mass.: The M.I.T. Press, 1968.
Rice, Edward. *Mao's Way*. Berkeley, Calif.: University of California Press, 1974.
Robinson, Thomas W. ed. *The Cultural Revolution in China*. Berkeley, Calif.: University of California Press, 1971.
Roots, John McCook. *Chou*. New York: Doubleday, 1978.
Rue, John E. *Mao Tse-tung in Opposition*. Stanford, Calif.: Hoover Institution, 1966.
Scalpino, Robert A. *Elites in the People's Republic of China*. Seattle: University of Washington Press, 1972.
Schram, Stuart, ed. *Chairman Mao Talks to the People*. Trans. John Chinnery and Tieyun. New York: Pantheon Books, 1974.
Schumann, Franz, and Orville Schell, *Communist China*. New York: Vintage Books, 1967.
Schwartz, Benjamin I. *Communism and China: Ideology in Flux*. New York: Atheneum, 1968.
Shelden, Mark. *The Yenan Way in Revolutionary China*. Cambridge, Mass.: Harvard University Press, 1971.
Sheng, Yueh. *Sun Yat-sen University in Moscow and the Chinese Revolution*. Lawrence, Kansas: The University of Kansas Press, 1971.
Sheridan, James E. *Chinese Warlord: The Career of Feng Yu-hsiang*. Stanford, Calif.: Stanford University Press, 1970.
Snow, Edgar. *Random Notes on Red China 1936-1945*. Cambridge, Mass.: Harvard University Press, 1957.
—————. *Red China Today*. New York: Vintage Books, 1971.
—————. *Red Star Over China*. New York: Grove Press, 1973.

——————. *The Long Revolution*. New York: Vintage Books, 1973.

Snow, Helen Foster. *The Communists*. Westport, Conn.: Greenwood Publishing Co., 1972.

Smedley, Agnes. *The Great Road*. New York: Monthly Review Press, 1972.

Solinger, Dorothy J. *Regional Government and Political Integration in Southwest China, 1949-1954*. Berkeley, Calif.: University of California Press, 1977.

Solomon, Richard H. *Mao's Revolution and Chinese Political Culture*. Berkeley, Calif.: University of California Press, 1974.

Tang, Peter S.H. and Joan M. Maloney. *Communist China: The Domestic Scene 1949-1967*. South Orange, N.J.: Seton Hall University Press, 1967.

Taylor, Jay. *China and Southeast Asia*. New York: Praeger Publishers, 1976.

Terrill, Ross. *Mao*. New York: Harper & Row Publishers, 1980.

——————. *The Future of China*. New York: Dell Publishing Co., 1978.

Thornton, Richard C. *China: The Struggle for Power 1917-1972*. Bloomington·, Ind.: Indiana University Press, 1973.

Townsend, James R. *Politics in China*. Boston: Little, Brown & Co., 1974.

Traeger, Frank N. and William Henderson, eds. *Communist China, 1949-1969*. New York: The New York University Press, 1970.

Trumbell, Robert, ed. *This is Communist China*. New York: David McKay Co., Inc., 1968.

Uhalley, Stephen Jr. *Mao Tse-tung*. New York: New Viewpoints, 1975.

Walker, Richard L. *China Under Communism*. New Haven: Yale University Press, 1955.

Wang, James C.F. *Contemporary Chinese Politics: An Introduction*. Englewood Cliffs, N.J.: Prentice Hall, 1980.

Warner, Denis. *Hurricane From China*. New York: The Macmillan Co., 1961.

Wheelwright, E.L. and Bruce McFarlane. *The Chinese Road to Socialism: Economics of the Cultural Revolution*. New York: Monthly Review Press, 1970.

Whitson, William W. *The Chinese High Command: A History of Communist Military Politics, 1927-1971*. New York: Praeger Publishers, 1973.

Wilson, Dick. *Anatomy of China*. New York: The New American Library, 1969.

Witke, Roxane. *Comrade Chiang Ch'ing*. Boston: Little, Brown &

Co., 1977.

Young, Marilyn B. and William G. Rosenberg. *Transforming Russia and China*. New York: Oxford University Press, 1982.

Zagoria, Donald S. *The Sino-Soviet Conflict 1956-1961*. New York: Atheneum, 1964.

Glossary of Names

(Wade-Giles and Pin-Yin)

A, B, no entry
C

Wade-Giles	Pin-Yin
Chang:	Zhang
Chang Ch'ien-yuan:	Zhang Qianyuan
Chang Ch'un-ch'iao:	Zhang Chunquia
Chang Hao:	Zhang Hao
Chang Hsueh-liang:	Zhang Xueliang
Chang Kuo-t'ao:	Zhang Guotao
Chang Mu-t'ao:	Zhang Mutao
Chang Tso-lin:	Zhang Zuolin
Chang Yun-i:	Zhang Yunyi
Chao Shih-yen:	Zhao Shiyan
Chao Tse-yang:	Zhao Zeyang
Chao Tzu-yang:	Zhao Zuyang
Ch'en Ch'ang-hao:	Chen Changhao
Ch'en Hao-jen:	Chen Haoren
Ch'en Hsi-lien:	Chen Xilian
Ch'en:	Chen Yi
Ch'en Keng:	Chen Geng
Ch'en Po-ta:	Chen Boda
Ch'en Tu-hsin:	Chen Duxin
Ch'en Yen-nien:	Chen Yannian
Ch'en Yun:	Chen Yun
Cheng Chieh-min:	Zheng Jiemin
Cheng-Feng Rectification:	Zheng-Feng Rectification
Chi Teng-k'uei:	Ji Dengkuei
Chiang Ching-kuo:	Jiang Jingguo
Chiang Ch'ing:	Jiang Qing
Chiang Kai-shek:	Jiang Jieshi
Ch'ien Hsin-chung:	Qian Xinzhong
Ch'ih Ch'un:	Chi Chun
Chin-Chi-Lu-Yu:	Jin-Ji-Lu-Yu
Chin-Chi-Lu-Yu region:	Jin-Ji-Lu-Yu region
Chin Wei-ying:	Jin Weiying
Ch'ing Ming Festival:	Qing Ming Festival
Cho Lin:	Zhuo Lin
Chou En-lai:	Zhou Enlai
Chou Jung-chin:	Zhou Rongjin
Chou T'ien-lu:	Zhou Tianlu
Chu Te:	Zhu De
Ch'u Ch'un-pai:	Chu Junbai
Ch'u Wu:	Chu Wu
Chuang people:	Zhuang people
Chung-shan:	Zhong-shan
Chungking:	Chongqing

F

Wade-Giles	Pin-Yin
Feng-ch'ing:	Feng-qing
Fen Ta-fei:	Fen Dafei
Feng Yu-hsiang:	Feng Yuxiang

H

Wade-Giles	Pin-Yin
Ho Ch'ang:	He Chang
Hsi Chung-hsun:	Xi Zhongxun
Ho Shih-ch'ang:	He Shichang
Ho Shu-heng:	He Shuheng
Ho Lung:	He Long
Honan:	Henan
Hsia Po-ken:	Xia Bogen
Hsiang Ching-yu:	Xiang Jingyu
Hsiao (wife of Ten Wen-ming):	Xiao
Hsiao Chin-kuang:	Xiao Jinguang
Hsiao Kan:	Xiao Gan
Hsiao Ming:	Xiao Ming
Hsieh Ching-i:	Xie Jingyi
Hsieh Fu-chih:	Xie Fuzhi
Hsieh Wei-chun:	Xie Weizhun
Hsieh-hsing:	Xie-xin
Hsien-ch'ing:	Xian-qin
Hsien-chung:	Xian-Zhong

Hsien-jung:	Xian-rong
Hsu-Hsiang-ch'ien:	Xu Xiangqian
Hsu Kuan-ying:	Xu Guanying
Hsu Li-ch'un:	Xu Lichun
Hsu Shih-yu:	Xu Shiyu
Hsu Te-Heng:	Xu Deheng
Hu Ch'iao-mu:	Hu Qiaomu
Hu Chung:	Hu Zhong
Hu Yao-pang:	Hu Yaobang
Hua Kuo-feng:	Hua Guofeng
Huang Yen-p'ei:	Huang Yanpei
Hu Pin:	Hu Bin

J

Jao Shu-shih:	Rao Shushi
Jen Cho-hsuan:	Ren Zhuoxuan
Jen Pi-shih:	Ren Bishi

K

Kan Tse-kao:	Gan Zegao
K'ang Sheng:	Kang Sheng
Kao-Jao case:	Gao-Rao case
Kao Kang:	Gao Gang
Kiangsi Province:	Jiangxi Province
Kiangsi:	Jiangxi
Ko Ch'ing-shih:	Ge Qingshi
Ko Lau Hui:	Ge Lauhui
Ku Cheng-kang:	Gu Zhenggang
Ku Chengting:	Gu Zhengding
Ku Po:	Gu Bo
Kuan Hsiang-ying:	Guan Xiangying
Kung-Ch'u:	Gong Chu
Kuo Mo-jo:	Guo Moruo
Kuomintang:	Guomingdang
Kwangsi Province:	Guangxi

L

Lei Ching-t'ien:	Lei Jingtian
Li Ch'ien:	Li Qian
Li Ching-ch'uan:	Li Jingquan
Li Cho-jan:	Li Zhouran
Li Fu-ch'un:	Li Fuchun
Li Hsien-mien:	Li Xianmian
Li Huan:	Li Huan
Li Huang:	Li Huang
Li Kan-hui:	Li Ganhui

Li Li-san:	Li Lisan
Li Ming-jui:	Li Mingrui
Li Shih-tseng:	Li Shizeng
Li Te-sheng:	Li Desheng
Li T'ien-yu:	Li Tianyu
Li Tsung-jen:	Li Zongren
Li Wei-han:	Li Weihan
Liang Ch'i-ch'ao:	Liang Qichao
Liao Mo-sha:	Liao Mosha
Lin Piao:	Lin Biao
Lin Chih-tan:	Liu Zhidan
Liu Hsiang-p'ing:	Liu Xiangping
Liu Nin-i:	Liu Ninyi
Liu Po-ch'eng:	Liu Bocheng
Liu Po-chien:	Liu Bojian
Liu Shao-ch'i:	Liu Shaoqi
Liu-Teng army:	Liu-Deng army
Liu Wen-hui:	Liu Wenhui
Lo Jui-ch'ing:	Luo Ruiqing
Lo Ming:	Luo Ming
Lo-Ming line:	Luo-Ming line
Lu Han:	Lu Han
Lu Ting-i:	Lu Dingyi
Lung-chou Soviet:	Long-zhou Soviet

M

Mao Tse-t'an:	Mao Zetan
Mao Tse-tung:	Mao Zedong
Mao Yuan-hsin:	Mao Yuanxin

N

Nanking:	Nanjing
Nanning:	Nanning
Nieh Jung-chen:	Nie Rongzhen

P

Pai Chung-hsi:	Bai Zhongxi
Pai Yu:	Bai Yu
Pai-se, City of:	Baise
Pan Tsu-li:	Pan Zuli
P'eng Chen:	Peng Zhen
P'eng Te-huai:	Peng Dehuai
P'i I-shu:	Pi Yishu
Po I-po:	Bo Yibo
Po Ku:	Bo Gu
Pu Cho-lin:	Bu Zhuolin

P'u Ch'iung-yin: Pu Qiongyin
P'u Tsai-ting: Pu Zaiding

S

Shansi: Shanxi, Shenxi
Shensi-Kansu Red Army:
  Shenxi-Gangsu Red Army
Shen Tse-min: Shen Zemin
Shensi-Kansu Soviet: Shenxi-Gansu
Shih Ko'-hsuan: Shi Kexuan
Shih Shu-yuan: Shi Shuyuan
Sian Incident: Xian Incident
Su Yu: Su Yu
Sun Yat-sen: Sun Yixian
Sung Jen-ch'ing: Song Renqing

T

T'an: Tan
T'an Chen-lin: Tan Zhenlin
T'ang To: Tang Do
T'ao Chu: Tao Zhu
Teng Chih-fang: Deng Zhifang
Teng Hsi-hsien: Deng Xixian
Teng Hsiao-ping: Deng Xiaoping
Teng Hsien-Yu Deng Xianyu
Teng Hsien-lich: Deng Xianlie
Teng Jung: Deng Rong
Teng Ken: Deng Gen
Teng Lin: Deng Lin
Teng-Mao-Ku-Hsieh anti-Party Group:
  Deng-Mao-Gu-Xie
Teng Ming-ch'iu: Deng Mingqui
Teng Nan: Deng Nan
Teng Pin: Deng Bin
Teng P'u-fang: Deng Pufang
Teng Shao-sheng: Deng Shaosheng
Teng shih-min: Deng Shimin
Teng Shu-p'ing: Deng Shuping
Teng To: Deng Duo
Teng Tzu-hui: Deng Zuhui
Teng Wen-ming: Deng Wenming
Teng Ying-ch'ao: Deng Yingchao
T'ien-an-men Square Incident:
  Tiananmen Square

Ts'ai Ch'ang: Cai Chang
Ts'ai Ho-sen: Cai Hesen
Tso Ch'uan: Zuo Quan
Tsun-i Conference: Zunyi Conference
Tung Pi-wu: Dong Biwu

W

Wan Li: Wan Li
Wang Chen: Wang Zhen
Wang Chia-hsiang: Wang Jiaxiang
Wang Ching-wei: Wang Jingwei
Wang Hung-wen: Wang Hongwen
Wang Jo-fei: Wang Rofei
Wang Tung-hsing: Wang Dongxing
Wang Ming: Wang Ming
Wang Pien: Wang Bian
Wang Tung-hsing: Wang Dongxing
Wei Kung-chih: Wei Gongzhi
Wei Kuo-ch'ing: Wei Guoqing
Wei Pa-ch'un: Wei Baqun
Wu Hsiu-ch'uan: Wu Xiuquan
Wu Pei-ju: Wu Beiru
Wu Te: Wu De
Wu Yu-chang: Wu Yuzhang
Wuhan: Wuhan

Y

Yang Hu-ch'eng: Yang Hucheng
Yang Shang-k'un: Yang Shangkun
Yang Te-chih: Yang Dezhi
Yang T'eng-hui: Yang Tenghui
Yang Yun: Yang Yun
Yao I-lin: Yao Yilin
Yao Lien-wei: Yao Lianwei
Yao Wen-yuan: Yao Wenyuan
Yeh Chien-ying: Ye Jianying
Yen Hsi-shan : Yen Xishan
Yu Hsiu-sung: Yu Xiu song
Yu Hui-hung: Yu Huihong
Yu Tso-po: Yu Zuobo
Yu Tso-yu: Yu Zuoyu
Yuan Jen-yuan: Yuan Renyuan
Yuan Yeh-lieh: Yuan Yelie

Index

A

"Against the Tide Campaign," 161, *see,* Mao Tse-tung, 162

Agricultural Producers Cooperative (APC), 112, *see,* Twelve-year Program, "12-year Draft Outline for Agricultural Development," 116, *see,* People's Communes, 120

All Patriotic Associations Union, 32

"Anti-Confucius Campaign," 160, *see,* Mao Tse-tung, 162

Anti-Confucius and Anti-Lin Piao Campaign, 162, *see,* Anti-Confucius Campaign

Anti-Japanese Military and Political University, 17, *see,* Cho Lin

Anti-Lin Piao Campaign, 162, *see,* Anti-Confucius and Anti-Lin Piao Campaign

Anti-Rightist Deviationism Campaign, 176, *see,* Mao Tse-tung, 180, *see,* Cultural Revolution, 185, *see,* "Criticize Teng and Anti-ightist Campaign," 201, *see,* Third Plenary Session of the Tenth Party Congress

Anti-Rightist Movement, 111, *see,* Hundred Flowers Campaign, Chinese Communist Party, 114, *see,* "12-year Draft Outline for Agricultural Development," 127, 206, *see,* Fifth Plenary Session of the Eleventh Central Committee

April Fifth Incident, 181, 182, *see,* Mao Tse-tung, Chiang Ch'ing, T'ien-an-men Square Incident, Ch'ing Ming Festival, 201, *see,* Third Plenary Session of the Tenth People's Congress

"August 7th Conference," 44, *see,* Chinese Communist Party Central Committee, 62

B

Battle of Huai-Hai, 86, 87, *see,* Kuomintang

Battle of Liao-Shen, 86, 87, *see,* Kuomintang

Battle of P'ing-Tsin, 86

Battle of Plin-Tsin, 88, *see,* Civil War

Building of Socialism, 116, *see,* Mao Tse-tung, "Three Red Banners"

C

Capital (Karl Marx), 138, *see,* Teng Hsiao-p'ing

Central China Bureau, 83, *see,* Chin-Chi-Lu-Yu People's Liberation Army, Teng Hsiao-p'ing, 85

Central Committee, 82, *see,* Seventh Party Congress, 106, *see,* Eighth Party Congress, 107, *see,* General Secretary of the Chinese Com-

tee, 107, 112, *see*, Twelve-year Program, 114, 150, *see*, Politburo Standing Committee, 202, *see*, Third Plenary Session of the Tenth People's Congress, 204, *see*, Second Plenary Session of the Fifth People's Congress

Cheng Chieh-min, 38, *see*, Sun Yat-sen University for Toilers of China, 38n, *see*, Nationalist Intelligence Agency

Cheng-Feng Rectification, 81, *see*, Teng Hsiao-p'ing

Chi Teng-k'uei, 191, *see*, Hua Kuo-feng, 200, 201, 205, *see*, Fifth Plenary Session of the Eleventh Central Committee, Politburo

Chiang Ching-kuo, 38, *see*, Sun Yat-sen University for Toilers of China, 38n, *see*, Republic of China

Chiang Ch'ing (wife of Mao Tse-tung), 7, 105, 106, *see*, Eight Party Congress, Teng Hsiao-p'ing, 125, 128, 142, *see*, Chinese Communist Party Central Cultural Revolutionary Group, 152, 153, 161, *see*, "Gang of Four," Tenth Party Congress, 162, 165, 166, 167, 178, *see*, Chang Ch'un-ch'iao, 179, *see*, Hua Kuo-feng, 181, 183, *see*, April Fifth Incident, 184, 185, 187, 189, *see*, Mao Tse-tung, 190, *see*, Politburo Standing Committee, "To Follow the Established Direction in Our Work," 191, *see*, "Gang of Four,"

Chiang Kai-shek, 42, *see*, Feng Yu-hsiang, Yen Hsi-shan, 48, 50, 51, 52, 56, 68, 73, *see*, Sian Incident, 85, *see*, Liu-Teng army

Ch'ien Hsin-chung, 186, *see*, Teng Hsiao-p'ing

Ch'ih Ch'un, 191, *see*, Chang-ch'ing

Chin-Chi-Lu-Yu People's Liberation Army (PLA), 82, *see*, 129th Div-

ision, Liu-Teng army, Teng Hsiao-p'ing, 85, *see*, Ch'en Keng

Chin-Chi-Lu-Yu region, 80, *see*, Liu-Teng army

Chin Wei-ying (second wife of Teng Hsiao-p'ing), 16, 66

Chinese Communist Party (CCP), 17, *see*, Cho Lin, 18, 29, 30, 31, 32, 40, *see*, Feng Yu-hsiang, 42, *see*, Wuhan, Kuomintang, 43, 44, 47, *see*, Sixth Party Congress, 48, 50, 52, *see*, Kwangsi Province, 56, *see*, Li Li-san, 74, *see*, Kuomintang, 75, *see*, Eighth Route Army, Shangsi, 82, *see*, Seventh Party Congress, Second United Front, 112, *see*, Anti-Rightist Campaign, 135, 206, *see*, Mao Tse-tung, 209, *see*, Twelfth Party Congress, 220

Chinese Communist Party Central Committee, 44, *see*, "August 7th Conference"

Chinese Communist Party Central Cultural Revolutionary Group, 142, *see*, Cultural Revolution

Chinese Communist Party Organization Department 100, *see*, Jao Shu-Shih, Teng Hsiao-p'ing, 197, *see*, Hu Yao-pang

Chinese Communist Party Southwest Bureau, 93, *see*, Southwest Region, Teng Hsiao-p'ing

Chinese delegation (to Russia), 133, 134

Chinese Republic, 37, *see*, Sun Yat-sen

Chinese Youth Party, 31, *see*, Statist Party, 32, *see* Li Huang

Ch'ing Ming Festival, 183, *see*, April Fifth Incident

Cho Lin (third wife of Teng Hsiao-p'ing), 17, *see*, P'u Ch'iung-ying Pu Cho-lin, 18, 23, 81, 153

Chou En-lai, 7, 12, 23, 26, 27n, 28, 29, *see*, Young Communist Party, 30, *see*, *The Youth*, 32, 34, 46, 47, 61, 64, 65, *see*, Lo Ming Line,

243

paign, 192, 194, 195, *see*, Mao Tse-tung, 196, *see*, Tenth Party Congress, 197, *see*, Eleventh Party Congress, Fifth National People's Congress, 201, *see*, Third Plenary Session, "New Leap Forward," 203, 206, *see*, Fifth Plenary Session of the Eleventh Central Committee, 208, 209, 214, 215, 216

Huang Yen-p'ei, 97, *see*, State Administrative Council

Hu Pin, 54

Hundred Flowers Campaign, 108, *see*, Mao Tse-tung, 109, 110, *see*, Supreme State Conference

J

Jao Shu-shih, 99, *see*, "Kao-Jao case," 100, 101

Japanese forces, 75, 78, 79, 80, 81, *see*, Hundred Regiment Battle, Liu-Teng army

Jen Cho-hsuan, 28, 28n, 38, *see*, Sun Yat-sen University for Toilers of China

Jen Pi-shih, 44, *see*, Chinese Communist Party Central Committee, 74, *see*, Eighth Route Army, Teng Hsiao-p'ing, 75

K

Kan Tse-kao, 12, *see*, Teng Hsiao-p'ing

K'ang Sheng, 134, (Chinese delegation (to Russia), 149, *see*, Politburo Standing Committee

"Kao-Jao case," 99, *see*, Kao Kang, Jao Shu-shih, Teng Hsiao-p'ing

Kao Kang, 41, 97, *see*, State Planning Committee, 99, *see*, "Kao-Jao case," 100, 101, 115

Kao Kang-jao Shu-shih case, 6, *see*, "Kao-Jao case"

Khrushchev, Nikita, 97, 101, 103, 115, 133

Kiangsi Province, 56, *see*, Seventh Army, Eighth Army, 58, 61, 62, *see*, Teng Hsiao-p'ing, 64, 68

Kiangsi Provincial Party Committee, 62, *see*, Teng Hsiao-p'ing

Ko Ch'ing-shih, 116, *see*, Fifth Plenary Session (1958)

Ko Lau Hui, 14, *see*, Teng Wen-ming

Ku Cheng-kang, 38, *see*, Sun Yat-sen University for Toilers of China, 38n, *see*, Kuomintang, Ku Chengting

Ku Chengting, 38, *see*, Sun Yat-sen University for Toilers of China, 38n, *see*, Ku Cheng-kang, Legislative Yuan

Ku Po, 62, *see*, Mao Tse-tung, 65

Kuan Hsiang-ying, 74, *see*, Eighth Route Army

Kuang-an, 11

Kung Ch'u, 49, 50, 53, 57

Kuo Mo-jo, 97, *see*, State Administrative Council

Kuomintang (KMT), 31, 32, 38, *see*, Sun Yat-sen University for Toilers of China, 38n, 39n, 40, 41, *see*, Feng Yu-hsiang, 42, 43, *see*, Wuhan, 44, 50, 52, 55, *see*, Left River Soviet, 56, 58, *see*, Seventh Army, 64, 65, 67, 73, 74, 75, 82, *see*, Second United Front, 84, 85, 86, *see*, Battle of Huai-Hai, 87, *see*, Battle of Liao-Shen, 89, 95, 213

Kwangsi Province, 6, 48, *see*, Teng Hsiao-p'ing, 49, 49n, 50, 51, 52, 56, 59

L

Left Army, 69, *see*, First Front Army, Teng Hsiao p'ing

Left River, 49, 50, 51, *see* Kwangsi Province, Chinese Communist Party, 52, 53, *see*, Eighth Red Army, 55

Left River Government, 54

Eleventh Central Committee, 207, 214-216, 221

Mao Yuan-hsin, 191, *see*, Chiang-h'ing

May Fourth Movement, 20, 26

"May Sixteenth Circular," 142, *see*, Cultural Revolution, "February Thesis"

Military Commission, 162, 163, *see*, Teng Hsiao-p'ing

N

Nanking (location of the right wing of the Kuomintang), 42, *see*, Chiang Kai-shek, Wuhan, 43, 88

Nanning, 49, 50

National Defense Council, 98, *see*, Teng Hsiao-p'ing

Nationalist Intelligence Agency, 38n, *see*, Cheng Chieh-min

New Fourth Army, 74, 83, *see*, Ch'en I

"New Leap Forward," 201, *see*, Hua Kuo-feng, Third Plenary Session of the Tenth Party Congress

Nieh Jung-chen, 26, 27, 74, 86, *see*, North China Field Army

Nixon, Richard M., 159

North China Field Army, 86, *see*, Nieh Jung-chen, 87

Northeast China Field Army, 86, *see*, Lin Piao, 87, *see*, Fourth Field Army

Northwest Field Army, 86, *see*, P'eng Te-huai, 87, *see*, First Field Army

O

"On the Resolutions of Certain Historical Issues," 66, *see*, Seventh Plenary Session, Lo Ming Line, Teng Hsiao p'ing

One Hundred Twenty-Ninth Division, 74, *see*, Fourth Front Army, First Front Army, Eighth Route Army, 75, 76, 77, *see*, Teng Hsiao-p'ing, 78, *see*, East China Field

Army, 82, *see*, Chen-Chi-Lu-Yu People's Liberation Army, Liu-Teng army

P

Pai Chung-hsi, 48, *see*, Kwangsi Province, 52

Pai Yu, 39n, *see*, Kuomintang, Legislative Yuan

Pai-se, City of, 52, *see*, Right River, Teng Hsiao-p'ing

Pai-se uprising, 65, *see*, Teng Hsiao p'ing

Pan Tsu-li, 134, *see*, Chinese delegation (to Russia)

Paris Manuscript (Karl Marx), 137-138, *see*, Mao Tse-tung

Party Central, 62, *see*, Teng Hsiao p'ing, Mao Tse-tung, 63, 68, 76, *see*, Liu Po-ch'eng, 94

P'eng Chen, 114, *see*, "12-year Draft Outline for Agricultural Development," 125, 134, *see*, Chinese delegation (to Russia), 140, *see*, Cultural Revolution, 141, *see*, "February Mutiny," 142, 143, *see*, "Four-family Shop," 145, 204, *see*, Second Plenary Session of the Fifth People's Congress, Fourth Plenary Session of the Eleventh Central Committee

P'eng Te-huai, 69, *see*, Left Army, Lin Piao, 70, *see*, Shensi-Kansu Red Army, 74, *see*, Eighth Route Army, 86, *see*, Northwest Field Army, 118, *see*, Mao Tse-tung, 119, 140, *see*, Cultural Revolution, 153, 201, *see*, Third Plenary Session of the Tenth Party Congress

People's Communes, 116, *see*, Mao Tse-tung, "Three Red Banners," Agricultural Producers Cooperative, 117, 128, 129, *see*, "Sixty Articles on Higher Education"

People's Daily, 181, *see*, Teng Hsiao-p'ing, 185, *see*, Mao Tse-tung, 186, 192, *see*, Hua Kuo-feng, 208

247

People's Republic of China, 89

People's Revolutionary Military Council, 89, *see*, People's Republic of China, Mao Tse-tung, Teng Hsiao-p'ing

P'i I-shu, 38, *see*, Sun Yat-sen University for Toilers of China, 38n, *see*, Kuomintang

Po I-po, 97, 112, *see*, Eighth Party Congress, Twelve-year Program, 201, *see*, Third Plenary Session of the Tenth Party Congress, 204, *see*, Second Plenary Session of the Fifth People's Congress

Po Ku, 61, *see*, "Twenty Eight Bolsheviks"

Politburo, 47, *see*, Sixth Congress of the Chinese Communist Party, 101, 101n, 106, 106n, *see*, Eighth Party Congress, 139, 140, *see*, Cultural Revolution, 146, *see*, Eleventh Plenum of the Eighth Central Committee, 161, *see*, Tenth Party Congress, 162, *see*, Teng Hsiao-p'ing, 184-185

Politburo Standing Committee, 149, *see*, Liu Shao-chi, Teng Hsiao-p'ing, 161, *see*, Tenth Party Congress, 163, 190, *see*, Chiang Ch'ing, 192, *see*, Eleventh Party Congress, 210, *see*, Twelfth Party Congress

Political Consultation Conference, 89, *see*, Teng Hsiao-p'ing

"Proposal Concerning the General Line of the International Communist Movement," 134, *see*, Teng Hsiao-p'ing, Mao Tse-tung, 146, *see*, Twenty-five Points, Eleventh Plenum of the Eighth Central Committee

Pu Cho-lin, 17, *see*, Cho-lin

P'u Ch'iung-ying, 17, *see*, Cho Lin

P'u Tsai-ting (father of Cho Lin), 17

R

Red Army, 48, 50, 56, 68, *see*, The Long March

Red Army Academy, 67, *see*, Teng Hsiao p'ing

Red Guards, 6, 7, 8, 13, 81, 141, *see*, Cultural Revolution, "February Mutiny," 144, 146, 148, 149, 150, 155

Reorganization Clique, 50, *see*, Wang Ching-wei, Kuomintang

Report Outline on Work of the Academy of Sciences, 170-171, *see*, Teng Hsiao-p'ing

Republic of China, 38n, *see*, Chiang Ching-kuo

Right and Left River Soviet, 55, *see*, Chinese Communist Party

Right Army, 69, *see*, Fourth Front Army

Right River, 49, 50, 51, *see*, Kwangsi Province, Chinese Communist Party, 52, *see*, Seventh Red Army, 54

Right River Government 54, *see*, Lei Ching-t'ien

Right River Soviet, 57, 59

S

Second Field Army, 87, *see*, Third Field Army, Nanking, 158, *see*, Teng Hsiao-p'ing

Second Front Army, 73, *see*, Ho Lung

Second Plenary Session of the Fifth People's Congress, 204

Second Plenary Session of the Tenth Party Congress, 166, 167

Second Ten Points, 129, *see*, "Some Concrete Policy Formulations of the Central Committee of the CCP in the Rural Socialist Education Movement," Teng Hsiao-p'ing, First Ten Points, Tenth Plenary Session, Mao Tse-tung, 130, 146, *see*, Eleventh Plenum of the Eighth Central Committee

Second United Front, 82, *see*, Kuomintang, Chinese Communist Party

248

(1965), 146, *see*, Eleventh Plenum of the Eighth Central Committee

V

Vietnamese Nationalist Party, 55, *see*, Lung-chou Soviet

W

Wan Li, 186, *see*, Teng Hsiao-p'ing, 195, 196, *see*, Eleventh Party Congress, 208, *see*, Third Plenary Session of the Fifth People's Congress

Wang Chen, 202, *see*, Third Plenary Session of the Tenth People's Congress

Wang Chia-hsiang, 67, *see*, Red Army Academy

Wang Ching-wei, 50, *see*, Chiang Kai-shek, Reorganization Clique, 51, 56

Wang Hung-wen, 161, *see*, "Gang of Four," Tenth Party Congress, 163, 166, *see*, "Feng-ch'ing" boat, Chiang Ch'ing, 167, *see*, Tenth Party Congress

Wang Jo-fei, 26, 27n, 28, 29, *see*, Chinese Communist Party

Wang Ming, 61 *see*, "Twenty Eight Bolsheviks"

Wang Pien, 39

Wang Tung-hsing, 191, *see*, Hua Kuo-feng, 199, *see*, Mao Tse-tung, 200, 201, 202, *see*, Third Plenary Session of the Tenth People's Congress, 203, 204, 205, *see*, Fifth Plenary Session of the Eleventh Central Committee, Politburo

Wei Kuo-ch'ing, 192, *see*, Teng Hsiao-p'ing

Wei Kung-chih, 41, 67, *see*, Red Army Academy

Wei Kuo-ch'ing (Wei Pa-ch'un's nephew), 54, 197, *see*, Eleventh Party Congress

Wei Pa-ch'un (leader of the Chuang), 52, 54, 56, 57, 58, *see*, Seventh Army

"Work and Study," 12, 19, 27, 35

Wu Han, 124, 125, *see*, P'eng Chen, Teng Hsiao-p'ing, 139, 140, *see*, Group of Five, Cultural Revolution, 142, *see*, "Three Family Village," 153

Wu Hsiu-ch'uan, 67, *see*, Red Army Academy

Wu Pei-ju, 40, *see*, Feng Yu-hsiang

Wu Te, 191, *see*, Hua Kuo-feng, 200, 201, 203, 205, *see*, Fifth Plenary Session of the Eleventh Central Committee, Politburo

Wu Yu-chang, 20, *see*, "Society of Thrift-Study in France"

Wuhan (location of the left wing of the Kuomintang), 42, *see*, Chinese Communist Party, Nanking, 43, 44, 56

Y

Yang Hu-ch'eng, 73, *see*, Sian Incident

Yang Shang-k'un, 134, *see*, Chinese delegation (to Russia), 141, *see*, Cultural Revolution, "February Mutiny," 143, *see*, "Four-family Shop," 145, 201, *see*, Third Plenary Session of the Tenth Party Congress

Yang Te-chih, 67, *see*, Red Army Academy

Yang T'eng-hui, 48, *see*, Yu Tso-po

Yang Yung, 54, 197, *see*, Eleventh Party Congress

Yao I-lin, 202, *see*, Third Plenary Session of the Tenth People's Congress, 204, *see*, Second Plenary Session of the Fifth People's Congress

Yao Lien-wei, 194, *see*, Hua Kuo-feng

Yao Wen-yuan, 140, *see*, Mao Tse-tung, Cultural Revolution, 161,